Museums in New York

Museums in New York
by Fred W. McDarrah

A descriptive reference guide to ninety fine arts museums, local history museums, specialized museums, natural history and science museums, libraries, botanical and zoological parks, commercial collections, and historic houses and mansions open to the public within the five boroughs of New York City

Foreword by Thomas P.F. Hoving

Special landmarks checklist edited by Gloria S. McDarrah

Third Edition 1978

New York, London, Tokyo

In a garden at The Cloisters, with the George Washington Bridge in the background.

ISBN: 0-8256-3112-2
LIbrary of Congress Catalog Number: 78-54604

In Great Britain: Book Sales Ltd., 78 Newman Street, London W1.
In Canada: Gage Trade Publishing, P.O. Box 5000, 164 Commander Blvd., Agincourt, Ontario M1S 37C.
In Japan: Music Sales Corporation, 4-26-22 Jingumae, Shibuya-ku, Tokyo 150.
Cover design by Iris Weinstein
Third Edition

For Timothy, Patrick and Gloria

Fred W. McDarrah was born in Brooklyn. He served in the paratroopers from 1944-1947 and in 1954 was graduated from New York University. He joined *The Village Voice* in 1958 and is now the Picture Editor and a photography critic. He has won numerous photo-journalism awards, including a Page One Award from Newspaper Guild of New York and a Guggenheim Fellowship for photography.

He is a member of ASMP, New York Press Photographers Association and The Author's Guild. His photographs have been widely published and exhibited and he is a regular contributor to *New York* magazine.

Among the many books published by Fred McDarrah are *Stock Photo and Assignment Sourcebook* and *Photography Market Place* (both R.R. Bowker, 1977); *The Artist's World* (E.P. Dutton, 1961); and *The Beat Scene* (Corinth Books. 1960). His biographical sketch appears in *Who's Who in America, Who's Who in American Art* as well as *The Writer's Directory.*

"Let us look at the art museum not as a collection of tangible artifacts, but rather as an expression of ideas and feelings about man and his most important work—art."

—Albert Ten Eyck Gardner

Foreword

There are plenty of guidebooks in the world. There are even a lot of guidebooks of New York. Some of these guidebooks are very good on logistics, or photographs, or descriptions, or any number of other things. This one is good for all of these purposes. It is a guide for museums, mansions, and mausoleums. If any of these venerable institutions captures your fancy, this is the book for you.

The guidebook can be used by any sort of New Yorker. For those who have ventured to the far corners of the city in quest of their heritage, this book will be a reminder that they have nevertheless not seen all there is to see. For those who have never ventured beyond the big mammas of New York museums, the Metropolitan, the Modern, or the Whitney, this book will give you an idea of what you are missing.

Have you ever been to the Poe Cottage, the South Street Seaport Museum, The Frick Collection, the American Numismatic Society, Richmondtown Restoration, Dyckman House, or the Cloisters? Get set for a new experience.

The remarkable thing about New York is that the art of the entire world may be seen here—and seen in a much more rounded and complete way than in any other city in the world. Here we have monster-sized museums, libraries, and zoos, as well as tiny out-of-the-way community museums in storefronts, brownstones, lofts, even warehouses—all serving to enrich our views of the past so that we can better understand and enjoy the future. Everything is right here—Dutch artifacts, Greek icons, Tibetan tankas, Eskimo totem poles, Japanese bonsai trees, Roman coins, California pottery, even moon rocks.

It has long been known to New Yorkers that there is more to the city than they suspect. There is more for children to do than to gloat morbidly over mummies, however delightful that may be. There is more local history encased between skyscrapers than even the most fervent students of New York suspect. And there are more subways and buses than anyone has ever ventured on, to take you to just these little off-beat places.

Museums in New York is the perfect guide for those who want to find out how to get there, what to expect, what to look for at the zoos, botanical gardens, historic houses and museums. It is an easy-to-use, simple handbook for the average person—a native New Yorker or out-of-town visitor—as well as the art buff.

Things to be seen are made very attractive by the photographs, which capture moods and ambiances so perfectly. Sometimes perhaps too revealingly perfect. But it is good that way, because you will have to find out for yourself what the best things in New York are. And you are tantalized to do so by the photography.

facing page: Portrait of the artist Juan de Pareja painted in Rome in 1650 by Diego Rodríguez de Silva y Velázquez and purchased by The Metropolitan Museum of Art in 1970.

One word about the biggest reason for going to any museum. Presumably, you are relatively aware of your daily surroundings. If you are also a bit curious as to how it is that your life runs along particular lines, and that you are surrounded by particular objects, and that certain things seem beautiful to you—if you are just a bit curious about the condition of man—then you are a museum person. Not every day, but every once in a while you feel like seeing something other than your four walls. These are the times that you go to a museum.

So swing yourself into a high gear, explore, and for enjoyment and reassurance, take along this excellent guide.

Thomas P.F. Hoving

Contents

Special Note: Every attempt has been made to have this volume as up to date as possible. But museum installations are in a constant state of change, and, as this volume is printed, some material will already be obsolete. Therefore, this museum guide is not intended to be a definitive catalogue of the art collections, but rather an introduction to the enormous pleasure that may be gained from a visit to any one of the museums in New York.

—Fred W. McDarrah, May 1978

Museums
in
New York

AMERICAN MUSEUM OF IMMIGRATION

Address: Liberty Island, New York, N.Y., 10004.
Phone: 422-2150 (Executive office); 732-1286

Days: Open daily, 9–5; open till 6 in summer.
Admission: Free.

Ferry: Leaves Battery Park landing for Liberty Island every hour on the
   hour. Round trip fare: Adults $1.50, Children $.50.
Subway: IRT 7th Ave. or Lexington Ave. to South Ferry station.
Bus: Broadway bus to South Ferry.
Auto: South to Bowling Green and State St. No cars on Liberty Island
   ferries. Public parking lots and meters at Battery Park.

Restaurant: Snack bar, vending machines near ferry. No picnics.

The American Museum of Immigration is under the administration of
the National Park Service of the United States Department of the Interior. It is on twelve-acre Liberty Island, at the base of the Statue of
Liberty, the first symbol of democracy visible to immigrants at the
threshold of the New World. The 150-foot-high female figure of Liberty enlightening the world stands amid the remains of Fort Wood.
   The museum is situated in a star-shaped rampart. Four exhibit halls
are at the center. Each of the ten sections of the rampart houses a
separate arm of the museum: auditorium, study collection, workrooms, library, hall of records, etc. The changing exhibit area is devoted to the innumerable contributions of the immigrants to the
building of America. Contributions to the fields of invention, engineering, science, art, music, industry, and crafts are illustrated by murals,
statuary, dioramas, photos, maps, charts, documents, and audio-visual
displays.
   The American Museum of Immigration tells the unique story of the
millions of men and women who came here from other countries, bringing the customs and traditions of their homelands. The Age of Immigration began about 1830 and lasted for over 100 years. During this
period, boatloads of immigrants arrived almost daily in New York harbor. They came for diverse reasons: some for economic opportunity;
others to escape the ravages of war or famine; and some to avoid per-
secution for their religious beliefs. Many came for pure adventure, to
see if the legend that the streets were paved with gold was true. The
Museum vividly recounts the immigrants' story in scenes from the past, 17
with many of the actual objects that accompanied their owners to the
new world. This is a visual account of those immigrants who earned
public acclaim, as well as those anonymous millions who braved the
unknown to make a new life in America.

The Statue of Liberty.

CASTLE CLINTON NATIONAL MONUMENT

Address: Battery Park at Broadway, New York, N.Y., 10004.
Phone: 344-7220

Days: Open Sundays through Thursdays, 8:30-4:30, Sept.—May; open every day during the summer.
Admission: Free.

Subway: IRT 7th Ave. or Lexington Ave. to South Ferry station.
Bus: Broadway bus to South Ferry.
Auto: South to Bowling Green and State St. Metered parking.

Anyone visiting the Statue of Liberty can hardly ignore the Castle Clinton National Monument in Battery Park. This ancient, round, red sandstone fortress presents a sharp contrast to the steel-and-glass, poured concrete, towering sky-monsters that blacken the lower Manhattan landscape. Ineffectual, shortsighted civic leaders and greedy real estate robber barons have succeeded in obliterating almost every last vestige of our New York City architectural heritage in the Battery Park area, except for this site, a few churches, and some row houses in Fulton and Front Streets.

Castle Clinton, like the Statue of Liberty and Federal Hall, is administered by the National Park Service of the United States Department of the Interior and was destined to be torn down in the 1940s to make way for the approach to the Brooklyn Battery Tunnel. But some fast civic maneuvering saved it, and Castle Clinton was put under Federal jurisdiction as a national monument.

From its beginning in 1811, this unusual structure served a variety of uses. It was first used as a fort, then as Castle Garden Theatre, as an immigrant depot, and then as the New York City Aquarium. Now it is a monument symbolizing American growth and change.

The original fort was built during the tense Napoleonic era when lower Manhattan was defenseless against the "enemy." Widespread "fortification fever" resulted in the building of Castle William on Governors Island, Fort Wood on Bedloe's Island, Fort Gibson on Ellis Island, and Castle Clinton, named in honor of three-time Mayor DeWitt Clinton.

As it turned out, the fort never saw combat, so it may be assumed that the sight of it successfully scared off the "invaders." Having served its noble purpose, it was given to the city, and in 1824 became Castle Garden, the setting for concerts, fireworks extravaganzas, balloon ascensions, and scientific demonstrations.

Its time as a center for public entertainments lasted for over thirty glamorous years in which many magnificent celebrations took place to honor various patriots, presidents, and heroic figures of the day who were wined and dined at huge public receptions.

18

Then in August, 1855, it was drastically changed and became an immigration landing depot to accommodate the extraordinary mid-century migration from Europe. In 1872, after processing eight million immigrants, the depot was moved to Ellis Island, and, four years later, Castle Clinton became the home of the New York Aquarium until 1941. Shortly thereafter it was declared a national landmark. A small museum and two barracks rooms are on view.

Castle Clinton National Monument.

SOUTH STREET SEAPORT MUSEUM

Address: 16 Fulton St. (near South St.), New York, N.Y., 10038.
Phone: 766-9020

Days: Open daily, 11—6.
Admission: Free. (Some ship-tour fees.)

Subway: IRT Lexington Ave., IRT 7th Ave. to Fulton St., or IND 8th
   Ave. to Nassau St.
Bus: Broadway or 2nd Ave. bus to Fulton St.
Auto: (1) South on Broadway, left at John St.
   (2) F.D.R. Drive, South St. exit; parking lots at Pier.

Restaurant: Outdoor snack bar on Pier 16.

Gift Shop: Souvenirs, prints, ship models, books, toys.

Special Events: Folk music concerts, children's theatre, Maritime Day
   programs, classes in coastal navigation.

Membership: Regular, $10.00 to $25.00; family $15.00.

If you "must go down to the sea again, to the lonely sea and the sky,"
as John Masefield put it, and it you want to see a tall ship and white
sails shaking, then the South Street Seaport Museum is the place for
you. Here you will see whaling ships, clippers, steamers, and square-
riggers dramatically situated in a "living museum" at Pier 16.

To stand at the end of the pier facing the city and see the tall masts,
rusted anchors, and carved figureheads of another age brings a nostalgic desire for a world long past when "men were men" and sailed the
seven seas for adventure, to return home in ships bulging with mys-
terious cargoes from India, Borneo, and Java. They sailed around Cape
Horn, the world's roughest seas, in ships like "The Chariot of Fame,"
"The Flying Cloud," "The Sea Witch," "Herald of the Morning" and
"Young America."

And now there is the reality of colossal skyscrapers going up, rivets
clanking into steel girders, the spinning blades of a helicopter as it spies
traffic snarls, sirens screeching on the highway, seagulls squabbling over
dead fish, and the busy hum of commerce in the canyons beyond.

In a jet-age world the South Street Seaport Museum is a door into
the past when, in the early nineteenth century, South Street was a
teeming port for waterfront trade. New York is a city built on commerce, and this museum captures the spirit and atmosphere of an era
when the waterfront was the center of that commerce.

When completed, the massive restoration will include numerous re-

Figurehead, U.S.C.G. training ship, "Eagle."

A view of Pier 16

Schermerhorn Row.

stored buildings encompassing a five-block area at Front and Fulton Streets. Ships and harbor craft, outfitted as closely to their original state as possible, will lie at the water's edge, once famous as the "Street of Ships." The museum building at 16 Fulton Street will tell the story of life on the waterfront, with its informative exhibits.

South Street Seaport Museum was conceived to tell the story of the young men in ships who built the city's greatness in the century that our young American republic came of age. The skills and disciplines of that time, now beyond our reach, are part of the story; so are the old buildings, the ships, and the essential quality of neighborliness of a city whose investors, craftsmen, traders and laborers worked side by side. The Seaport is intended to weave back into the fabric of city life some of the warmth and accessibility that have been lost.

23

Front Street was a thriving area in 1797; it housed merchants, coopers, tobacconists, and tanners, as well as being a marketplace for produce, fish, meat, game, books, farm implements—an incredible variety of goods from the North River sloops, Erie Canal boats, Liverpool packets, Levant traders, China and San Francisco clippers, coasting schooners, fishing smacks, and oyster boats that came into the waterfront there. Eventually the Fish Market crowded out the other functions, thrived, and then passed away in recent times.

It is this neighborhood around the old Fulton Fish Market that comprises the five-block complex of the South Street Seaport Museum. These include Fulton Street, known as Schermerhorn Row with the earliest buildings dating from 1811; and South, Front, and Water Streets to Peck Slip. A number of the oldest landmarks along Front Street date back to 1798 and are in various stages of restoration.

The waterfront restoration is based on real ships with a real story to tell; reality is more complex, more unknown, and has more to tell us than anything we can re-create in its name. South Street's real ships today are "The Peking" sailing ship of 1911; the "Ambrose" lightship of 1907; "The Lettie G. Howard" fishing schooner of 1891; the great full-rigged ship "Wavertree" of 1885; "The Major General William A. Hart" ferryboat; and, from time to time, the Hudson River sloop "Clearwater and the schooners "The Pioneer" and "The Harvey Gamage."

The Seaport program of walking tours, visiting ships, street fairs, concerts, festivals, seminars, European excursions, and vast outdoor events involving numerous flotillas in the rivers and bays of New York are what make the museum one of the most lively, interesting and educational in all of New York.

FRAUNCES TAVERN
Address: 54 Pearl St. (at Broad), New York, N.Y., 10004.
Phone: 425-1776

Days: Open weekdays, 10—4; and on Washington's Birthday.
Admission: Free.

Subway: (1) IRT Lexington Ave. to Bowling Green station. (2) BMT Brighton (local) to Whitehall St.

24 *Bus:* Broadway bus to Pearl St. Walk east to Broad St.

Auto: South on Broadway into State St., left to Bridge St. to Broad St. Metered parking.

Restaurant: Restaurant and bar on main floor.

Special Events: A presentation history of lower Manhattan, concerts, lectures, courses in conjunction with Columbia University.

Fraunces Tavern takes its name from Samuel Fraunces, a West Indian of French antecedents who was the tavern's proprietor and a steward to George Washington. The first announcement advertising the establishment appeared in the New York weekly *Independent Gazette* of April 4, 1763: "At Queens Head Tavern near the exchange or Long Bridge by Samuel Fraunces an **ORDINARY** dinner every day to be served at half after one."

The history of the tavern began on April 11, 1700, when Stephanus van Courtlandt gave the parcel of land to his son-in-law Stephen Delancey, who erected a three-story mansion on it. In 1759 it was converted into an office and a warehouse. Samuel Fraunces bought the building in 1762 and opened a tavern that became very popular because of its central location. The New York City Chamber of Commerce was founded there in 1768, and Fraunces held the property until the British occupied the city in 1776.

The building has gone through numerous alterations and its architectural history is extensively documented in a Museum display. Fraunces Tavern became a significant landmark at the close of the Revolutionary War. Before leaving for Annapolis to resign his commission on December 4, 1783, George Washington hosted a noontime gathering to bid farewell to his officers. Samuel Fraunces was one of those in attendance. The occasion is documented in the memoirs of Colonel Benjamin Tallmadge, who attended the event, and it was reported to be an emotional leave taking. According to the December 6, 1783 *Independent Gazette,* Washington's farewell was attended by Governor George Clinton, Mayor James Duane and Baron Friedrich Wilhelm von Steuben. "At his departure he was saluted with a discharge of 13 cannon from the fort."

Washington was rowed across the Hudson River to Paulus Hook (now Jersey City). He traveled to Philadelphia and Annapolis, and then to his estate in Virginia. Tallmadge sensed it was unlikely "that we should see his face no more." In 1789 Washington returned to New York to take the oath of office as president.

Washington's farewell took place in the Tavern's Long Room. There are numerous nineteenth century engravings that record the event, which took place on the second floor where public inns' dining rooms were usually located. The public restaurant today is on the first floor.

The Fraunces Tavern Museum is administered by the Sons of the American Revolution in the State of New York, a society whose basic purpose is to inspire interest in the ideas upon which America was founded. Membership in the society is "open to men whose ancestors actively assisted in establishing American Independence during the War

Fraunces Tavern.

of the Revolution between April 19, 1775 and April 19, 1783."

The society also works to generate interest in the events and personalities which helped found the republic. This is admirably accomplished in this unique and distinctive museum where the exhibits and programs are informative and educational.

26   This is one of the few museums that specializes in the Revolutionary period. Its period rooms, furnishings, paintings depicting major battles of the Revolution, flag displays and historic and military artifacts on exhibit fulfill its objective of being an educational center for American history.

NEW YORK STOCK EXCHANGE EXHIBIT HALL

Address: 20 Broad St., New York, N.Y., 10005.
Phone: 623-5168

Days: Monday through Friday, 10–4.
Admission: Free.

Subway: IRT Lexington Ave. to Wall St. station.
Bus: Broadway bus to Wall St. East one block.
Auto: South on Broadway to Wall St. Limited meter parking.

Tours: Continuous guided tours available including a film showing.

Special Restriction: No cameras allowed. Visitors' gallery partitioned
from trading floor by bullet-proof, 1-1/16th-inch-thick glass.

The New York Stock Exchange, in close proximity to Trinity Church
and Federal Hall, was founded on May 17, 1792, after a group of mer-

The New York Stock Exchange.

chants and auctioneers decided to meet regularly to buy and sell securities under an old buttonwood tree on Wall Street. In 1793, the twenty-four original members of the Exchange moved their operation indoors to the Tontine Coffee House. In succeeding years the Exchange occupied various quarters, until 1863, when it settled in its present location. The Exchange is now preparing to move again, this time about eight blocks south on Broad Street near Front Street, to a site recently cleared of its historic buildings.

The present building, a landmark building in the style known as Beaux Arts Eclectic, was designed by George B. Post and finished in 1903. Behind the six four-story Corinthian columns, an all-glass curtain wall provides light for the huge floor of the Exchange. The pediment sculpture group by John Quincy Adams Ward, when viewed from the street, looks like the downtrodden slaves of oppression, an incongruous choice for a building epitomizing American enterprise. The additional twenty-two stories of the Exchange hardly seem noticeable above this striking facade.

Every working day the main entrance on Broad Street sees a constantly moving crowd of stock clerks, tellers, office boys, secretaries, bankers, brokers, uniformed chauffeurs, and guards transporting securities in distinctive black valises on roller skates.

The Stock Exchange Exhibit Hall is on the third floor. The vivid story of capitalism is unfolded by means of documents, films, displays, ticker tape, and the Big Board. "Own a Share of American Business" exhorts an explanatory chart. Guided-tour lectures on what is a share of stock, how to read a stock table, and how an order is executed are presented by attractive hostesses. A number of interesting exhibits are by those who sell stock on the Exchange—Bristol Myers, Union Oil of California, Northern Natural Gas, I.B.M., and Avon products.

MUNICIPAL REFERENCE AND RESEARCH CENTER
Address: 31 Chambers St., New York, N.Y., 10007.
Phone: 566-4284

Days: Monday through Friday, 9—5.
Admission: Free.

28

Subway: IRT Lexington Ave. or BMT (local) to City Hall station.
Bus: Broadway bus to Chambers St. Limited parking lots.
Auto: South on Broadway to Chambers St. Limited parking lots.

The Municipal Reference and Research Center is a research library of published documents pertaining to New York City history, laws, codes and rules. It has all the reports of the Bureau of the Budget and the Board of Estimate, biographies of city officials, a complete file of street names, all the Valentine manuals, legislative reference material dating back to 1653, Stokes' *Iconography of New York,* volumes of O'Callaghan's *History of New York State,* and bound volumes of press releases from city agencies and the Mayor's office.

The Municipal Archives and Records Center, at 31 Chambers Street, 566-4292, is a reference resource that contains original unpublished documents such as land maps, deeds, birth certificates before 1897, and original records of Manhattan buildings demolished before 1866. Eventually both agencies will be combined as *The Department of Records and Information Services.*

The Municipal Archives has directories of prominent New Yorkers dating from the 1700s.

Aaron Burr, Efqr. 10, Little Queen-ftreet
Alexander Hamilton, Efqr. 57, Wall-ft.
Brockholft Livingfton, Efqr. 12, Wall-ft.
Wm. S. Livingfton, Efqr. 52, Wall-ftreet
Thomas Smith, Efqr. 9, Wall-ftreet
Wm. Cock, Efqr. 66, Wall-ftreet
Robert Troup, Efqr. 67, Wall-ftreet
Morgan Lewis, Efqr. 59, Maiden-lane
John Rutherfurd, 50, Broadway
George Bond, Efqr. attorney and notary-
    public, 5, William-ftreet;
William Wilcocks,   , Broad-ftreet
Richard Varick, Efqr. 46, Dock-ftreet
James Giles, Efqr. 65, Maiden lane
John M'Keffon, Efq. 49, Maiden-lane
John Keeffe, Efq. not.-pub. 227, Q.-ftreet
Peter Ogilvie, 144, Queen-ftreet
—— Depeyfter, Efq.   , Queen-ftreet
—— Cozine, Efq. 55, Beekman-ftreet
C. J. Rogets, Efq. 42, Beekman-ftreet
Jacob Remfen, Efq. 55, Broad-ftreet
John Ricker, Efq. corner of St. James-ft.
John Shaw, Efq. 19, Cliff-ftreet
Daniel C. Verplanck, Efq. 3, Wall-ftreet
R. Morris, Efq. 1, Wall-ftreet
Jas. M. Huges, Efq. conveyancer and no-
    tary public, 20, Wall-ftreet
Jofeph Winter, Efq. 184, Water-ftreet
John Kelly, Efq. conveyancer, land, and
    money-broker, 56, Smith-ft.

FEDERAL HALL NATIONAL MEMORIAL

Address: Corner of Wall and Nassau Sts., New York, N.Y., 10005.
Phone: 264-8711

Days: Open Sundays to Fridays, 9–4:30, Sept. to May; open every day in the summer. Closed major holidays.
Admission: Free.

Subway: (1) BMT (local) to Fulton St. station. (2) IRT Lexington Ave. to Wall St. station. (3) IND 8th Ave. to Fulton St.
Bus: Broadway or Second Ave. bus to Wall St.
Auto: South on Broadway to Wall St. Limited meter parking.

Tours: Guided tours available for groups; call in advance.

Federal Hall, with its great Doric columns and massive bronze statue of George Washington staring down Broad Street amid the newer buildings of metal and glass, still possesses a classic majesty.

Old City Hall was built in 1699. In 1765 the Stamp Act Congress met there; and in 1774, the first Continental Congress. The building was altered in 1788 and renamed Federal Hall before the first Congress under the Constitution convened. Washington took his presidential oath of office on the balcony on April 30, 1789. The Departments of State, War and the Treasury were created, and the Bill of Rights was adopted on this site. In July, 1790, Washington, D.C. was chosen as the permanent capital of the nation, and by 1812 Federal Hall had been sold for salvage for $425.

The present Greek Revival structure was built in 1842 as a customs house. It was remodeled in 1862, and thereafter housed offices of the Subtreasury, Federal Reserve Bank, State Department, Passport Agency, Public Health Service, and other Federal departments until May, 1939, when it was designated a National Historic Site. Finally, on August 11, 1955, the building became a National Memorial administered by the National Park Service for "the inspiration and benefit of the people of the United States commemorating the founding of the Federal Government and related historic events."

The most significant object associated with Federal Hall is the Washington Stone in the rotunda room. It is a large rust-colored slab of sandstone (5' x 9½'), recovered from the balcony of the old Federal Hall, on which Washington stood while taking the oath of office. The Bible used in the inaugural ceremony is now owned by St. John's Masonic Lodge.

The Washington Room contains material pertaining to the first sixteen months of the Presidency—April 30, 1789, to August 30, 1790—in beautifully designed modern displays in well-illuminated cabinets.

Federal Hall.

Miniature paintings, medals, snuffboxes, signed receipts, and bills of sale are in glass-covered pull-out drawers that contain the Messmore Kendall Collection of Washingtoniana. They were designed especially for the National Park Service.

The Bill of Rights Room is a gift from the American Bar Association. There is a translation from the Latin of the Magna Charta, and a diorama shows the debate over the Bill of Rights. Congress finally adopted twelve amendments on September 25, 1789, and sent them to the states for approval. Two were rejected, but the other ten became part of our Constitution on December 15, 1791.

The John Peter Zenger Room is dedicated to the journalist-printer who began his career as an apprentice to New York's first newspaper publisher (William Bradford, who is buried in Trinity churchyard). In 1733, Zenger founded his own *New York Weekly Journal.* After he exposed the corrupt administration of New York's Governor William Cosby, he was charged with seditious libel, imprisoned, and tried in the old City Hall building. Zenger's acquittal in 1735 was a landmark in the struggle for a free press in the Colonies.

31

Entrance to the Governor's Room in City Hall.

CITY HALL GOVERNOR'S ROOM

Address: City Hall, Broadway and Park Row, New York, N.Y., 10007.
Phone: 566-5525

Days: Open daily, 10—4. Closed Saturdays, Sundays, and holidays.
Admission: Free.

Subway: (1) IRT Lexington Ave. to Brooklyn Bridge station. (2) BMT
   Brighton (local) to City Hall station.
Bus: Broadway bus to City Hall Park.
Auto: South on Broadway to Chambers St. Limited meter parking.

The Governor's Room in City Hall is a museum within a museum. The
City Hall was designed by Joseph Francois Mangin and John McComb,
Jr. McComb, who supervised the job, was paid $6 a day, a considerable
wage at that time. Construction was begun in 1803 and completed in
1812. A harmonious combination of French Renaissance and American Colonial influences, the building's two wings balance a central portico. Over the portico are the five arched windows of the Governor's
Room.

The interior of City Hall is particularly fine. The first-floor rotunda
is dominated by a superb double curving staircase with wrought-iron
railings. The marble staircase leads to a ring of fluted Corinthian columns on the second floor. At the head of the stairs, on April 24th and
25th, 1865, the bier of Abraham Lincoln was placed. Over 100,000
citizens climbed the winding staircase to view the martyred president.

The executive branch of the city's government occupies the first
floor. The mayor's office is in the west wing, and the City Council
president's is in the east wing. On the second floor the legislative arm
is represented by the City Council in the east wing and the Board of
Estimate in the west wing. The Board's public hearing room conveys
the flavor of New York in the 1800s because of its white benches
trimmed with dark mahogany. They are similar to the pews of the
same period in historic St. Paul's Church.

The Governor's Room, on the second floor, is actually one large
room with two small chambers on each side. It was originally set aside
for use by the governor as a personal office when in the city. Long
used for ceremonies, such as Lafayette's reception in 1824, it is now
maintained as an important showcase for City Hall's antique furnishings and fine portraits of celebrated public officials associated with
New York. Special conferences are still held in these chambers.

Recently, doubt was raised regarding the authenticity of the furnishings in the Governor's Room. The City Art Commission, after extensive
research, uncovered documents, letters, and bills of sale that showed
proof of their age and origin. The Washington Writing Table, chief

33

Inside the Governor's Room.

cause of the controversy, was in use prior to 1790 at Federal Hall, the capital building of the new nation. The writing table, directly in the center of the Governor's Room, is considered the most notable object in the city's possession, and ranks with the foremost antique pieces in the country.

34   The John Trumbull portraits of George Washington (1790), George Clinton (1791), Alexander Hamilton, and John Jay (1805) were also originally installed in Federal Hall. Many of the exceptional portraits hang in various restricted areas of City Hall, but can be seen on application to the Art Commissioner's office.

FIRE DEPARTMENT MUSEUM
Address: 104 Duane St. (near Broadway), New York, N.Y., 10007.
Phone: 570-4230

Days: Open weekdays, 9–4; Saturdays, 9–12. Closed Sundays and all holidays, and Saturdays in July and August.
Admission: Free.

Subway: (1) IND 8th Ave. to Chambers St. station. (2) BMT Brighton (local) to City Hall station. North 3 blocks.
Bus: Broadway bus to Duane St.
Auto: South on Broadway to Duane St. Limited meter parking.

Tours: For guided tours, obtain permission from the museum at least one month in advance.

35

A famous 19th-century fire engine from New York City.

36

*Bright paint and brass
spangle another elaborate engine.*

The Fire Department Museum occupies three floors of a building that would be an obvious choice for these collections—a firehouse. It is about three blocks north of City Hall. The museum, filled with engines, ladder trucks, tools, trophies, photographs, and documents, is a poignant memorial to the gallant and dedicated efforts of the New York City firemen, whose motto is "Prevent Fires! Save Lives!"

All the colorful, fascinating fire-fighting apparatus displayed was used in actual fire service during the nineteenth and early twentieth centuries. On the ground floor there are hand-drawn pumpers, horse-drawn and early motorized fire engines. A hand-drawn and hand-operated pumper, the Washington No. 1, built in 1820, has a leather hose with seams that are riveted together, a technique similar to that in the sewn hoses used in Holland as early as 1672.

A steam engine, the Silsby Steamer, in gleaming silver plate, was known as the queen of her day, and once pumped for thirty-nine hours continuously in a 1904 fire. There are also a La France steam engine with a pumping capacity of 700 gallons a minute, and a 1920 Model-T Ford for a deputy fire chief. One of the horse-drawn vehicles, built in 1853, is decorated with landscapes of Indian reservations and portraits of Indians in full headdress. The ground floor also has the first firebell, cast in England in 1796 and installed in a stone house that stood at Fulton and Front Streets. In the rear courtyard are alarm boxes, hose nozzles, gongs, and decorative stone sculpture portraits of firemen that appeared over early firehouse entrances.

The second floor has gooseneck hand pumpers, golden trumpets used by chiefs to issue orders, cases of medals, trophies, badges, uniforms, hatchets, fire helmets, and portraits of fire officials. There is also a section of the first water main constructed of wooden logs, laid in lower Manhattan in 1829.

In the center of the third floor in the Huguenot hose reel originally used in Staten Island. There are a number of torchlights, axes, firemen's diving hoods, and fireboat equipment. There is also a fire chief's sleigh, used until the turn of the century. A cut-away model of a firehouse shows the kitchen, bunks, brass sliding poles, and drying racks for hoses. The walls are hung with photographs of great fires which serve as a reminder that the purpose of the museum is to create public cooperation in fire prevention.

CHINESE MUSEUM

Address: 8 Mott St., New York, N.Y., 10013.
Phone: 964-1542

Days: Open daily, 10–6, all year.
Admission: Adults, $.50; children, $.35. Group rates available.

Subway: (1) BMT to Canal St. station. Walk two blocks east to Mott St. (2) IRT Lexington Ave. to Brooklyn Bridge station. North one block, east to Mott St.
Bus: Third Ave. bus to Mott St.
Auto: South on 3rd Ave. to Chatham Sq. Ample parking lots.

Gift Shop: Novelties and souvenirs.

Special Services: Tours and meals arranged for groups.

Lectures: Lecture tours for school groups recommended.

The Chinese Museum is on one of the busiest streets in New York's most exotic community, directly inside a penny arcade. The mixture of ancient Chinese culture in the museum and Pop-Art culture in the arcade has attracted thousands of school children, groups of Scouts, and visitors in the past ten years.

When the museum was started by Herbert H. Weaver, his intention was to provide an educational facility for New York school children, whose field trips to Chinatown would be more meaningful if they had some idea about the Chinese—their cultural contributions, their history, theatre, music, religion, and even what and how they eat. The museum offers a tour of its exhibits, a tour of the Chinese community, and will even make luncheon and dinner arrangements for groups.

The museum has about ten exhibits that demonstrate Chinese culture clearly and simply. The main exhibit shows the course of Chinese history and what the Chinese have contributed to the progress of the world. All of the articles exhibited are still in use today, and instead of showing historic artifacts, the display contains such contemporary articles as modern playing cards, a dish of rice, firecrackers, etc.

A display of ancient Chinese musical instruments incorporates a fascinating sight-and-sound device: the viewer pushes a button and then watches and hears a color film of the instrument being played. This unique technique offers a dramatic educational lesson. One of the best exhibits reproduces the window of a Chinatown food store that has wax examples of every item that you can find in a typical Chinatown market. Over 200 Oriental foods are thus shown and identified.

The Chinese began to use chopsticks 2,500 years ago.

The other exhibits show flowers and fruits and their symbolic meaning in Chinese culture, Chinese parade masks, the story of incense, of rice, etc. A Buddhist temple altar over 100 years old and a figure of Confucius are also included.

THE OLD MERCHANT'S HOUSE
Address: 29 East 4th St. (at the Bowery), New York, N.Y., 10003.
Phone: 777-1089 (may be closed for restoration)

Days: Open Tuesdays through Sundays. Escorted tours at 2, 3, and 4
o'clock. Closed holidays and August. Phone in advance.
Admission: $.50. Special rates for public school classes.

39

Subway: IRT Lexington Ave. to Astor Place station. South to 4th St.,
then east 2 blocks.
Bus: Broadway or 3rd Ave. bus to 4th St.
Auto: Ample parking lots.

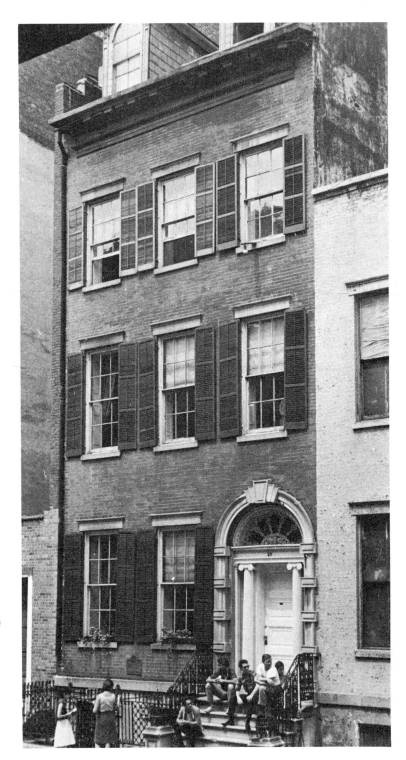

The street where the Old Merchant's House stands was once very fashionable, lined with beautiful town houses. Now there are trucking garages, factories, run-down lofts, and an occasional rooming house on the block.

The building is one of the finest examples of Classic Greek Revival architecture in the city. The only group of such town houses remaining intact stands along Washington Square North, a few blocks west. The Old Merchant's House is distinguished from the Washington Square buildings by its preservation of original furnishings and interiors, left exactly as they were in 1835 when Seabury Tredwell, a merchant and hardware importer, moved into the house, which had been built five years earlier by Joseph Brewster.

When Gertrude Tredwell, Seabury's last child, died in 1933, the Tredwell house and its contents were scheduled for public auction to satisfy debts and the mortgage. George Chapman, a distant relative, created the Historic Landmark Society to rescue the house. His purpose was to preserve it as a public museum displaying the family's entire belongings—paintings, furniture, china, lamps, books, even the framed diplomas from the fashionable girls' schools of the time.

In the house are trunks full of clothes, gowns, gloves, hats, Chantilly lace, paisley shawls, satin dancing slippers, even an exquisitely embroidered christening bonnet. Many of the trunks are not open, but may be seen on request.

With the exception of worn rugs and a number of broken cane chairs, most of the furniture and accessories are in good condition, particularly on the main floor, which is a huge double drawing room, cut in half with Corinthian columns and a sliding double door.

The principal bedrooms on the second floor have matching four-poster beds. All beds have canopies of silk and wool damask. The hall bedroom has a small pine tester bed with an arched chintz canopy. Although the surroundings seem elegant today, they were not considered luxurious a hundred years ago. Seabury Tredwell was an ultra-conservative person whose restrained good taste is evident throughout his house.

THE MUSEUM OF HOLOGRAPHY
Address: 11 Mercer St., New York, N.Y., 10013.
Phone: 925-0526

Days: Wednesdays through Sundays, 12—6; Thursdays until 9.
Admission: $1.50 adults; $.75 children.

41

Subway: All subways to Canal St.
Bus: Broadway bus to Canal St.
Auto: South on Broadway to Howard St.

The Old Merchant's House.

A hologram, "Kiss II," by Lloyd Cross.

Special Events: Traveling exhibits, seminars, library, workshops.

Membership: Patron $1,000; family $45; individual $25.

This is the only museum of its kind. It is in a cast iron building in the center of the Soho arts district south of Greenwich Village. Holography is a relatively new photographic art that was discovered in 1947 by Dr. Dennis Gabor, who received the Nobel Prize in physics for his invention. Hologram is from the Greek "holo" meaning whole, and "gram" meaning message.

Holography is a sophisticated, complex informational medium. It represents the space in front of, and behind, the plane of traditional visual recording. It is revolutionary because its form is not two-dimensional, where images exist in a static relationship to each other, such as in a flat photograph. Holographic images are three-dimensional, and the images change in relationship to each other when viewed from different positions.

Holography does not employ a camera. It uses laser light to record the patterns of light waves reflected from an object onto the emulsion of light-sensitive film. When that film is developed and re-exposed to laser light, it recreates the object. The image, either behind or in front of the holographic plate (or cylindrical viewer), appears to float in space and looks real.

Artists were first introduced to holography in the late 1960s. As an art form, it exhibits unique creative possibilities that expand the entire concept of visual art.

The purpose of The Museum of Holography is to create an environ-
 ment in which the public becomes acquainted with holography as an art form. The Museum has regular exhibitions showing historic works as well as survey shows on the art of holography. Traveling exhibitions, a reference library, films and publications are also among the Museum's activities.

THEODORE ROOSEVELT BIRTHPLACE, N.H.S.

Address: 28 East 20th St. (between Broadway and 4th Ave.), New York, N.Y., 10003.
Phone: 260-1616

Days: Open daily, 9—4:30. Closed Mondays and Tuesdays, Christmas, and New Year's Day.
Admission: $.50. Children under 16 free. Advance arrangements for group visits.

Subway: IRT Lexington Ave. to 23rd St. station, south to 20th St.
Bus: Madison Ave., 5th Ave., or Broadway bus to 20th St.
Auto: Limited meter parking.

Gift Shop: Commemorative medals, books on Theodore Roosevelt.

A block west of Gramercy Park stands the massive five-story brownstone where Theodore Roosevelt, twenty-sixth President of the United States, was born and lived until he was fifteen years old. The only remaining brownstone on the street, its well-kept exterior is within steps of a "hero" sandwich shop, lofts, factories, a towel-supply company, and wholesalers of office equipment.

The Greek Revival house was built by Roosevelt's father. It is set back from the building line just enough to be almost unnoticeable from a distance. Only the American flag juts out, distinguishing the birthplace as a National Historic Site, under the supervision of the National Parks Service of the Department of the Interior, with the cooperation of the Theodore Roosevelt Association, "to keep alive for future generations the life, the standards and the ideals of Theodore Roosevelt."

Five rooms and two museums are open to the public. The lower-floor museum presents a chronology of Roosevelt's life, from his birth on October 27, 1858, to his death on January 6, 1919. In about fifty desk-sized glass cases the display tells the story of the major events of Roosevelt's life: early childhood, college days to assemblyman, police commissioner, rancher, author, Assistant Secretary of the Navy, Rough Rider in the Cuban campaign of the Spanish-American War, Governor, President, hunter, and explorer. The array of memorabilia is staggering: his personal diaries, bits of baby clothing, faded sepia family pictures and tintypes, zoological notebooks showing the animals captured and skinned, newspaper clippings highlighting significant events, political cartoons, sealskin caps, uniforms, bugles, mementos of the Inaugural Ball, relics of World War I, flowered teacups, and an elaborate selection of tin campaign buttons and emblems of miniature Rough Rider hats, whiskbrooms, eyeglasses, and elephants.

43

44

Theodore Roosevelt's birthplace.

The parlor.

45

Roosevelt's accomplishments are highlighted in the Canal Zone commemorative postage stamps and the Nobel Peace Prize awarded him in 1906 for his efforts to end the Russo-Japanese War. A most unusual item on display is the book through which a bullet passed during an attempt to assassinate Roosevelt in 1912 in Milwaukee.

Roosevelt was born on the third floor. The bedroom, reached now by means of an elevator, is furnished in rosewood and satinwood. Next door, a charming nursery is set up with a little sleigh bed, dolls, and a child's tea set.

The furnishings on the elaborate parlor floor are the epitome of interior decoration in the Victorian era, "a period in which men of substance liked to have their homes reflect the dignity and solidity of their traditions and lives." These three rooms—parlor, library, and dining room—are furnished entirely in the style of that period, including the wallpaper, draperies, and carpets. In the library, the side chairs and sofa are upholstered in the expensive black horsehair so fashionable in Victorian homes. Taken as a whole, this house-museum is a fascinating tribute to the colorful and important man born there.

POLICE ACADEMY MUSEUM
Address: 235 East 20th St., New York, N.Y., 10003.
Phone: 477-9753

Days: Open weekdays, 8—4. Closed Saturdays, Sundays, and holidays.
Admission: Free.

46   *Subway:* IRT Lexington Ave. to 23rd St. station. South to 20th St.
Bus: Second Ave. or 3rd Ave. bus to 20th St.
Auto: Limited meter parking.

Tours: Groups must make appointment in advance.

A "tommy gun" hidden in a violin case.

The purpose of the Police Academy Museum is to "inform the public, gain their support, emphasize the duties and obligations of the police, and to create a cooperative atmosphere between the police and the public."

New York City Patrolman Fred J. Levine, who was largely responsible for developing the concept of the museum, pointed out that the police must have public support and understanding in order to carry out their responsibilities: "It is true that Crime Does Not Pay, but only a small part of police work is devoted to chasing gangsters. The greatest percent is of a regulatory nature, that of being the protector of life and property, and the prevention of crime. In this museum we have developed a facility for people to come and learn the true role and function of the police."

The museum plays host to elementary-school children, teen-agers, adults, visiting law-enforcement officers, students of law and sociology, and it attempts to reach school dropouts, antisocial youths, and the underprivileged.

The exhibits cover gambling, counterfeiting, unlawful weapons,

47

prostitution, suicide, homicide, historical memorabilia, and the training and recruitment of policemen. Two authoritative, outstanding exhibits illustrate the weapons used by youthful gangs and the narcotics racket.

Gang weapons, displayed in four glass cases, include machetes, meat cleavers, brass knuckles, ice picks, and an assortment of home-made zip guns. The narcotics display includes the plants from which drugs are obtained, and all the paraphernalia used by addicts: needles, syringes, rubber bands, bent spoons, pipes, and so on.

In addition to the museum on the second floor of the new building of the Police Academy, visitors are encouraged to tour the entire building, where they are shown the work of the ballistics and bomb squads, the police-evidence laboratory, emergency service division, gymnasium, and the firing range where demonstrations are given.

Various displays in the Police Museum.

BOXING HALL OF FAME

Address: 120 West 31st St. (between 6th and 7th Aves.) New York, N.Y., 10001.

Phone: 564-0354

Days: Open weekdays, 10–4. Closed Saturdays, Sundays, and holidays.

Admission: Free.

Subway: (1) IND 6th Ave. to 34th St. station. (2) IRT 7th Ave. to 34th St. station. South 3 blocks.

Bus: Sixth Ave. or 7th Ave. bus to 31st St.

Auto: No parking available.

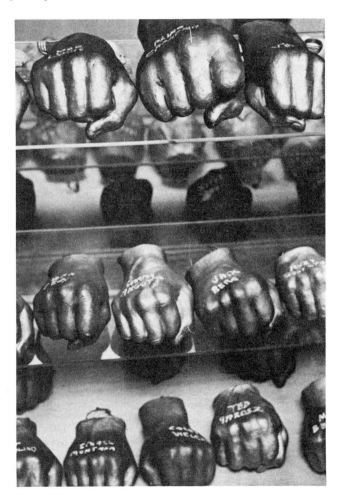

49

Casts of famous boxers' fists.

Perhaps the most offbeat museum in New York is the Boxing Museum, located in an old loft building on the edge of the garment district. The principal attraction here is fist sculpture, arranged row on row in show-cases in the reception room of *The Ring* magazine. The museum also displays collections of fighters' photographs, gongs, timers, pocket watches donated by famous boxers and sportsmen, a wide array of boxing gloves, punching bags, and championship belts.

The fist sculpture, created by Dr. Walter H. Jacobs, a dentist, shows in fifty bronze colored plaster casts the huge fists of Primo Carnera, Joe Louis, Muhammad Ali, Rocky Graziano, Jack Johnson, Floyd Patterson, and others. Another memento is a typed letter addressed to the magazine's founder, Nat Fleischer, dated Paris, January 27, 1916, in which Jack Johnson confessed he faked the fight with Jess Willard. Mr. Fleischer, who saw the contest, said it was legitimate. He claimed Johnson spun the yarn in order to make some money on the story.

As there are no other archives of this type, it can be said that this collection of memorabilia has real historical value for boxing buffs.

THE PIERPONT MORGAN LIBRARY
Address: 29 East 36th St., New York, N.Y., 10016.
Phone: 685-0008

Days: Tuesdays through Saturdays, 10:30–5; Sundays, 1–5; closed
Sundays and Mondays in July; closed in August.
Admission: Suggested contribution $1.00.

Subway: IRT Lexington Ave. to 33rd St. station.
Bus: Fifth or Madison Ave. bus to 36th St.
Auto: North on Madison or Park. Limited garage parking.

Special Restrictions: No cameras allowed.

Sales Desk: Books, cards, slides.

The Pierpont Morgan Library serves as a reminder of the Victorian era
when Murray Hill was a fashionable residential section containing, in
the last decades of the nineteenth century, dwellings of many of New
York's Four Hundred—the Belmonts, Rhinelanders, Tiffanys, Have-
meyers, and its leading citizen, J. Pierpont Morgan, financier and
collector.

Morgan began collecting from the time he went abroad to school in
1854. Wealthy and educated, he felt no need to rely on the taste or
judgment of art experts. He bought what he liked. Morgan believed the
surest way to learn about art was to keep looking at it. His father,
Junius Morgan, had also been a collector. He owned a six-page letter
written by George Washington in 1788 expressing his hopes for the new
nation. The letter is in the library today.

It was not until 1890, when Junius Morgan was killed in a carriage
accident on the Riviera, that Pierpont Morgan began to collect in
earnest, and on a grand scale. He bought a copy of the Gutenberg Bible
on vellum, four Shakespeare folios, and manuscripts by Keats, Dickens,
and Byron, to name a few. Eventually he began to accumulate whole
libraries of other collectors. In ten years his collection assumed monumental proportions. At that point he commissioned the architectural
firm of McKim, Mead and White to provide a beautiful setting for his
treasured manuscripts and works of art. Charles F. McKim undertook
the assignment himself, and in 1906 finished the Renaissance palazzo
built in the classic Greek manner of fitted marble blocks. The building
has become one of New York's classic landmarks.   51

By the time of Morgan's death, in 1913, his library was renowned
as the finest private collection in the United States. In his will, Morgan
said, "It has been my desire and intention to make some suitable dis-
position of my collections which would render them permanently

available for the instruction and pleasure of the American people." His son continued the collections with the assistance of Miss Belle Da Costa Greene, library director for forty-three years. In 1924, believing that the library had achieved too important a position to remain in private hands, J. P. Morgan transferred it to a board of trustees, with an endowment to provide for maintenance. It was incorporated as a public reference library.

In the mansion around the corner, at Madison and 37th, Pierpont's son, J. P. Morgan lived. The landmark was apparently slated for demolition. In 1945, two years after J. P. Morgan died, the Lutheran Church in America bought the building for $245,000. The old mansion is a forty-five-room Victorian brownstone, built in the 1840s, in Renaissance revival style, with graceful balconies and wrought-iron grillwork. It is separated from the library by a small garden.

The main entrance to the Morgan Library is through the Annex, at the corner of Madison and 36th Street. This was originally the site of Pierpont's house. A scholars' reading room, on the right, is open for study and research by accredited students and research workers. The library issues a four-page folder of stringent rules pertaining to the use of its material.

The only manuscripts that can be seen by the general public are those on exhibition, under glass, to the side of the reading room. Except for periods during the summer, there are frequent exhibitions of varying duration. The long corridor that leads to the two principal galleries contains exhibitions of drawings, manuscripts, prints, and book bindings, and a literature sales section.

In the West Room, the study, Pierpont Morgan was host to royalty, politicians, ecclesiastical figures, foreign dignitaries, art dealers, collectors, scholars, intellectuals, writers, and the group of bankers whom Morgan assembled there to stem the financial panic of 1907. The walls are hung with a silk damask of intense red that provides a magnificent background for the paintings, sculpture, massive furniture, stained-glass windows, marble mantelpiece, and decorated ceiling. A handsome marble vestibule separates the West Room from the East Room.

The East Room is stacked from floor to ceiling with three tiers of bookcases. A huge tapestry hangs over a monumental marble fireplace, and stairs used to reach the two upper tiers of books appear when the bookcases nearest the doors are half turned, like a revolving door. A modern electronic fire-detection system and an atmospheric control system protect some of the greatest literary treasures in the Western Hemisphere.

53

The library is outstanding in the fields of English, American, French, and Italian autograph manuscripts and medieval and Renaissance manuscripts from the sixth to the sixteenth centuries. The books date from the inception of printing, and include many from the press of the first

The Pierpont Morgan Library.

East Room, The Pierpont Morgan Library (Ezra Stoller photo).

English printer, William Caxton. There is also a collection of etchings by Rembrandt.

The library maintains an active acquisition program. Its most recent achievement was the purchase of the second edition of the Book of Hours made for Catherine of Cleves. These books of the fourteenth and fifteenth centuries were commissioned by individuals for their private devotions and were profusely illuminated with miniatures. For over a hundred years it was believed that this Book of Hours, belonging to the Guennol Collection on Long Island, was complete. It was then found that another part existed. The two parts of the book were united permanently at the Morgan Library and are on exhibition from time to time. With its 157 dazzling miniatures, it is the finest Dutch manuscript in existence.

GUINNESS WORLD RECORDS EXHIBIT HALL
Address: 350 Fifth Ave. (at 34th Street), New York, N.Y., 10001.
Phone. 947-2335

Days: Daily 9:30—7, April through September; 10—5:30 October through March.
Admission: $1.50 adults; $1.25 children (also family rates).

Subway: All subways to 34th Street station.
Bus: Fifth Ave. bus or 6th Ave. bus to 34th St.
Auto: Limited side street parking garages.

Lectures & Tours: Arranged by calling 532-7160. Teachers free with groups.

The Guinness World Records Exhibit Hall has the good fortune to be conveniently located in one of New York's greatest tourist attractions, The Empire State Building. The building was completed in 1931 and holds a world record of sorts with a million and a half visitors annually and has a lifetime visitors record, to date, of 52,793,429. It has the world's tallest TV tower, 1,472 feet, and the structure is still one of the modern wonders of the world.

The Guinness Exhibit Hall was inspired by Norris and Ross McWhirter, authors of *The Guinness Book of World Records* (Sterling Publishing, New York), and the exhibits are highlights from the book. There is no shortage of adjectives to describe these records: the world's largest and smallest, slowest and fastest, zaniest and cleverest, cheapest and costliest, heaviest and lightest, most unusual, most fascinating, most dramatic, the finest, longest, fastest and, of course, the greatest.

The 200 plus exhibits are categorically arranged under a compendium of oddities that comprise human, animal and natural phenomena. The exhibits are scaled to life size. One entire wall has informative and amusing framed certificates issued by *The Guinness Book of Records:* to those who have achieved a world record for such bizarre things as most times struck by lightning (five times); holding breath underwater (13 minutes, 42½ seconds); walking backwards (8,000 miles); needle-threading (3,795 strands through a No. 13 needle in two hours); cars wrecked (1,958 career record) and voracious smoking (110 cigarettes for 30 seconds in the Oddball Olympics of 1974).

THE NEW YORK PUBLIC LIBRARY

Address: Fifth Ave. at 42nd St., New York, N.Y., 10018.
Phone: 790-6262

Days: Mondays, Tuesdays, Wednesdays, Fridays and Saturdays, 10—6; closed Thursdays, Sundays and holidays.
Admission: Free.

Subway: (1) IND 6th Ave. to 42nd St. station, then east. (2) IRT Lexington Ave. to 42nd St. station, then west.
Bus: Fifth Ave. or Madison Ave. bus to 42nd St.
Auto: No parking available.

Gift Shop: Publications sales desk in main lobby.

56 It is difficult to imagine the time when anything else was on the site where the New York Public Library now stands. But before this monumental library was built in 1911—taking 14 years—the enormous high-walled brick basin of the Croton Reservoir stood on the corner of what is now one of the busiest intersections in the United States. The library,

The Guinness World Records Exhibit Hall is in the Empire State Building.

designed by Carrere & Hastings, is deeply set back from Fifth Avenue, ornamented with Corinthian columns, sculpture, water fountains, urns, and the two famous library lions, of the species that appears in civic architecture from Trafalgar Square to Baltimore to Fifth Avenue.

The New York Public Library is second in size in America only to the Library of Congress. The entire system consists of eighty community branches, four mobile units, the main reference building on Fifth Avenue, general reference at Mid-Manhattan on East 40th Street, and the Newspaper Collection on West 43rd Street. The Donnell Library Center on West 53rd Street features an extensive art library, children's section and foreign language library. The Library for the Blind and Physically Handicapped at Avenue of the Americas and Spring Street has over 80,000 talking books, 3,500 tapes, and 12,000 volumes of braille. The library is a result of the consolidation of three private libraries founded separately by John Jacob Astor, James Lenox, and Samuel Jones Tilden. These original libraries constitute the Research libraries, largely supported today by private funds. The daily attendance is over 8,500.

Among its invaluable holdings are the handwritten copy of Washington's Farewell Address, the first Gutenberg Bible brought to America, Jefferson's early draft of the Declaration of Independence, the Dongan Charter of New York City, dated 1686; and a copy of the New York *Gazette* dated 1726, the first newspaper published in New York. The library itself regularly publishes bibliographies, facsimiles, and material concerning literary research.

The library has an invaluable collection of pamphlets, many of which are the only ones in existence. The same is true for its countless periodicals, journals, broadsides, scrapbooks, song sheets, and other documents.

A logical starting point to see the exhibits is the entrance hall at the top of the stairs at the Fifth Avenue entrance. In the enormous lobby are a series of display cases in which a wide variety of books are regularly exhibited. "The Bible and Its Illustrators," "Illustrations from Dante," "Gaelic Books," "Music of the Shakers," and "Images of America" are titles of exhibitions in recent years.

A comprehensive explanation of the development of printing is displayed along the left corridor. At the right side of the lobby a large sales shop carries a wide range of publications pertaining to book research, techniques, and the art of printing and letters.

Halls on the third floor are lined with Currier & Ives prints of the "Life of the Fireman" and colored stone engravings of a number of American cities. These early views are from the Phelps Stokes Collection.

The Exhibition Room (318) is open to the public. It offers changing displays of manuscripts, mainly from the Berg Collection of English

59

and American literature. Original manuscripts are often illegible and bear numerous corrections, but they are of special interest to students and scholars who may see here manuscripts by many famous authors.

Paintings by John Trumbull, Gilbert Stuart, and Joshua Reynolds are in the library's collection. In the central hall hangs a classic example of the Hudson River School of painting by Asher Brown Durant, who depicted two of his friends, William Cullen Bryant and Thomas Cole, standing on a rocky ledge overlooking a peaceful gorge. The works of art are changed from time to time.

In the south corridor are the Print Gallery, the Print Room (308), and Art and Architecture (313), which are open to the public. Some of the other rooms, such as the Berg Collection (320), Arents Collec-

Entrance hall of the library.

tion (324), Manuscripts (319), and Rare Books (303), require a special admission card from the director's office. But for the most part, the general visitor strolling through the building would be sufficiently occupied by the rooms and resources open to the public.

The Central Card Catalogue (315) has eight million file cards, in ten thousand card trays, that cover every imaginable subject. After a specific book title has been found in the card file and a call slip filed, it is then routed through pneumatic tubes to the proper section of the stacks. Books are then located along the eighty miles of shelves, sent upstairs on electric lifts, announced on an electric indicator, and then picked up by the reader in either one of the huge main reading rooms. They are two blocks long, fifty feet high, cover a half acre and seat nearly eight hundred readers. On the open shelves there are two thousand dictionaries, encyclopedias, reference guides, and a copy of every phone book in the country. Also near the reading rooms are the history and genealogy rooms.

The second floor occasionally has an exhibition relating to New York history, with maps, manuscripts, and documents. It also houses the Jewish, Slavonic, and Oriental Literature departments and the Economics ànd Sociology divisions. The first floor, in addition to exhibitions, houses the Science and Technology departments and Periodicals and Maps. The Popular Library and Picture Collection are on the ground floor reached by an entrance on 42nd Street.

The New York Public Library is a unique American institution—responsive to the needs of the diverse population that pursues knowledge. Generations of disadvantaged Americans have made use of its treasures, enriching both themselves and their society.

Perhaps the best way to describe the value of the New York Public Library is to quote from one of its own booklets, written by Richard W. Couper. "The quality that makes the Library great is one that runs deeper than men and books. It is the quality of freedom. This is a building that takes no sides because it presents all sides. It grants its visitors the dignity of free access to information . . . [and] operates on the belief that free men will find the truth."

MUSEUM OF BROADCASTING

Address: 1 East 53rd St., New York, N.Y., 10022.
Phone: 752-7684 (administration, 752-4690; groups, 752-0577)

Days: Tuesdays through Saturdays, 12—5.
Admission: $1.00 adults, $.50 children.

Subway: IND "E" or "F" train to Fifth Ave.
Bus: Fifth or Sixth Ave. bus to 53rd St.
Auto: Limited garage parking; no meters.

Membership: Residents, $30; students, $20.

The Museum of Broadcasting is dedicated to the study and preservation of the more than 50 year history of American radio and television broadcasting. It has been housed in a small building next to Paley Park since its opening in 1976.

The Museum's collection of taped programs spans the entire period from the 1920s to the present. It provides a living document of this era's changing arts, attitudes and technologies. The Museum also maintains a library of rare scripts, as well as books and periodicals on broadcasting.

This is the first collection of its kind designed specifically for public use. All program material is preserved on either audiotape or videotape, with each entry described in an extensive computer-generated cross-indexed card catalogue. Once a program is selected, it can be monitored at one of the eight broadcast console booths.

The uses of this fascinating museum are varied: a student of journalism compares the style of reporters from Ed Murrow to Barbara Walters; a sociologist studies the portrayal of women in 1950 commercials; a mother and her children watch Mary Martin as Peter Pan; a space age cultist revels in Orson Welles' "War of the Worlds"; a popculture critic studies the Beatles' first tour in America and a political analyst watches Joe McCarthy's self-defense on "See It Now." The riches of the Museum of Broadcasting are many.

Most of the radio and television programs are available for public study for the first time here since they were originally broadcast. Some of the earliest Presidential broadcasts in existence are in the collection. There are early speeches by Warren G. Harding as well as campaign and inaugural speeches by Hoover, Roosevelt, Kennedy and Jimmy Carter.

62   Rare musical, comedy and dramatic material from the 1920s includes the Rhythm Boys with Paul Whiteman's Orchestra and "Jack Oakie's College" featuring 13-year-old Judy Garland. There are numerous broadcasts from World War II plus propaganda messages made by Lord Haw Haw, Axis Sally, and Tokyo Rose. Other highlights of the

Radio reporting in the 1930's from the New York American.

Museum's radio collection include a full catalogue of the Columbia Workshop, the earliest version of Amos 'n' Andy, and radio coverage of Charles Lindbergh's triumphant return to the U.S. in 1927. There is also a fully indexed file of vintage commercials.

63

THE MILL AT BURLINGTON HOUSE
Address: 1345 Avenue of the Americas, New York, N.Y., 10019.
Phone: 333-3622

Days: November through April, Tuesdays through Saturdays, 10–6; closed Sundays and Mondays.
Admission: Free. Group tours available.

A textile mill in the heart of New York City.

Subway: (1) IND 6th Ave. to 49th St. station. (2) IND 8th Ave. to 7th Ave. station.
Bus: Sixth Ave. or 7th Ave. bus to 54th St.
Auto: North on 6th Ave. Limited garage parking.

At Burlington House a trip through The Mill lets you see the operation of many textile mills under one roof, shows you how fibers are made from the raw materials of nature, and in a colorful slide display tells some of the ways in which textiles serve man.

When you enter The Mill you find yourself on a moving walkway, longest of its kind. It moves at twenty feet per minute for a 155-foot tour through the world of textiles; it is probably the most compact eight minutes of information dispensed anywhere in Manhattan.

The moving walkway progresses through a total education in textile manufacturing in which you see the various raw materials of textiles and the unique machinery and methods of processing them.

Many manufacturing processes and machines are to be seen here: spinning frame, dye vats, warper, circular doubleknit machines, hosiery-knitting machines, hosiery-boarding machines, Jacquard loom, shuttleless loom, raschel machine, and the carpet-tufting machine.

A third section of this educational exhibit shows in a dazzling display of images some of the ways in which Burlington fabrics serve us. This sound-slide presentation consists of seventy rear-view slide projectors, all moving to the beat of a lively rock sound.

There are more than 5,000 color slides in this display, and each sectioni is programmed on a punched tape to flash in a certain sequence. You see these images at the rate of 1,500 a minute and quickly get the Burlington message—"We're glad you made the trip through The Mill and we hope that the next time you put on a shirt of a pair of socks or a dress you'll realize that a lot of skill, a lot of knowledge, a lot of complex machinery, and a lot of people made them possible."

MUSEUM OF AMERICAN FOLK ART
Address: 49 West 53rd St., New York, N.Y., 10019.
Phone: 581-2474

Days: Open daily, except Mondays, 10:30—5:30.
Admission: $1.00; students, $.50

Subway: IND 8th Ave. "E" train or 6th Ave. "F" train to Fifth Ave. station (53rd St.).
Bus: Fifth Ave. or 6th Ave. bus to 53rd St.
Auto: Limited garage parking.

Membership: Annual membership $18.00 up. Benefits include admission to all exhibitions for two persons, newsletters, invitations to special lectures and films.

The Museum of American Folk Art was opened in 1963. It is the first museum in New York City devoted exclusively to the exhibition and study of the work of untutored native artist-craftsmen. The fascination of folk art and its universal appeal to housewives, children, collectors, businessmen, artists, designers, and teen-agers have already established this museum as a permanent and useful member of the art community.

Aside from providing entertainment and education, the museum has another purpose: "To display and collect the arts which embody the creative individuality of our people and to offer a historical background for the contemporary American scene." The museum acts also as a clearinghouse for research and information on folk artists, known by name or by style, and eventually hopes to establish a folk-art index of photographs, slides, and manuscripts documenting the works of American folk artists.

The museum occupies one floor of a spacious studio building on the same street as the Museum of Modern Art and the Museum of Contemporary Crafts. Although its quarters, by comparison with other museums, could be considered small, the quality and depth of its exhibitions more than compensate. In its short lifespan the museum has offered impressive exhibitions. "Turning in the Wind" displayed rare and unusual nineteenth-century weathervanes, hand-carved weather devices, and wind toys in such forms as angels, butterflies, chickens, soldiers on horseback, all painstakingly carved and sensitively colored. These objects showed the strength and individuality of the folk tradition in American art and design.

Other exhibits have been "Rubbings from New England Gravestones," one of the oldest forms of folk art; "The Art of the Decoy"; "The American Image," paintings and sculpture featuring American symbols and Presidents; the paintings of Erastus Salisbury Field, one of the most famous of nineteenth-century American folk artists; "Religion in Wood: A Study in Shaker Design"—an outstanding collection of Shaker furnishings; and "Santos: The Religious Folk Art of New Mexico," in which carved figures and painted panels expressed in naive, colorful terms the splendor and horror of Christ's Passion, together with figures of Spanish saints.

From its members and from private donors the museum is gradually accumulating its own permanent collection. Notable acquisitions have been two limestone sculptures of Will Edmondson, a Nashville folk carver; a wooden gate of c. 1872 made to look like a contemporary American flag; a huge yellow weathervane in the form of an Indian chief and called "Chief Tammany"; a carved and painted eagle made about 1900 by Bernier of Maine, some decoys, Sunday-school samplers, and early tin toys.

As the museum grows its programs expand. Five new shows, historic village and house tours, lectures and movies, and folk-art tours of Central Europe are part of its future plans.

67

The angel Gabriel blows his horn
in the Museum of American Folk Art.

MUSEUM OF CONTEMPORARY CRAFTS

Address: 29 West 53rd St. (between 5th and 6th Aves.), New York, N.Y., 10019.
Phone: 977-8989

Days: Open Tuesdays through Saturdays, 11—6; Sundays, 1—6. Closed Mondays. Library open Tuesdays through Fridays, 12—5.
Admission: Adults, $1.00; children, $.25

Subway: IND 8th Ave. "E" train or 6th Ave. "F" train to 5th Ave. station (53rd St.).
Bus: Fifth Ave. or 6th Ave. bus to 53rd St.
Auto: Limited garage parking.

Membership: Membership categories start at $18.00. Privileges include subscription to *Craft Horizons,* other discounts.

The Museum of Contemporary Crafts has gradually elevated public consciousness of crafts as a true form of artistic expression. Its presentations offer living craft art, changing exhibitions of ceramics, woven and printed textiles, metalwork, enameling, and fibers. The museum also encourages and stimulates working artists, and has shown the work of thousands of craftsmen since it was opened in 1956 by its parent organization, the American Craftsmen's Council.

The museum offers about five shows a year, which have attracted some 110,000 visitors annually. Their variety is indicated by their titles: "Stage Design Models," "Louis Comfort Tiffany," "World of Puppets," "1000 Years of Pottery in America," "Contemporary French Bookbinding," "Glass: Czechoslovakia and Italy," "The Art of Personal Adornment," "Plastics as Plastics," and "The Great American Foot." A series of Participatory Exhibition/Events "Acts, for Total Involvement" included phosphorescent inflatables and evanescent shadow sculptures.

Much of the success of recent exhibitions can be attributed to the dynamic and inspiring leadership of Paul J. Smith, Director. One of the recent shows that drew a record attendance was entitled "Made with Paper," an unusual experimental exhibition technique that invited and encouraged visitor participation and involvement.

Usually there are three exhibitions held at once, a group show, a one-man show, and a survey show with a special theme. The main gallery on the first floor and second level is used for the leading exhibit. The Little Gallery, a large alcove on the second floor, is set aside for showing the work of one craftsman. The third-floor museum gallery is also used to display the crafts of a single artist or a theme exhibition. The Research and Education Department, the Service and Information

69

Example of early American folk art.

*Thirty-foot legs advertising
"The Great American Foot" exhibition.*

*New forms in ceramics from California
at the Museum of Contemporary Crafts.*

Center of the museum, and the Crafts Council Headquarters and Research Library are at 44 West 53rd Street.

The council is a nonprofit national membership organization chartered by the Board of Regents of New York and was founded in 1943 by Mrs. Vanderbilt Webb. The museum opened in 1956. Primarily, the council acts as an educational and professional service organization "to promote every aspect of craftsmanship and the use of craft products for the enrichment of our lives and culture." It receives no government support other than tax exemption.

Although there is nothing for sale in the museum, crafts can be purchased through its affiliate, The Museum Shop, across the street. The Council also keeps up-to-date files on craftsmen with examples of their work. These files are open to the public on request. It is a unique repository of biographic and pictorial information on twentieth-century craftsmen. There are also a catalogue and file on craft schools. Another council service is a Portable Museum, consisting of slide kits, films, and other visual aids about crafts and craftsmen. These kits may be rented.

The Council also sponsors lectures and conferences. It is responsible for the formation of the World Crafts Council, an international organization for facilitating communications in the world of crafts; and it founded the School for American Craftsmen at the Rochester Institute of Technology. It is the publisher of *Craft Horizons*.

71

THE MUSEUM OF MODERN ART

Address: 11 West 53rd St., New York, N.Y., 10019.
Phone: 956-7070 and 956-7078 (Films)

Days: Monday through Saturday, 11–6; Thursdays until 9; Sundays, 12 noon to 6. Closed Wednesdays and Christmas Day.
Admission: Adults $2.00, children under 16, $.75. Student group rates by advance arrangement. Tuesdays by contribution.

Subway: IND 8th Ave. "E" train or 6th Ave. "F" train to 5th Ave. station (53rd St.).
Bus: Fifth Ave. or 6th Ave. bus to 53rd St.
Auto: Limited garage parking.

Restaurant: Garden restaurant has complete luncheons, tea. Dinner on Thursday only. Members' restaurant in Penthouse.

Gift Shop: Museum shops in lobby and 23 and 27 W. 53rd St. are well stocked with books, catalogues, reproductions, stationery, posters, slides, Christmas cards, and toys.

Special Events: Extensive film program, art-lending service, concerts, symposia, lectures, avant-garde events; see calendar.

Membership: $25.00 and up; student, $12.50 and up. Benefits include free admission to museum, invitations to previews, exclusive use of Penthouse restautant, free publications, discounts on books; call museum.

Tours: Gallery talks as announced; Acoustiguides available.

At the Museum of Modern Art trends are launched, tastes formed, and the social scene is set. The museum is the place to view a Picasso, have lunch in the Sculpture Garden, listen to a lecture, see a classic film, steep yourself in jazz, drink champagne at an opening, meet your wife or friends, take your children, and, of course, see the avant-garde art of America and Europe. As an important contemporary influence, the museum has made its mark on New York by making a new level of aesthetic standards available to a popular audience.

72   The Museum of Modern Art was the product of three pioneering collectors: Abby Aldrich Rockefeller, wife of John D. Rockefeller, Jr., Lillie P. Bliss, and Mrs. Cornelius J. Sullivan. They were joined by A. Conger Goodyear, Frank Crowninshield, Mrs. Murray Crane, Dr. Paul J. Sachs, Stephen C. Clark, Chester Dale, Duncan Phillips, and Sam Lewisohn in forming the museum. In July, 1929, the Regents of the

"St. John the Baptist" by Francois Auguste Rodin.

University of the State of New York granted a charter for "establishing and maintaining a museum of modern art, encouraging and developing the study of modern arts and furnishing popular instruction." The founders intended to establish a collection of the immediate ancestors of the modern movement and the most important living masters. Forming a collection of contemporary art was in itself a gamble, but to attempt to establish a museum of modern art was a daring commitment during the beginning and worst years of the Great Depression.

Alfred H. Barr, Jr., who was then twenty-seven, was appointed director of the museum. The first exhibition opened on November 7, 1929, in the Heckscher Building at 730 Fifth Avenue.

This landmark exhibition contained 35 Cézannes, 28 van Goghs, 21 Gauguins, and 17 Seurats, and attracted 47,000 visitors during the first month. Until this significant moment not one museum in Manhattan owned a single canvas by these artists, most of whom had been dead for forty years. Despite the Armory Show of 1913, America was still hostile to modern art.

"Guernica" by Pablo Picasso.

In 1939, Mrs. John D. Rockefeller, Jr., and her husband (who hated modern art) deeded to the museum the land for its present buildings. Ultimately, she gave the museum 2,000 objects of art—190 paintings, 1,630 prints, 137 drawings, and 44 pieces of sculpture. Lillie P. Bliss also left the museum the greater part of her masterpieces by Cézanne, Matisse, Picasso, Seurat, Redon, Gauguin, and other artists. When Mary Sullivan died, her collection was auctioned at the Parke-Bernet Galleries. One painting by Derain was bought by Mrs. Rockefeller and given to the museum in memory of Mrs. Sullivan.

During the 1930s the collections grew through acquisition funds made possible by Mrs. Simon Guggenheim, whose generosity for over thirty years provided the largest purchase fund for works of exceptional importance. Mainly through the generosity of some nine hundred donors, the museum has acquired the most important collection of twentieth-century painting and sculpture in the world.

The collections have grown from 2,600 items to nearly 33,000 works of art. Among its finest and most popular examples of paintings are Picasso's "Les Demoiselles d'Avignon" and the antiwar "Guernica," Rousseau's "The Dream," Matisse's "The Moroccans" and "The Dance," Marc Chagall's "I and the Village," Braque's "Woman with a Mandolin," Max Beckmann's "The Departure," Edward Hopper's "House by the Railroad" (the first painting acquired), Joseph Pickett's "Manchester Valley," Joan Miró's "Composition," Monet's "Water Lilies," and Jackson Pollock's "Number 1." The collections also include masterpieces by Bonnard, Toulouse-Lautrec, Cézanne, Kandinsky, Modigliani, Mondrian, Nolde, Léger, Rouault, Shahn, Tchelitchew, van Gogh, Weber, Gorky, de Kooning, Magritte, Newman, Wyeth, Davis, Vasarely, Rothko, and Albers— to name just a very few.

The museum's collections are intended to help the visitor to understand modern art. The great innovations in style, technique, subject matter, and aesthetic goals that characterize modern art may be seen in about forty galleries on the second and third floors. These permanent collections progress in clearly defined categories of art with works of a particular artist often grouped to show significant periods of development.

Starting in the Alfred H. Barr galleries, there are works by Impressionists, Postimpressionists, Anti-Impressionists, Neo-Impressionists, the Fauves, the German Expressionists, Early and Late Cubists, Italian Futurists, Expressionist Abstractionists, Geometric Abstractionists, and Primitive Realists. There is a sampling of Fantasy (di Chirico), Dada (Duchamp), Surrealism (Dali) and Realism (Wyeth). Some of these works of art may not be in exact location described.

75

Nearly a third of the collections are devoted to the post World War II Americans known as The New York School of Painting, which includes Jackson Pollock, Hans Hofmann, Clyfford Still, Bradley Walker

Tomlin, Franz Kline, Willem de Kooning, Robert Motherwell, Mark Rothko, Adolph Gottlieb, Ad Reinhardt, Mark Tobey, Alfonso Ossorio, Jack Tworkov, Barnett Newman, and Philip Guston. *The Artist's World* by Fred W. McDarrah, an E. P. Dutton paperback published in 1961, was a pictorial documentation of this art movement.

Many of these artists had a profound influence on art communities throughout the world. Authorities admit that these postwar American artists, and the daring judgment, evaluation and selections of Alfred H. Barr, Jr., ex-Director, and Dorothy C. Miller, retired Senior Curator, established New York as the art capital of the world.

The Museum of Modern Art also collects second-generation Abstract Expressionism, Hard-Edge Abstractions, Pop Art, Op Art, kinetic constructions, combines, collages, assemblages, and conceptual pieces. There are works by Jasper Johns, Robert Rauschenberg, Robert Indiana, Ellsworth Kelly, Frank Stella, Jim Dine, Donald Judd, Larry Rivers, Lucas Samaras, Andy Warhol, Claes Oldenburg, Richard Anuszkiewicz, Allan D'Arcangelo, Roy Lichtenstein, and James Rosenquist.

In sculpture the museum excels in works by Constantin Brancusi, Alexander Calder, Gaston Lachaise, Jacques Lipchitz, Henry Moore, Auguste Rodin, David Smith, Marino Marini, Aristide Maillol, Julio Gonzalez, Naum Gabo, Pablo Picasso, David Hare, Herbert Ferber, Alberto Giacometti, George Segal, and Mark di Suvero.

In the sculpture collection are also pieces by Seymour Lipton, Theodore Roszak, Ibram Lassaw, Isamu Noguchi, Richard Lippold. A number of well-known classic works including Lachaise's "Standing Woman," Rodin's "St. John," and Matisse's "Four Reliefs of Backs," are in the Abby Aldrich Rockefeller Sculpture Garden of the museum.

The Philip L. Goodwin Galleries of Architecture and Design include architectural material, graphic design, furniture (especially chairs), and industrial objects. Some of the twentieth-century designs include Thonet bentwood chairs, Art Nouveau Tiffany glass, Bauhaus textiles, machine art, kitchenware, tableware, and crafts. Amont the designers are Ludwig Mies van der Rohe, Marcel Breuer, Alvar Aalto, Eero Saarinen, and Charles Eames. The collection comprises over a thousand examples selected for quality and historical significance.

The Abby Aldrich Rockefeller Print Room, which can be visited by appointment, can be entered from the third-floor galleries. Her gift of 1,600 prints formed the nucleus of this study collection, now grown to 10,000 original prints by some 1,700 artists from 55 countries. The collection is supplemented by over 800 illustrated books and 3,000 posters and graphics, some on exhibition in the Paul J. Sachs Galleries.

The Edward Steichen Photography Center emphasizes the historic phases of photography. The museum has exhibited photographs since 1932 and it was the first art museum to accord photography a regular

Abstract-Expressionist paintings by Still, Gottlieb, and Kline (left to right).

and important share of its program. Its memorable exhibits have included one-man shows of photographs by Walker Evans, Eugene Atget, Dorothea Lange, Bernice Abbott, and Henri Cartier-Bresson, as well as the historic "Family of Man" show.

The museum's other major programs cover the range of popular culture including the presentation of vintage Hollywood films, such as *Intolerance, Duck Soup, The Invisible Man, King Kong, Citizen Kane,* and other classics that marked distinct stages of cinematic development. Approximately 3,500 films and 1,000,000 stills and other unique archival material have been acquired by the Film Department since it was founded in 1935.

The Lillie P. Bliss International Study Center makes available to scholars, students, and artists concerned with the visual arts a unique combination of 50,000 original works of art in the museum collections in flexible open exhibition-type storage space located in the north wing.

Paintings not on public exhibit are hung on specially designed sliding aluminum panels, sculptures are placed on low pallets, and large hanging works are suspended from ceiling hooks for quick and easy viewing. This remarkable exhibition-style storage area can be conveniently seen and studied.

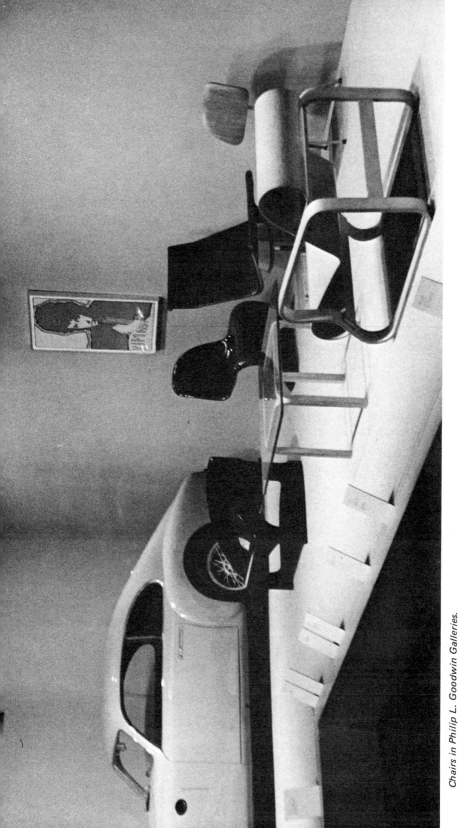

Chairs in Philip L. Goodwin Galleries.

"The River" by Aristide Maillol.

Multigravitational performance.

"Water Lilies" by Claude Monet.

The museum reference library has an electrically operated revolving file that brings files containing up-to-date material on individual artists, including exhibition announcements, press releases, art reviews, catalogues, and cross-reference notices to the researcher when he pushes a button.

The library also has a collection of scrapbooks of the 1913 Armory Show including the official publications, together with postcards, posters, and even examples of the lapel button designed by Arthur B. Davies, which members wore during the exhibition.

The street-level galleries are usually devoted to the changing exhibition program, a principal activity of the museum. The influence and magnitude of the institution's aesthetic experiments reach far beyond the art community, and frequently affect everything from fashions to fiction.

Today the museum's total annual attendance is about a million people, equal to the total of its first ten years' attendance. Unlike most museums, it receives no regular city, state, or Federal funds, and is supported primarily by admissions, publication sales, earnings from endowments and contributions, and membership dues, of which there are now about 40,000.

Since its founding in 1929, the Museum of Modern Art has redefined for the benefit of succeeding generations the concepts and ideas that constitute "modern" art. It has broadened modern sensibility to include not only the traditional aesthetics of a painter or sculptor, but also of a photographer, a filmmaker, an architect, and a designer. This renewal and refreshment of our perceptions at the cutting edge of contemporary artists' imagination are what keeps the Museum of Modern Art uniquely modern.

81

Retrospective of Pop Art by Claes Oldenburg.

JAPAN SOCIETY

Address: 333 East 47th St., New York, N.Y., 10017.
Phone: 832-1155

Days: Open daily, 9—5.
Admission: Free.

Subway: IRT Lexington Ave. to 51st St. station.
Bus: First or Second Ave. bus to 47th St.
Auto: Limited garage parking.

Membership: Patron $100; family $40; individual $25; student $10.

The purpose of The Japan Society, founded in 1907, is to advance a mutual understanding and appreciation between the United States and Japan and to generate a cooperative spirit between the two nations. Energy, experience, and dedication combined with innovation have earned the Society international stature both in Japan and the U.S. Symbolic of this recognition was the recent visit to Japan House by Their Majesties, the Emperor and Empress of Japan.

Japan House, headquarters of The Japan Society, was designed by Tokyo architect Junzo Yoshimura. Construction materials are almost entirely American in origin, while treatment and finishes are Japanese in style. The four-story building contains the Lila Acheson Wallace Auditorium, a library, museum gallery, conference rooms, a spacious reception area and two beautiful gardens blending Eastern and Western motifs.

A typical calendar of Japan Society activities is rich in variety, visual beauty and intellectual stimulation with programs that encourage the cultural and intellectual exchange between the two countries. The Japan Society has brought city planners, architects and urban experts of New York and Tokyo together to discuss the urban crisis in both cities. Discussion of Japan's budget, trade and economy, the oil crisis, security and detente, relations with China and northeast Asia, anti-trust laws and legal aspects of corporate responsibility to Japanese society are discussions that brought politicians, lawyers and businessmen together.

Forums have also been held on the Japanese press and public opinion, the role of the intellectual in society, Marxism in Japan, and attitudes toward the West. Japanese women have met to discuss the special adjustments faced by families living in New York, the cultural differences, Japanese food, the educational system and medical problems.

Media-related activities of The Japan Society include briefing sessions by leaders and policymakers to furnish background on current issues.

A print by Suzuki Harunobu (1725-1770) at Japan House.

Another project of The Japan Society is The Sumitomo Fund for Policy Research Studies that provides grants to American institutions for projects on problems affecting U.S.-Japan relationships. The Intellectual Interchange Program fosters understanding through individual exchange of American and Japanese scholars, writers, and public leaders who visit each other's countries and meet with intellectual leaders.

The Japan Society's visual arts program has attracted thousands of visitors to Japan House Gallery to see exhibits such as "The Art Treasures from the Imperial Household," "Tagasode: Whose Sleeves" (the kimono collection of the Knaebo corporation of Osaka), and "Nippon-to: Art Swords of Japan," the first exhibition of sword blades in America. The blades were from the Society for the Preservation of Japanese Art Swords and the National Treasure "Kunimune."

The performing arts program includes classical and avant garde dance concerts, contemporary drama, shakuhachi concerts, lectures, poetry readings based on No drama, and Japanese electronic music.

Foreign film buffs are familiar with the programs at Japan House, which serves as a premiere showcase for new directors and new releases as well as revivals and retrospectives. One recent film premiere featured *The Man Who Skied Down Everest,* a fascinating adventure that showed Olympic Champion Yuichiro Miura in the extraordinary feat of skiing down the south face of Mount Everest. Mr. Miura appeared in person to share his experiences with the audience and to comment on the new film.

Education at The Japan Society means furthering the understanding between Japanese and Americans. The Society distributes audio-visual teaching films and video cassettes and maintains a library of 6,000 volumes. Japanese periodicals arrive daily from Japan. *The Japan House Newsletter* covers art, architecture, education and film, while *The Japan Interpreter* covers social, political and literary ideas and opinion. Japanese grammar and conversation classes are also available.

UNITED NATIONS
Address: First Ave. at 46th St., New York, N.Y., 10017.
Phone: 754-1234

Days: Open daily, 9—4:45 (UN sessions held on weekdays only).
Admission: Free (tours: $2.00, adults; $1.50, students).

Subway: All trains to Grand Central Station.
Bus: Crosstown 42nd St. bus to First Ave.
Auto: First or Second Ave. Limited garage parking.

Restaurant: Delegate's dining room; coffee shop and vending machines in public concourse.

Gift Shop: (1) Postal Counter, (2) Gift Center, (3) Souvenir Shop, (4) Bookshop (5) UNICEF Counter all located in public concourse.

Special Events: World Health Day (April 7); Namibia Day (August 26); United Nations Day (October 24); Human Rights Day (December 10); General Assembly Special Disarmament Session (1978); UN Decade for Women (1976—1985); World Conference to Combat Racism (1978); International Year of the Child (1979); International Year for Disabled Persons (1981).

Film Library: Extensive 16mm film library for rental or purchase.

Lectures & Tours: Advance reservations call 754-7713.

The United Nations is probably the greatest tourist attraction in New York. At this juncture, well past its first quarter century, it is a bona fide museum attraction with an artistic, social and humanistic identity. Its concerns go beyond ordinary exhibits of artifacts, parchment documents or heroic sculpture—it is the world's diplomatic assembly symbolizing the brotherhood of all people, with a spiritually uplifting message that goes far beyond the perimeter of its glass and concrete walls. When a visitor goes to the United Nations, it is almost a sacred pilgrimage to a global shrine that embodies the hope that a community of nations can find a way to live in comfort, peace and harmony.

It is not that the Fernand Leger murals, the tapestries, the garden sculpture, or the stained glass windows by Marc Chagall are unimportant. These works are simply overshadowed by the mission of the United Nations, which is uppermost in the minds of visitors.   85

The United Nations came into being on October 24, 1945. The aims and principles of the U.N. remain today as they were then: to maintain international peace and security; to develop friendly rela-

The United Nations.

General Assembly Building.

tions among nations; to achieve international cooperation in solving economic, social, cultural and humanitarian problems and in promoting respect for human rights and fundamental freedom for all. The United Nations is not a world government or a super-state, nor does it legislate. All 149 member states are sovereign and equal.

The main work of the U.N. takes place in the General Assembly and its working organizations: The Security Council, Trusteeship Council, Secretariat, Economic and Social Council, and the International Court.

The visitors' entrance, in the General Assembly building, faces onto the plaza, overlooking the parklike grounds. The General Assembly Hall is the hub of the building. The blue, green and gold hall is 165 feet long and 115 feet wide, with a 75 foot high ceiling. A circular skylight four feet in diameter admits a single shaft of sunlight onto the Assembly floor. At the Italian marble podium are three places for the President of the General Assembly, the Secretary-General and the Under Secretary-General.

Lots drawn before each Assembly session determine which delegation will occupy the first seat in the first row. Delegations then follow in English alphabetical order. All 2,070 seats are equipped with earphones allowing the listener to hear the language being spoken or any of the simultaneous translations.

United Nations headquarters is the diplomatic crossroads of the world and has drawn kings and queens, presidents and prime ministers as well as millions of other people from all corners of the earth.

The U.N. is situated on a 16-acre site overlooking the East River, between 42nd and 48th Streets, in an area formerly occupied by slaughterhouses. Along United Nations Plaza the flags of all member countries fly in a row more than 500 feet long.

Tons of topsoil and fertilizer were brought to the site to provide a planting place for the many varieties of trees, shrubs and flowers. There are some 2,000 prizewinning rose bushes, 185 flowering cherry trees, 52 dwarf fruit trees, as well as hawthorns, sweet gum, pin oaks, sycamores and honey locust trees. Lining the asphalt walks are ilex, myrtle, wisteria, rambler roses and a ground cover of English ivy and plain grass. The site has a cathedral-like quality.

American Bible Society.

AMERICAN BIBLE SOCIETY
Address: 1865 Broadway, New York, N.Y., 10023.
Phone: 581-7400, ext. 367

Days: Mondays through Fridays, 9—4:30; closed holidays.
Admission: Free.

Subway: (1) IRT 7th Ave. to 59th St. station. (2) IND 6th Ave. or 8th
   Ave. to Columbus Circle 59th St. station.
Bus: Eighth Ave. bus to Columbus Circle, or Broadway bus to 63rd St.
Auto: West Side Highway to 57th St. exit, or north or south on Broad-
   way. Garage parking.

Gift Shop: Bibles, testaments, portions, selections.

88   *Tours:* Available for individuals and school or church groups.

Bible House, home of the American Bible Society, quartered in an
ultramodern structure near Columbus Circle, is a nonprofit organization supported by voluntary contributions from individuals and or-

Listening booths at Lincoln Center Library.

ganizations and seeks to make available to *every person on earth* "without note or comment" the Holy Scriptures in the language he can read and understand.

This Herculean task is slowly being accomplished with the aid of IBM computers, which process 30,000 donor transactions a day, store inventories of Scriptures and literature on magnetic tape, computer-process thousands of daily orders, and computer-mail millions of volumes each week. Its annual world circulation is over 100 million copies. These supersophisticated techniques of marketing a single ancient book only emphasize that the Holy Bible is as pertinent to life today as it was a thousand years ago.

Since Bible House was founded in 1816 it has produced over 750 million Bibles in 1,431 translations. Its modern library contains 29,280 volumes in 1,337 languages and dialects, the largest collection of its kind in the Western Hemisphere. A handwritten copy of the Latin Vulgate completed around the year 1250 and a Hebrew scroll 72 feet long sewn together with flaxen thread are its prized possessions.

The Bible House staff is pleasant, and informed escorts will guide both individuals and groups through its computer banks, translation facilities, and art gallery where changing exhibits feature everything from modern paintings to the Dead Sea Scrolls.

LIBRARY AND MUSEUM OF THE PERFORMING ARTS 89
(NEW YORK PUBLIC LIBRARY AT LINCOLN CENTER)
Address: Lincoln Center Plaza North, 111 Amsterdam Ave. at 65th St., New York, N.Y., 10023 (2 entrances).
Phone: 799-2200

Days: Mondays and Thursdays, 10–8; Tuesdays and Wednesdays, 10–6; Fridays and Saturdays, 12–6.
Admission: Free.

Subway: IRT Broadway-7th Ave. to 65th St. station.
Bus: Broadway bus to 65th St. and Broadway.
Auto: Parking garage in Lincoln Center.

Gift Shop: Film and theatre books, souvenirs.

The Library and Museum of the Performing Arts, designed by Eero Saarinen, is in the new Vivian Beaumont building in the Lincoln Center architectural complex. The main entrance is on Amsterdam Avenue and 65th Street. Another entrance on the theatre plaza faces the central pool containing Henry Moore's monumental bronze.

The nucleus of the collection in this library was supplied by the main Reference Branch of the New York Public Library at Fifth Avenue and 42nd Street, where these archives were originally located. The research materials now at Lincoln Center comprise half a million books, pamphlets, periodicals, sheet music, scores, manuscripts, phonograph records, photographs, theatre programs, clipping files, scrapbooks of reviews and memorabilia. A recent addition to the theatre collection are Florence Vandamm's prints and negatives of over 2,000 professional theatre productions between 1925 and 1950.

A unique section of the Library and Museum of the Performing Arts is the Rodgers and Hammerstein Archives of Recorded Sound, the first major sound library. It contains over 200,000 records that reflect the development of recorded sound from its beginnings to the present.

The library also contains the Dance Collection, the world's only archive devoted solely to the literature and iconography of the dance. The Music Division, covering classical, jazz, pop, musical comedy, and experimental ventures, contains over 200,000 volumes.

The museum section is primarily for semipermanent and loan exhibitions of material from library collections, other Lincoln Center institutions, and the collections of other New York City museums. It has been suggested that the museum also house and exhibit the Society of Strings collections of great and rare violins.

The Main Gallery is devoted to thematic exhibitions dealing with various aspects of the arts. The Astor Gallery features exhibitions of autograph scores, original costume designs, models for dance productions, and manuscripts. The gallery was dedicated by Mrs. Vincent Astor in memory of her late husband, who played a major role in the development of the New York Library. The Amsterdam Gallery is devoted to various art exhibitions.

The plaza gallery level has circulating books, records and a gift

90

Henry Moore's great bronze sculpture dominates the plaza in front of the museum.

shop of material related to the performing arts. The Mezzanine contains a children's library intended to develop a child's interest in, and appreciation of, the performing arts. The Heckscher Oval is a functional playhouse area where children attend story hour, Punch and Judy shows, fairs, festivals, and other activities for the pleasure and education of young people.

CENTRAL PARK ZOO

Address: 64th St. and Fifth Ave., New York, N.Y., 10021.
Phone: 360-8213

Days: Open daily. Buildings open 11—5. Gates close at dusk.
Admission: Free. (No pets allowed in zoo.)

Subway: BMT Astoria train to 60th St. station. North 4 blocks.
Bus: Fifth Ave. or Madison Ave. to 64th St.
Auto: Two hours' free parking in Central Park Boathouse and Rambles parking lots behind zoo. Commercial garages on crosstown streets between 5th and Park Aves.

Restaurants: Terrace Cafeteria and Outdoor Café: hot dishes, sandwiches, snacks. Carretinas: snacks, soft drinks. Beer garden.

Gift Shop: Toys and small souvenirs at carretinas near sea-lion pool.

Children's Facilities: Pony cart rides $.25. Children's Zoo: Open daily, 10—5; for children's birthday parties, call 360-8213.

The interest, excitement, and charm of the zoo lie only partly in the exhibits. Visible also on any day are the many strata of New York society—the visitors from foreign lands in native dress, very proper ladies and gentlemen, stiff-backed and starched nannies, bearded strangers, blue-jeaned teen-agers, young lovers, and mobs of scrambling children. Eventually everyone in New York goes to the Central Park Zoo—to see the lions, the tigers, sea lions, and monkeys.

In the fascinating monkey house are the forever-swaying gibbon of southeast Asia; the fantastic red-nosed, white-eyed, Halloween-masked, goat-bearded Mandrill; South American spider monkeys; Guinea baboons with their piercing screech; the sloe-eyed white-crowned West African mangabey; and the stump-tail monkey from Malay; and the orangutan, a large, long-armed anthropoid ape that is less closely related to man than are the gorilla and chimpanzee.

92

Children meet barnyard animals at Central Park Zoo.

The Central Park Zoo has its share of lions, tigers, jaguars, leopards, pumas, African camels, elephants and rhinos. But the most fun at the zoo is usually watching the sea lions being fed every afternoon in the center pool below the terrace restaurant.

At the Terrace Cafeteria and Café the food is above average City Park Department fare. The chief virtue of the café is the vantage point it offers to viewers of the passing scene. Seats are at a premium both in winter and summer.

Another principal attraction is the Herbert Lehman Children's Zoo. Old McDonald's Farm, Three Little Pigs, Alice's White Rabbit, and other storybook figures appear in an imaginative setting where city children may encounter domesticated and farm animals in a warm and inviting way.

Girl Scouts admire the Arabian camel.

This jovial whale delights children at the zoo.

The nonanimal attraction at the zoo is the Delacorte clock, which is over the archway between the monkey house and the lion and tiger house. It has bronze animals that tell the hours by striking a big bell.

ABIGAIL ADAMS SMITH MUSEUM
Address: 421 East 61st St. (at York Ave.), New York, N.Y., 10021.
Phone: 838-6878

Days: Mondays to Fridays, 10—4.
Admission: $1.00; school groups and children free.

Subway: IRT Lexington Ave. to 59th St. station.

Bus: First Ave. bus to East 61st St.
Auto: North on First Ave. or East River Drive to 61st St. exit. Ample parking lots.

This landmark was originally a carriage house on the estate of Colonel William Stephens Smith, aide-de-camp to George Washington and husband of Abigail Adams, the daughter of President John Adams.

The house is set on a high embankment about ten feet above 61st Street. Because it is located so far east the house is familiar mainly to the drivers taking the 61st Street exit off the East River Drive.

Abigail Adams Smith Museum.

The estate, once known as "Smith's Folly," dates to 1795. The original twenty-three acre property with its huge mansion facing the East River was considered one of the finest estates in Manhattan. A map of the farm from a survey in 1806 by Joseph F. Mangin is in the New York Historical Society.

In the early 1900s the property was purchased by the Colonial Dames of America, who have made it their headquarters and maintain the exhibition rooms—a music room, dining room, bedrooms, and parlors. Most of the authentic furnishings date from 1810 to 1820.

THE ASIA SOCIETY
Address: 112 East 64th St. (between Park and Lexington Aves.), New York, N.Y., 10021.

Phone: 751-4210

Days: Open Mondays through Saturdays, 10—5; Sundays, 1—5; Thursdays, until 8:30.

Admission: Free.

Subway: IRT Lexington Ave. to 68th St. station. South 4 blocks.
Bus: Madison Ave. or Lexington Ave. to 64th St.
Auto: Limited street parking.

Gift Shop: Catalogues of gallery shows on sale.

Membership: Membership privileges include attendance at lectures
and special publications. Membership fees are: resident $50; con-
tributing $100; sponsor $500; sustaining $1,000.

The modern Asia Society building, designed by Philip Johnson, is situated between Victorian brownstones on a tree-shaded residential
street. The front of the building is faced entirely with a charcoal-
colored glass. From the street the facade appears opaque, but from
inside the building the glass is translucent. The building has seven
floors. The library and lounge are on the first floor, the huge thirty-
five by sixty-foot Gallery is on the second; and the 170-seat lecture
hall and auditorium are in the basement, all open to the public. The
third floor is occouped by the offices of the Japan Society.

The Asia Society is "a non-profit, non-political membership organization founded in 1957 in the belief that there is a continuing need for
greater knowledge of Asia among Americans." The society sponsors
programs dealing with the cultural heritage of Asia. Covering contemporary economic, political, and social questions, these programs are
given by the society's various Country Councils. Each council is composed of Americans familiar with a particular Asian country. The
Country Council programs are open to the membership and invited
guests in the Lecture Hall. The society also presents films, and dance
and music recitals.

The Asia House Gallery exhibits the arts of Asia. It presents three
loan exhibitions each year. Exhibitions have dealt with Rajput paintings,
tea taste in Japanese art, the art of Nepal, and relics of ancient China.
Tape-recorded half-hour lectures by the gallery director, designed to
enlarge the viewer's understanding of each exhibition, may be rented
by visitors for a small sum.

The Asian Literature Program acts as an unofficial and unpaid literary agency for Asian writers by encouraging American book and magazine editors to publish their works. This program handles more than
three hundred manuscripts and proposals a year. The society has also
developed the Asia Library, a series of books designed to acquaint the
general reader with basic historic and contemporary facts on Asian
nations.

In the Education Department, American teachers are invited to im-

97

prove their knowledge of Asian peoples and cultures. The department offers free literature and a course on the peoples and cultures of Asia. The Information and Reference Service answers general questions on Asian topics, and maintains a service for Asian visitors to enable them to make professional and business contacts while visiting New York.

THE FRICK COLLECTION
Address: 1 East 70th St., New York, N.Y., 10021.
Phone: 288-0700

Days: Open daily, 10—6; Sundays, 1—6. Closed Mondays and holidays.
Closed Tuesdays in summer.
Admission: $1.00. Children under 10 not admitted without adult.
Group visits by appointment only.

Subway: IRT Lexington Ave. to 68th St. station. East to 5th Ave.
Bus: Fifth Ave. or Madison Ave. bus to 70th St.
Auto: North on Madison or Park Aves. Limited street parking.

Gift Shop: Postcards, reproductions, greeting cards, slides, books.

Special Events: From October to May illustrated lectures daily, call
museum. Sunday-afternoon chamber music concerts.

Special Restriction: Absolutely no cameras allowed.

The building housing the Frick Collection is a fine example of how
people of extreme wealth lived in New York in the early part of this
century. It is one of the few museums specifically built as a residence.
With slight variations to accommodate the public, the mansion was
opened as a museum in 1935. It appears much as it was when Henry
Clay Frick, the steel magnate, lived there. It was built in 1913 by Carrere & Hastings, who specialized in French Classic Eclectic, and was
occupied until 1931, when Mrs. Frick died. The building replaced the
Lenox Library, which formerly occupied the site.
   The mansion is much like a Louis XVI chateau that might be seen
in the Loire Valley. The first floor is the only one of the three open
to the public, and has about fifteen rooms, not including the enclosed
garden court. There are about forty rooms in the entire house.
   The priceless collection displayed in this magnificent house contains
works of art bought by Henry Frick over a period of forty years, and
bequeathed in trust to a board of trustees empowered to set up the
collection and the house as a center for the study of art and kindred
subjects. The financier, who grew up near Pittsburgh, began collecting
art seriously on his first trip abroad in 1880 with his friend Andrew
Mellon. By 1900, he had acquired about sixty pictures, principally of
the Barbizon School. During the next few years he obtained his first   99
Old Masters, and in the decade after 1900 formed the basic character
of the collection. There were one hundred thirty-one paintings among
the works bequeathed in 1919 to form the Frick Collection. Many
additional paintings have been acquired by the trustees.

Asia House; Philip Johnson, architect.

The Frick Collection.

The collection is not arranged according to any rigid classification of date or school, but possesses a harmonious freedom that retains the intimate atmosphere of a private home.

100   In the Boucher Room is a set of eight wall panels that depict cherubic figures representing the sciences and occupations of man. These were created by Francois Boucher to decorate the boudoir of Madame de Pompadour's chateau. Eighteenth-century British paintings dominate the handsome corner dining room.

An unusual feature near the South Hall is the massive organ, set near the stairs leading to the upper floors. The organ itself is a work of art.

The Fragonard Room contains magnificently colored panels representing the Progress of Love that Madame du Barry commissioned for her pavilion at Louveciennes. In the Living Hall are "St. Jerome" by El Greco and "St. Francis" by Giovanni Bellini. The former hangs between two Holbeins, the latter between two Titians.

The spacious wood-paneled library has a number of paintings by Gainsborough, Reynolds, Romney, Lawrence, Constable, and Turner. Over the mantel is a portrait of Henry Clay Frick. The porcelains are Chinese vases, chiefly of the type known as Black Hawthorn. Some of the furniture is Queen Anne.

Paintings by 18th-century English artists.

The Colonnade Court at the Frick Collection.

The masterpieces hanging in the West Gallery are colorfully set off by Turner's lemon-yellow scenes of Cologne and Dieppe. At the far end of the gallery hang Veronese's "Wisdom and Strength" and "Choice of Hercules." Rembrandt's "Self-Portrait" and portrait of "Nicolaes Ruts," Velázquez' "Philip IV" and El Greco's "Vincente Anastagi" are highlights of the gallery. Certainly this is a magnificent setting for some of the world's greatest art.

In the small Enamel Room are French painted enamels of the late fifteenth, sixteenth, and seventeenth centuries from the Limoges workshops of Nardon Penicaud and others.

In the East Gallery are the portrait of Conde de Teba by Goya and Claude Lorrain's "Sermon on the Mount." Of the four portraits in the Oval Room, two are by Van Dyck and two by Gainsborough.

102   The last gallery is the beautiful Colonnade Court. Originally an open carriage drive, its arched-glass roof was put on when the museum was remodeled under the guidance of John Russell Pope. At some time during a visit, most people will enjoy sitting on a stone bench in this lovely court and watching the bronze frogs spouting water into the fountain.

WHITNEY MUSEUM OF AMERICAN ART

Address: 945 Madison Ave. (at 75th St.), New York, N.Y., 10021.
Phone: 794-0600; 794-0630 (films); 483-0011 (Water St.)

Days: Open Tuesdays, 11–9; Wednesdays through Saturdays, 11–6;
Sundays and holidays, 12–6; closed Mondays.
Admission: $1.50; Tuesdays, 6–9, free.

Subway: IRT Lexington Ave. to 77th St. station. West to Madison Ave.
Bus: Madison Ave. or 5th Ave. bus to 75th St.
Auto: North on Madison Ave. or Park Ave. Metered street parking.

Restaurant: Cafeteria-style light luncheon, open various hours.

Gift Shop: Catalogues, selected art books, reproductions.

Membership: Annual fee $15.00.

The works in the Whitney Museum of American Art are generally painting, sculpture, and graphic arts of the United States created after 1900. Anyone viewing the collections will find the significant developments in American art from "The Eight" to the first wave of Modern Painting, Figurative artists of the 1920s, the Social Realists, the Hard-Edge Abstractionists, Magic Realists, New Abstractionists, New Naturalists, New Realists, Pop Artists, Conceptualists, and all the other schools that helped create rather than conserve a tradition that has put the Whitney in the front ranks of American museums.

Whitney Biennials are considered the most significant surveys and forecasts of trends in American art. Over the years more than 1,500 artists have appeared in the shows. The museum has never awarded prizes or medals. It believes that first-, second-, or third-place awards are arbitrary and meaningless, misleading to the public and unfair to the artists. Instead of awarding medals, the Whiteney buys works of art, a policy that has had a wide influence on other museums. In most of its exhibits works are for sale, a small commission is charged. In addition to the Biennials, there are shows built around a particular school, period, subject, region—like "200 Years of Indian Art."

The museum is open to the new, young, and experimental; it has always regarded the artist as the prime mover in aesthetic matters, and has respected artistic individuality. The superb avant-garde film programs in which the artist can show just about anything he creates is but one example of how the Whitney absorbs the new and young. 103

Visible proof of the museum's exciting growth is its superb new building on Madison Avenue, its third major move since it was officially opened in 1931. Gertrude Vanderbilt Whitney, a wealthy sculp-

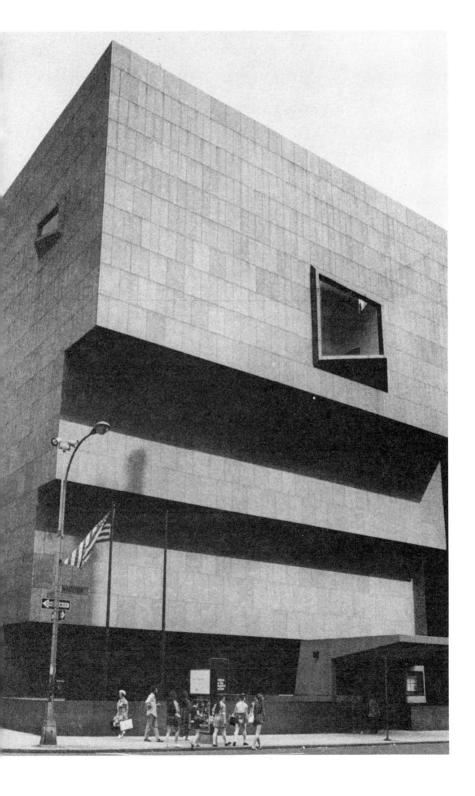

George Bellows' "Dempsey and Firpo." Collection of
The Whitney Museum of American Art, New York;
photo by Geoffrey Clements.

tor, founded and endowed the museum. She first showed the work of
fellow artists in her MacDougal Alley studio in Greenwich Village. Later
she converted an adjoining house at 8 West 8th Street into a gallery to
hold regular exhibitions. Mrs. Whitney also allotted funds to send
promising artists abroad and to purchase their works. She was, in a
sense, a one-woman foundation for the arts.

In 1915 she formed the Friends of the Young Artists to give youthful talent in this country an opportunity to show its work under a system without juries or prizes. Instead, works of art were purchased.
Those purchases form the nucleus of the present Whitney Collection.

The Whitney Museum of American Art;
Marcel Breuer, architect.

The entrance ramp at the Whitney.

By 1918 the Whitney Studio Club on 8th Street had been organized as an exhibition center. At the clubhouse, 147 West 4th Street, artists met socially and to plan, discuss, and execute their vigorous campaign to persuade the public to buy works of art from living Americans. The only requirement for admission to the club was talent; any serious artist who was introduced by a member could join. Membership included the leading young independent artists; eventually the club grew to a membership of over three hundred.

Cow-print wallpaper at
Andy Warhol retrospective.

From 1916 to 1930 the artists who exhibited at the Whitney Studio Club did become the heroic figures in American art—John Sloan, Stuart Davis, Edward Hopper, Joseph Stella, William J. Glackens, Reuben Nakian, Reginald Marsh, Ernest Lawson, Walt Kuhn, Guy Pené duBois, Charles Demuth, and dozens of others. From almost every exhibit Mrs. Whitney bought works for her collection. Annuals were held from the beginning, and so grew in size, quality, and scope that by the middle twenties the Whitney Club was the most active and influential center of liberal art in the country.

By 1928 the club had achieved victory in the fight to gain acceptance for young artists with fresh ideas about art, and it disbanded. Twenty years later, a similar organization, also called "The Club," was formed by the generation of Postwar Abstract Expressionists. At its peak, about 130 artists belonged. The Club did not hold exhibitions, but conducted a perpetual Friday-night dialogue from season to season. Its dedication was to promote the acceptance of Abstract-Expressionist paintings in America. By the early sixties it became evident that there had been a breakthrough, and, like the club before it, this one, too, saw a great rebellion come full circle. In 1962, without quarters and interested younger members to assume leadership, The Club automatically dissolved, unable to absorb the psychological impact caused by the death of one of its leaders, Franz Kline. Achievements of both clubs are evident in the galleries at the Whitney.

After the Whitney Studio Club disbanded, the Whitney Museum opened on 8th Street on November 18, 1931, with Gertrude Whitney's collection of over five hundred artworks. The museum's activities were much the same as today: to hold exhibitions, acquire works for the permanent collection, lend works to other institutions, and publish works on American art. The publication program has produced extensive catalogues, monographs, and broad histories by Lloyd Goodrich and John I. H. Baur, both formerly of the Whitney. The museum is maintained by the income from an endowment left by Mrs. Whitney. It does not receive any subsidy from the government, but does have a regular membership and receives financial support from "Friends of the Whitney."

The Whitney was a landmark in Greenwich Village for twenty-five years, its quarters providing an atmosphere of intimacy and charm. But then it moved uptown. In a benevolent gesture, John Hay Whitney, Nelson A. Rockefeller, and Stephen C. Clark of the Museum of Modern Art offered land on West 54th Street for a new museum building. It opened in 1954. It was never large enough to handle the greatly increased number of visitors, caused in part by the juxtaposition of the two museums, which were back to back. On 8th Street the average attendance at the Whitney was about 70,000 persons a year; on 54th Street it increased by 200,000; it is now about 300,000.

In late September 1966 the Whitney moved to its spectacular new building designed by Marcel Breuer, architect of the UNESCO Headquarters in Paris. This magnificent structure has very much the appearance of a gigantic work of sculpture. It is a five-story, inverted pyramid of flame-treated gray granite and concrete, punctuated with seven fascinating sculptural windows of random size. The museum has 30,000 square feet of exhibition space with movable floor-to-ceiling partitions, making it possible to create a wide variety of space patterns for exhibition purposes. The floors are made of flagstone for more comfortable walking, and the floodlights are equipped with diffusion lenses and tiny mirrors to spread the light evenly on the art objects.

Duane Hansen tableau.

Avant-garde dance concert at the Whitney Museum.

One enters the building by crossing a concrete bridge, constructed over a sunken sculpture garden, into the street-level lobby. In the words of Ada Louise Huxtable, architectural critic for *The New York Times:* "Mr. Breuer's stark and sometimes unsettling structure may be less than pretty, but it has notable dignity and presence, two qualities not found uniformly in today's art. . . . The building has an extraordinary urbanity, which masquerades as a kind of 'back-to-structure' crudeness. . . . It stresses masses of stone, largely unpolished—in this case a truly beautiful gray granite outside and in—raw concrete complete with board marks of the forms, rugged bush-hammered concrete aggregate

"Iron Year," a sculpture by Laurace James.

for interior walls, bluestone and split-slate floors." There is an auditorium on the second floor for special events, such as lectures and symposiums, and there is a public restaurant on the lower level.

The Whitney has begun to expand again by going out to the public and establishing branch museums. Its downtown branch at 55 Water Street has attracted a wide audience from the Wall Street business community. As museums and their collections outgrow their buildings as physical expansion becomes increasingly costly and difficult, this concept may be the best solution for making creative use of art, which otherwise is locked in storage and never seen.

CHINA INSTITUTE IN AMERICA
Address: 125 East 65th St., New York, N.Y., 10021.
Phone: 744-8181   111

Days: Mondays through Fridays, 10—5; Saturdays, 11—5; Sundays, 2—5.
Admission: Free.

A class at the China Institute in America. Photo by Sheldon Dix.

Subway: IRT Lexington Ave. to 68th St.
Bus: Third Ave. or Lexington Ave. bus.
Auto: Limited garage parking.

Membership: Associate $50; patron $1,000.

China Institute in America, a non-political, tax-exempt organization, was founded in 1926 to promote better understanding between the American and Chinese peoples and to serve the Chinese ethnic minority in the United States.

The permanent headquarters of the Institute is known as China House. In 1945, Henry R. Luce, the Shantung-born son of China missionaries Dr. and Mrs. Henry Winters Luce, donated the imposing townhouse as a memorial to his father. Luce's parents devoted their entire lives "to the purpose of seeking understanding and friendship among peoples of the East, of discovering the source of their greatness, and trying to intrepret the West to the East, and the East to the West."

Institute services include a full curriculum on China and Chinese civilization; exhibitions of classical Chinese art; a counseling and social program for young Chinese and their families; lectures; forums, conferences and seminars on cultural, political and economic issues; and audio-visual and print materials developed to provide accurate information about contemporary China and its ancient civilization.

China House Gallery presents exhibitions dealing with unusual facets of classical Chinese art. A guest curator organizes each of the Gallery's biannual exhibitions around a particular theme, material or period and prepares a fully-illustrated catalogue for the show. Some of these distinguished exhibitions have been on the "Dragon in Chinese Art," "Yi-Hsing Ware," "Chinese Embroidery," "Ceramics in the Liao Dynasty," "China Trade Porcelain," and "Tantric Buddhist Art."

The Center for Community Studies and Service conducts research and social action programs. Throughout the Center, the Institute collects basic data about the Chinese in the United States and provides counseling and supportive services for Chinese-Americans. The Institute is an educational and social center for Chinese youth in the New York metropolitan area. Courses offered by the Institute cover Chinese culture, history, philosophy, literature, geography, painting, calligraphy, art, language, opera, music, dance, and Taichichuan, the ancient Chinese art of health training.

China Institute also conducts a combined study and vacation program of visits to Japan, Taiwan, Hong Kong, and Thailand in the summers. Its program in practical arts includes such interesting courses as "The Art of Cooking Chinese Dim Sum," "Gourmet Cooking," and "Chinese Vegetarian Cooking."

A comprehensive film series, "China: The Enduring Heritage," produced for the Institute by Wan-go H. C. Weng, portrays Chinese civilization from prehistory up to the overthrow of the Ch'ing Dynasty. Using art objects, artifacts, still photographs, maps, charts, animation and live photography, these films provide a comprehensive chronological overview of Chinese civilizations.

The Institute has developed a Bilingual Vocational Training Program for unemployed Chinese with limited English-speaking ability to prepare for professional restaurant careers. Combining classroom instruction with in-service training at leading restaurants in New York, this program has a job placement rate of over ninety percent.

In its half century of service, China Institute has been a symbol of 113 the world's most numerous people and its oldest civilization. It seeks to provide unromanticized, undistorted information about China and its people. The Institute has illuminated the cultural achievements, triumphs and subleties of Chinese civilization for thousands of Americans.

CENTER FOR THE STUDY OF THE PRESIDENCY

Address: 926 Fifth Ave., New York, N.Y., 10021.
Phone: 249-1200

Days: Mondays through Fridays, 9—5.
Admission: Call for an appointment.

Subway: IRT Lexington Ave. to 77th St. station. West to Fifth Ave., south to 74th St.
Bus: Fifth Ave. or Madison Ave. bus to 73rd St.
Auto: North on Madison Ave. or Park Ave. Metered street parking.

The Center for the Study of the Presidency, founded in 1965, is located in a Fifth Avenue townhouse. Its purpose is to provide a political background and an interpretation of critical issues relating to the American presidency. The Center is primarily a research library and annually answers several hundred inquiries from primary school children as well as post-doctorate fellows. The founding group, which includes a cosmetics manufacturer, a publisher, a philanthropist, a public relations official, and an attorney, chose New York because of its concentration of scholars and libraries, massive population and transportation facilities. Programs of the center include lectures, films, symposia, seminars, fellowships, publications, clearinghouse, and student series.

The center collects original documents and reproductions of all the existing papers of all the presidents. The collections are then indexed and stored in the library, where reading and study rooms are available to scholars. By means of these archives the center hopes to facilitate the study of history by providing a central source of information, thereby eliminating the necessity of traveling throughout the United States to individual presidential libraries.

Copies of documents are also available for loan to other libraries, educational institutions, and individual scholars unable to visit the building. There is a nominal fee charged for this service. A series of lectures and meetings with government figures now gives anyone interested a chance to learn about politics from practicing politicians. Some scholarships also enable university graduates to serve internships in particular fields of government at Federal, state, or local level. The center is planning to produce exhibits for young students that will "stimulate interest in the Presidency by recalling the details of the man who held the job." These exhibits will be lent to other institutions.

The Center for the Study of the Presidency concentrates its fields of concern to over a dozen research areas. These include such topics as the Federal Constitution, the President and Congress, decision-

114

Center for Study of the Presidency.

making in the executive and legislative branches, reorganization of the 115
executive branch of the government, mass media, political parties and
pressure groups, memoirs and biographies of the presidents and cabinet
officers, White House aides' memoirs, and techniques in political anal-
ysis.

THE METROPOLITAN MUSEUM OF ART

Address: Fifth Ave. and 82nd St., New York, N.Y., 10028
Phone: 535-7710 (Information), 879-5500 (Office)

Days: Tuesdays, 10—8:45; Wednesdays through Saturdays, 10—4:45;
Sundays, 11—4:45; closed Mondays.
Admission: By contribution.

Subway: IRT Lexington Ave. to 86th St. station. Walk three blocks
west to 5th Ave., south to museum.
Bus: Fifth Ave. or Madison Ave. bus to 82nd St.
Auto: North on Madison Ave. or Park Ave. Museum parking lot for
visitors, fee $1.75 to $4.00.

Restaurant: Fountain restaurant has cafeteria-style service in a beautiful water-garden atmosphere. Complete luncheons, dinner, and
snacks. Alcoholic beverages. Call museum for hours open.

Museum Book Shop: Art books, museum catalogues, bulletins, guides.
Print Shop: Posters, color prints, reproductions, color slides.
Gift Shop: Silver, glass, jewelry, art objects, and reproductions.
Post Card Shop: Art postcards, Christmas cards, jewelry.

Special Events: Concerts, lectures, gallery talks, films.

Library: Art Reference Library open 10—4:45 Tuesday to Friday, open
to qualified research workers and museum members. Photo and
Slide Library, including sales of museum photographs, open
10—4:45 Tuesday through Friday.

Membership: Annual membership, $35.00 up. Special privileges include
six free issues of museum bulletin, calendar, annual garden party at
the Cloisters, library privileges, Saturday art classes, and other special activities for members' children.

As a critic once said, the Metropolitan Museum of Art is the supermarket of American museums, where you can find enough art to satisfy any appetite. Although almost any segment of its contents could
occupy a student or scholar for a generation of study and contempla-
tion, the museum is particularly noted for its Egyptian, Greek, and
116   Roman art, European paintings, arms and armor, and American paintings. Primarily a museum of retrospect, it also endeavors to relate its
collections to the present and to the civilizations that produced the
works of art.

The Metropolitan is the largest and most important treasure house of

The Great Hall of the Metropolitan Museum of Art.

Greek sculpture of the 5th century B.C.

art in the United States and the fourth largest in the world—after the British Museum, Leningrad's Hermitage, and the Louvre in Paris. It contains the largest number of galleries (248), with the most floor space (20 acres), catering to astronomical annual attendances (6,281,162), served by the biggest staff (828), with the most curators (165), making the most spectacular purchases ($5,544,000 for one painting), with the most impressive collections in the Western Hemisphere (500,000 works of art), and is also the richest by far ($121 million, excluding the art) of any museum in the United States.

The museum houses two concert halls, four restaurants, two photographic studios, four bookshops, three restoration laboratories, a photo-slide library, and a foundry with a complete set of seventeenth-century armorer's tools.

Because its collections are so overwhelming, it is impossible to see everything in a few hours or even days. The most sensible plan is to select just a few sections on which to concentrate during a single visit. Following a somewhat straight and narrow route, a first tour could begin with the Cesnola group of Cypriote antiquities in the corridor at the left of the entrance, then on to the interior of the Peri-nebi tomb to the right of the entrance. Proceed from there to the Bluementhal Spanish patio, then down the hall to the hall of Medieval Sculpture to see the heroic wrought-iron Spanish choir screen, and then the Equestrian Court. On the second floor outstanding features are the musical instruments and the Arthur M. Sackler Far Eastern Gallery. A visit might close with a long look at the rooms containing eighteen paintings by Rembrandt. One of them is the world-famous "Aristotle Contemplating the Bust of Homer," whose much-publicized purchase price at auction ($2,300,000) makes it the second costliest work of art in the museum. The costliest: Diego Velázquez' portrait of Juan de Pareja, purchased by the Metropolitan Museum of Art for over $5,000,000 in 1970.

Owing to the size of the Metropolitan and the number of people it attracts, these galleries alone could occupy a visitor for the better part of a long afternoon. The best place for some rest and refreshment is the beautiful canopied restaurant on the main floor.

The Metropolitan is divided into some eighteen curatorial departments, including the Cloisters at Fort Tryon, the Costume Institute, and the Junior Museum. The last two have their own entrances at the north and south wings along Fifth Avenue. The entire complex of buildings includes at least seventeen units, incorporating wings, galleries, many hallways, and historic houses. The museum's first structure, in 1874, has been added onto every ten or twenty years. When the museum opened, it owned no art, no building, and had no funds, and no provisions were made for the future. Since the first building plans were drawn, not a year has passed without some part of the structure being in the hands of an architect for redesigning, improvement, alteration, or addition. The Templer of Dendur is the latest. Future construction includes the Michael C. Rockefeller Wing of Primitive Art and the new American Wing.

At least twice in the past forty years responsible individuals have suggested that the building be abandoned. Solomon R. Guggenheim in 1933 offered a sizable donation toward a new building. During World War II the museum entertained the idea of moving, but Robert Moses, then Commissioner of Parks, made it clear that the Museum had to stay where it was. The land and the building belong to the City of New York; the art collections belong to the Metropolitan.

In 1967 Thomas P. F. Hoving, former Commissioner of Parks, was named Director. He served ten years. Previously he had been Curator

Bas-relief from the palace of Ashurnasirpal II, King of Assyria (883–859 B.C.), at Kalhu (modern Nimrud).

of the Cloisters, before going to the Parks Department. His responsibility as the director of America's largest museum complex covered the complete range of matters legal, financial, architectural, and curatorial. He was also responsible for the security of the collections, and personnel, engineering, (including superintendence of the buildings), purchase of supplies, management of the membership program, production of publications, development of new installations and exhibits, operation of the library, the care of museum documents and archives, conservation, restoration, and for good measure, fund raising.

Under Mr. Hoving a new philosophy of acquisition, exhibition, and public service evolved, plus a vast program to rehabilitate the museum. He not only made America more culture conscious, but vastly improved the archaic, dusty atmosphere of museums. His personal accomplishments are too numerous to mention, but many are visible to the regular museum visitor. Mr. Hoving resigned in 1978. He demonstrated more clearly than any previous director that a museum's character is determined largely by the personality of the person running it.

121

Claes Oldenburg's "Giant Pool Balls" as seen in Curator Henry Geldzahler's exhibition "New York Painting and Sculpture: 1940–1970."

Through the munificent philanthropy of the Metropolitan's chief benefactors the collections have grown to their present scope and importance. Among these benefactors have been J. Pierpont Morgan, Benjamin Altman, Horace O. Havemeyer, Samuel P. Avery, Edward C. Moore, Julian X. Bache, Lord Carnarvon, John Taylor Johnston, William K. Vanderbilt, Isaac D. Fletcher, Theodore Davis, Mrs. Russell Sage, William T. Walters, Brayton Ives, Michael Dreicer, and Dr. Eugene Bolles. Growth still depends heavily on individual bequests and gifts from philanthropic citizens. Benefactors have also sponsored expeditions and excavations, such as those in Egypt that were handsomely supported by the generosity of Edward S. Harkness.

Egyptian art is displayed on the main floor, to the right of the entrance, beginning with the white limestone tomb of Peri-nebi, a Fifth Dynasty Lord Chamberlain. The collection continues through numerous galleries, all of which have been renovated and reinstalled for chronological clarity. The collection reveals the civilization of the Nile Valley as it developed in an unbroken story of human progress, beginning some 6,000 years ago and lasting until Egypt was absorbed into the Roman Empire. The art objects found in these galleries reflect daily life, customs, and beliefs. It is the largest and most comprehensive Egyptian collection in America, and is complemented by the collections in the Brooklyn Museum.

The chronology of ancient Egypt is conveniently divided into thirty dynasties, each representing successive generations of ruling families. The dynasties are grouped into broad periods known as Early Dynastic, the Old Kingdom, Middle Kingdom, New Kingdom, and Late Dynastic.

The most familiar example of Egyptian architecture in the museum is the tomb of Peri-nebi, Lord Chamberlain in the Fifth Dynasty. In 1913, almost 4,500 years after it was constructed, it was disassembled, and reconstructed in the museum. The Egyptian Department is now assembling 651 stones from the Temple of Dendur.

In the galleries surrounding the massive sepulcher are funerary models from the tomb of the nobleman Meketre. Unearthed in Egypt, the miniature, brightly colored, carved figures appear to belong in a dollhouse. Intended to aid the nobleman in his life after death, the models are documentary evidence of daily life, showing the nobleman's tree-sheltered pool, his "yachts" on the Nile, servants harpooning fish, and scenes in a granary and carpenter shops.

The Egyptian jewelry collection is unequaled outside Cairo. There are also some displays of the toiletries of the ancient Egyptians: metal mirrors, bronze razors, little pots and jars for perfumes, rouge, and eye paint. A variety of tools represents various arts, crafts, and professions.

123

Some embalmed mummies when on view are in adjoining galleries. During the process of preparing a mummy, the body was disemboweled, cured or tanned, dehydrated with soda, and then packed with sawdust

The Equestrian Court.

124

Monumental sculpture of a Bodhisattva in polychromed sandstone from Shansi, China, Northern Ch'i Dynasty, A.D. 550-577.

and wrapped in resin-soaked linens. Rolled in layer upon layer of bandages, sheets, and pads, the body was finally placed in the coffin, with the head facing the East.

The Egyptian collection also includes temple sculpture, sarcophagi, limestone reliefs, altars, offering tables, a papyrus captital, and a number of enormous standing, seated, and kneeling statues of Queen Hatshepsut. She was frequently portrayed in the garb of a man, including a ceremonial beard—because as a woman she was not qualified to rule. When she died her successor ordered all her monuments defaced and destroyed. The fragments were discovered by the museum's expeditions of 1921, and were laboriously pieced together. Not all of these monumental Egyptian sculptures are on view.

Ancient Near Eastern Art is another of the Metropolitan's fine collections. A large portion of one wall is covered with Assyrian relief sculpture. The arched doorway is guarded by two great human-headed beasts from the palace of Ashurnasirpal II, King of Assyria. The cuneiform inscriptions and figures in relief were worked by vigorous and expert sculptors in stone. An inscription states that Ashurnasirpal built

South Italian red-figure vases, 4th century B.C.

the city of Kalhu (modern Nimrud) and that "in white limestone and alabaster I fashioned beasts of the mountains and of the seas and set them up in its gates. I adorned it, made it glorious and put knobs all around it. . . ." Only a portion of the collection is open to the public.

About a dozen galleries containing Greek and Roman art start at the left of the main entrance and lead directly to the museum restaurant. The upper and lower portions of a huge marble Ionic capital from the Temple of Artemis at Sardis are placed at the foyer of the restaurant. The hall arcade holds the important Cesnola collection of antiquities from Cyprus, acquired in 1874, that formed the beginning of the museum's collections. The stone and terra-cotta sculpture, vases, limestone reliefs, bronzes, gold jewelry, silver—more than five thousand items—were excavated by General Luigi Palma di Cesnola. An Italian soldier of fortune, he won his rank in our Civil War. He excavated in Cyprus while serving as the American consul there. He sold his collections of antiquities to the Metropolitan and became its first director in 1879, eight years after the state granted a charter to the museum. Recalling this colorful personality, the former curator of prints, A. Hyatt Mayor, wrote in the Museum *Bulletin:* ". . . since the General liked to find everybody alert and on the job, his shoes had steel heels that could be heard several galleries away. When his military tidiness was offended by the headless bodies and bodiless heads among the sculpture that he had dug up, he set any head on any body that it would approximately fit, plastering up the chinks in the necks with a paste of lime-dust and honey. The Cypriot gods and goddesses endured the mixture all winter, but when the windows were opened in summer they put on collars of flies."

The collection of Greek and Roman art continues in the galleries directly above, on the second floor. Comprising the work of several civilizations, Greek art, including Roman copies of Greek originals, is arranged by material, such as stone sculpture. Roman sculptures and paintings are displayed together. Gold, silver, glass, and coins are grouped by material without ethnic distinction, but Etruscan art is shown as an entity. There is an elegantly tarnished bronze chariot from a tomb in Spoleto, terra-cotta fragments, vases, and other Etruscan relics. The arts of Cyprus and Sardis, on the first floor, are confined to one gallery.

The earliest works of art in the museum are from the Cyclades, a group of islands in the Aegean Sea. Principally marble statuettes of women, these simple forms with arms bent at the elbows and held across the chest suggest peasant art. The Mycenaean period is represented by glossy black terra-cotta vases that show marine life and chariot scenes. The priceless collection of Greek pots contains some 1,450 items. The Greek Geometric period takes its name from the geometric vase patterns that contrast with the figurative decorations of the Mycenaean period. Most of these vases, such as the three huge kraters that served as tomb monuments, were used in burial rites.

Greek art made rapid advances in the techniques of rendering the human figure. The outstanding collection in the second-floor galleries shows Greeks at home, working, at play, at festivals, and at war, all depicted on the black- and red-figure vases of Attica. In one display case forty-five different vases have been assembled in an effective exhibit of storage and water jars; vases for cosmetics, oils and perfumes; drinking cups; wine jugs and bowls for mixing wine and water.

The earliest Greek marble statue in the museum, and one of the earliest extant, is the Archaic period figure of a young man, which probably stood over his tomb. A variety of styles and techniques in Greek coinage reveal the development of types and symbols—the Pegasus of Corinth, the Owl of Athens, the Tortoise of Aegina.

Marble imperial portrait sculptures from Rome are in the first gallery to the left of the main hall. The colossal portrait of Emperor Constantine marked a significant phase of Roman art, when the sculptor strove for an exact likeness of his subject. The museum owns the greatest group of Roman paintings to be seen outside Italy. Monumental frescoes from a villa at Boscoreale on Mount Vesuvius show rustic scenes and architectural cityscapes painted in the vivid red so often identified with wall paintings from Pompeii. The most impressive addition to the collection is a complete bedroom with magnificent frescoes and a tile floor.

The Thomas J. Watson Library and Blumenthal Patio are on the ground floor to the left of the main stairway. The library, with 175,000 volumes and over 1,200 periodicals, contains the greatest independent reference and research collection of art publications in America. Entrance to the library, study rooms, print collections, and print gallery is through the Patio. The Watson Library, founded in 1881, is privately endowed and is the most complete art and archaeology library in the Western Hemisphere. Its volumes include biographical works, monographs, museum guide books, auction catalogues, museum bulletins from around the world, and file clippings on individual artists.

Originally built around 1506, the Blumenthal Patio was brought from Spain in the early 1900s and formed a magnificent inner hall in the George Blumenthal house at 70th Street and Park Avenue. Mr. Blumenthal was president of the museum from 1934 to 1941. When the house was torn down shortly after his death, the entire patio was dismantled, and each marble carving, column, window, doorjamb, frame, and two thousand blocks of marble were stored in the museum. 127

This beautifully proportioned court follows as closely as possible its original appearance in the castle of the Fajardo family, near the southeastern coast of Spain. The original setting was poetically described by Olga Raggio, the museum's curator of Renaissance arts, who visited the

Colonial furniture of the 17th century in the American Wing.

site to secure the photographs and measurements necessary to the re-construction in New York: "The traveler who, after having admired the beauties of Granada, braves the dusty road winding eastward through the desolate ranges of the Sierra Maria and reaches the village of Velez Blanco, discovers the svelte silhouette of the castle of the Fajardos standing upon a rocky spur and dominating a vast plain. The warm yellow glow of its walls proudly rising against the stony gray mountains and the southern blue sky, the whitewashed houses of the village clustering at its foot, and the vast expanse of the valley, dotted with olive trees and vine groves, make a truly unforgettable sight."

In 1904, the owners of the castle decided to sell the marbles to a French interior decorator, who transported the pieces to Paris, where

In the Blumenthal Patio.

French porcelains and furniture of the 18th century.

they were offered for sale to prominent American collectors. The richly carved Renaissance patio, a unique example of Spanish and Italian architecture, was first offered to Archer M. Huntington for possible use as a building to house the Hispanic Society of America, but without result. In 1913, George Blumenthal purchased the marbles for his New York mansion. From the time the patio left Spain until it was reinstalled in the Metropolitan, exactly sixty years had elapsed.

Medieval art is displayed in one of the enormous single galleries directly to the rear from the main entrance, reached by passing through either to the right or to the left of the stairs. The collection shows Early Christian art, Byzantine and Ottoman art, and Romanesque and Early Gothic sculpture and furniture. In the Tapestry Hall hang fourteen textile panels depicting the Sacraments of the Church with parallel scenes from the Old Testament. The immense Medieval Sculpture Hall is dominated by a breathtaking 45-by-47-foot wrought-iron choir screen, weighing 60,000 pounds, from the Cathedral of Valladolid, Spain. Made in 1668 to separate the choir from the congregation, this monumental example of Spanish ironwork, the only one of its type in a public museum, was a gift of the William Randolph Hearst Foundation. When the famous "Mona Lisa" (on loan from the Louvre in Paris) was displayed in the museum in 1963, it was placed against this three-story-high screen.

The Western European Arts section encompasses works of art made in Europe from the beginning of the Renaissance to the present. It is the largest and most varied department of the museum, with entire rooms from palaces, hotels, and country estates, together with all their accessories and furnishings from floor to ceiling. The objects illustrate the changes in taste and style that have succeeded one another for some five hundred years—early Renaissance, mannerism, seventeenth-century baroque, eighteenth-century rococo, neoclassicism, the period of Louis XVI, and so on.

European ceramics, glass, and metalwork are displayed on the ground floor, in fifteen galleries. To reach them, take the stairway in the Tapestry Hall. This vast collection of art offers French, German, and Dutch ceramics, eighteenth-century French and English silver, the art of Fabergé, gold lapidary work, early German timepieces, compasses, portrait miniatures, China trade porcelain, miniature silver sets, and Venetian glass. Rare examples of Medici porcelain, made in Florence about 1580, represent early European attempts to imitate Chinese porcelains.

The main exhibit of Renaissance arts is a bedroom from the Segredo Palace in Venice that is decorated with at least twenty-five cherubs on the walls and ceiling. Although early Renaissance architecture can be seen on a grand scale only in Italy, the Metropolitan has a small fifteenth-century chamber of intarsia work from the chapel and oratory of the Castle of La Bastie D'Urfe in France. A glazed terra-cotta altarpiece by Andrea Della Robbia and some handsome Italian bronzes are noteworthy in this collection.

The galleries of French art also contain complete rooms with characteristic examples of the extravagant decorative art of the period as well as signed works by the greatest French cabinetmakers of the late 1700s. The Wrightsman Rooms are two magnificently installed and furnished rooms from the Hotel de Varengeville in Paris and the Palais Paar in Vienna. The carved and painted paneling of these rooms exemplifies an earlier and later phase of the Rococo style. A shopfront from 3 Quai Bourdon on the Ile Saint-Louis displays Sèvres "Rose Pompadour" vases and objects from the Samuel H. Kress Foundation collection, together with superb examples of Louis XVI furniture inlaid with porcelain plaques painted with flowers by Martin Carlin, a master cabinetmaker who worked in Paris about 1766.

The Robert Lehman Collection is presented in a magnificent pavilion with a glass pyramid roof. The Lehman Wing was designed by Roach &

Set of coffins of the Priest of Amun, Men-Kheper-re.

Dinkerloo and is a unique setting for the Renaissance painting and decorative arts in surrounding bays and period rooms. It is a stunning architectural achievement that is a fitting tribute to one of America's great art collectors.

English art is in the last set of galleries. These are mostly late-seventeenth and eighteenth-century furnishings. Of noteworthy interest is a staircase carved by Grinling Gibbons in 1677. It is the only known example of this type by the famous woodcarver.

Entering the exhibits of arms and armor, you are immediately confronted by a jousting knight, ready for the charge. The extraordinarily comprehensive collection in the Equestrian Court illustrates the technical and artistic evolution of weapons and protective equipment in Europe. Some of the armor was so ingeniously designed that it was virtually impregnable. A man's armor might weigh as much as 85 pounds; that of a horse, up to 92 pounds. The galleries surrounding the hall display swords, ceremonial spurs, kidney daggers, maces, crossbows, firearms, great basinets, helms, gauntlets, toe and elbow caps, and mail shirts tailored to fit the body loosely, but linked so closely that they could not be penetrated with a dagger. A unique tournament book of 126 watercolors shows how jousting armor was worn.

An outstanding example of the armorers' art is the parade suit of Henry II of France. It is estimated that a skilled metalworker would have needed two years to accomplish the forging, embossing, damascening, leaf-gilding, silvering, punch work, and blueing done on the armor. It is truly fit for a king. Many pieces of armor are signed by the artisans. There is also a section devoted to Oriental arms and armor.

The American Wing displays the early domestic arts of the United States. Period rooms, removed from original dwellings, were brought to the museum and arranged chronologically on three floors. The American Wing may be temporarily closed for restorations.

133

*A metallophone
from Java in the
Crosby Brown Collection
of Musical Instruments.*

The Metropolitan Museum has the earliest examples of Colonial craftsmanship covering the period 1640–1750. Gothic influence on the construction of the central room is evident in the roughly hewn trusses and beams. The earliest American table known to exist, a trestle type of pine and oak from New England, stands in the middle of the room.

The rooms on the second floor date from 1750 to about 1790. Characteristic of the era are the increasing use of mahogany, and the hand-cut leaves, flowers, vines, and naturalistic detail on highboys, lowboys, chairs and tables. The main central gallery re-creates the assembly room from the City Tavern in Alexandria, Virginia, in 1793, then a major East Coast stopping place between North and South.

The first floor of the eighteenth- and early-nineteenth-century interiors is notable for the splendid Van Rensselaer Room taken from a great mansion built in Albany in 1765. The unusual English wallpaper, made especially for the room, consists of large panels of romantic landscapes and seacoast scenes encircled by a scroll frame. The Van Rensselaer house was a striking example of Georgian architecture in the Middle Atlantic Colonies.

American painting and sculpture are displayed on the second floor, as well as twentieth-century decorative arts. Among the most spectacular works on view is a large wall of glass panels, which were part of the Grand Salon on the luxury liner *Normanie.* The mural depicts historical images of navigation, and it was painted in 1934 in silver, gold and black after designs by Jean Dupas. There is also Art Deco furniture and glass.

The Metropolitan held an outstanding exhibition of its American Collection in 1965, when 425 paintings were on view in 22 galleries. With the exception of American paintings of the seventeenth century, the museum's collection of the work of native painters and sculptors is the most complete and significant in existence, touching on every artist and style important to the history and development of art in America. Owing to limitations of space, only a fraction of its 1,250 works by nearly 625 artists are on display. The extraordinary collection is described in detail in three very informative catalogues: *American Sculpture,* by Albert Ten Eyck Gardner; *American Paintings* (painters born by 1815), by Mr. Gardner and Stuart P. Field; and *American Painting in the 20th Century,* by Henry Geldzahler.

Far Eastern and Islamic art are on the second floor. Chinese sculpture is impressively displayed in two large galleries named for Arthur M. Sackler, a collector of Oriental art. A spectacular fresco of a Buddha surrounded by his disciples dominates one gallery. Monumental heads and full figures of Buddha, one standing fourteen feet high, of stone, bronze, and wood, date from the second century after Christ to the fourteenth century. A stone pagoda, considered the oldest and most important Chinese architectural monument in a Western museum, is

The Lehman Wing.

"Washington Crossing the Delaware" by Emanuel Gottlieb Leute.

carved with guardians, dragons, floral motifs, animal masks, and countless figures of Buddha.

Among the most beautiful of the Metropolitan's vast holdings is the
Crosby Brown Collection of Musical Instruments on view in the Andre
Mertens Galleries overlooking the Armor Court. Over 800 instruments
are on exhibit including many extraordinary examples from the Far and
Near East, Oceania, Africa, the Americas, and Europe. The galleries are
divided according to geographical origin, and instruments are shown
both in the open and in glass cases. The collection was begun in the
1870s by Mrs. John Crosby Brown, a banker's wife, who formed one of
the richest and most systematic collections in the world. The chronological development of many instruments is shown; and many have in-
triguing shapes and are lavishly decorated. As unique works of visual
and musical art they are a vital complement to the other art treasures
in the museum.

136

Room from house in Damascus, Syria, A.D. 1707.

The Harry Paine Galleries containing European paintings are displayed in thirty-five galleries. Over seven hundred masterpieces present the evolution of painting in Europe from the thirteenth century through the first quarter of the twentieth century. Byzantine, Spanish, Italian, Dutch, Flemish, British, French, and German paintings are arranged by historical periods and schools.

Among the great masters and works in the collections are: Benvenuto Cellini ("Rospigliosi Cup"), Franz Hals ("The Merry Company"), Rembrandt van Rijn ("Aristotle Contemplating the Bust of Homer"), Lucas Cranach ("The Judgment of Paris"), Peter Paul Rubens ("The Fox Hunt"), Nicolas Poussin ("Rape of the Sabine Women"), Georges de La Tour ("The Fortuneteller"), El Greco ("View of Toledo"), Diego Velázquez ("Juan de Pareja"), Giovanni Paolo Pannini ("Renaissance Room"), Antonio Canale Canaletto ("Scene in Venice"), Eugène Delacroix ("Abduction of Rebecca"), J. M. W. Turner ("The Grand Canal"), Jean Antoine Watteau ("Mezzetin"), Pieter Brueghel ("The Harvesters"), Vittore Carpaccio ("The Meditation of the Passion"), Edouard Manet ("Boating"), Vincent van Gogh ("Mme. Ginoux"), and Paul Cézanne ("The Cardplayers").

The European collection typifies the multiple facets of the museum's personality. Its roles of presentation and use, education and entertainment give the institution a vitality evident the moment you step inside. It should be all of what it has become: a place for pure scholarship, an arena of popular instruction, a unit for experimentation, a place for the refreshment of the mind, eye, and soul, an attraction for tourists, a center for learning, and area for pure enjoyment.

COSTUME INSTITUTE OF
THE METROPOLITAN MUSEUM OF ART
Address: Fifth Ave. and 82nd St., New York, N.Y., 10028.
Phone: 535-7710 or 879-5500 (Office)

Days: Exhibition galleries open to the public during museum hours, see previous listing for hours. Research facilities, study, storage, workrooms open by appointment only.
Admission: By contribution.

138 *Subway:* IRT Lexington Ave. to 86th St. station. Walk three blocks west to 5th Ave., south to museum.
Bus: Fifth Ave. or Madison Ave. bus to 83rd St.
Auto: North on Madison Ave. or Park Ave. Museum parking lot for visitors open daily, fee $1.75 to $4.00.

Restaurant: See listing for Metropolitan Museum.

The Costume Institute of the Metropolitan Museum offers exhibits of public interest that show the social, technical, and aesthetic values of costumes. Its collections, considered works of art, are among the most comprehensive in the world in quality, range and variety. There are almost 30,000 articles of dress. These include European and American urban costumes and accessories dating from the sixteenth century through the twentieth century and regional costumes representing different cultures in Europe, Asia, Africa, and the Americas. The library has 22,000 items as well as collections of original fashion plates and sketches, pattern books, photographs, and thousands of clippings.

For the general visitor the most important part of the Costume Institute are the ten ultramodern galleries where different parts of the

The Costume Institute of the Metropolitan Museum.

collections are shown periodically thus emphasizing costume as an art form.

Those with special interests have available, usually by appointment, the Irene Lewisohn Costume Reference Library, five Dorothy Shaver Designer rooms, three study-storage rooms, a classroom, and hundreds of racks and drawers that hold thousands of articles—shoes, skirts, trousers, dresses, robes, vests, hats, even fans—for private study.

These collections are a practical and priceless source of information and inspiration for high-fashion designers; theatre, motion picture, and television wardrobe designers; artists; photographers; students and apparel manufacturers from Seventh Avenue.

Among the oldest costumes in the museum's collection is an English, gilt-embroidered wool gown dating from about 1690. It was acquired by the museum in 1933 and has been restored to its original design.

The contemporary collection includes clothes designed by Americans like Blass, Galanos, Mainbocher, Norell, Tiffeau, and Trigere. The Europeans are represented in the Institute's collections by Balenciaga, Cardin, Dior, Galitzine, Givenchy, Gres, Pucci, and Ungaro.

JUNIOR MUSEUM OF THE METROPOLITAN MUSEUM OF ART
Address: Fifth Ave. and 81st St., New York, N.Y., 10028
Phone: 535-7710 or 879-5500 (office)

Days: Open Tuesdays through Saturdays, 10—5; Sundays and holidays, 11—5.
Admission: By contribution.

Subway: IRT Lexington Ave. to 86th St. station. Walk three blocks west to 5th Ave., south to museum.
Bus: Fifth Ave. or Madison Ave. bus to 81st St.
Auto: North on Madison Ave. or Park Ave. Museum parking lot for visitors open daily, fee $1.75—$4.00.

Restaurant: Cafeteria and lunchroom.

Lectures and Tours: For school groups; auditorium available.

Gift Shop: Well stocked with art merchandise especially suited to young people; assembly kits, school picture sets.

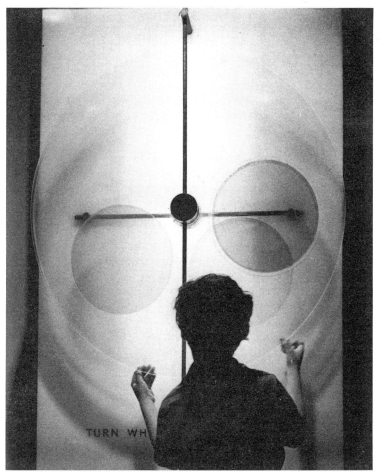

Color wheel at the Junior Museum.

The Junior Museum was established in 1941 and now occupies the entire South Wing on the first floor, with three entrances. It is a separate arm of the Metropolitan, pleasantly informal for children, who may roam through it freely. The main purpose of the Junior Museum is to contribute to the realization of the chartered purpose of the Metropolitan, "encouraging and developing the study of the fine arts . . . and furnishing popular instruction. . . ." In accomplishing this, the staff seeks to introduce children to the Metropolitan and to help them to know and enjoy its collections. It is confidently expected that these

141

young people will be the students, artists, designers, architects, interested laymen, and perhaps patrons of the future.

Upon entering the building, children find a self-service checking rack for coats and parcels, supermarket carts for their box lunches, washrooms, and a registration desk. The lobby gallery that adjoins the Junior Museum contains the Color Print Shop. There is a large variety of prints of classic works from the Metropolitan collections as well as those of contemporary artists. The shop also sells frames, color slides, and superb plastic-coated pictures ready for hanging.

The young visitors are well provided with a choice of activities and exhibits in the modern and spacious setting wherein the staff provides hospitality and interpretation. Usually there is one major exhibit, such as "The Age of Discovery," which began with Marco Polo and progressed through the opening of the New World. Another exhibit, "Archaeology and the World," showed archaeological tools and how artifacts were buried under layer upon layer of succeeding civilizations. The display was made vivid with an example of a cutaway section from lower Manhattan showing some fascinating Indian artifacts. Another exhibit, "The Artist's Workshop," concentrated on tools and techniques.

In addition to the many displays and exhibitions specifically scaled to the junior world, there are art classes, and Saturday programs that combine live performances, music, films, and demonstrations based on the collections. The Junior Museum also has a well-stocked and imaginatively decorated library, and a senior-size snack bar seating 204.

THE SOLOMON R. GUGGENHEIM MUSEUM
Address: 1071 5th Ave. (between 88th and 89th Sts.), New York, N.Y., 10028.
Phone: 860-1300

Days: Open daily, 10—6; Sundays and holidays, 11—5. Closed Mondays and Christmas. Open Tuesday evenings until 8.
Admission: $1.50, free Tuesdays, 5—8.

Subway: IRT Lexington Ave. to 86th St. station. Walk west to 5th Ave., north to museum.
Bus: Fifth Ave. or Madison Ave. bus to 88th St.
Auto: North on Madison Ave. or Park Ave. Limited street parking.

Restaurant: Lunch and snacks plus wine and beer.

143

The Solomon R. Guggenheim Museum;
Frank Lloyd Wright, architect.

Gift Shop: Publications and reproductions for sale in bookstore.

Membership: Annual fee $125–$250.

Solomon R. Guggenheim was the fourth of seven Guggenheim brothers from a remarkable family which, upon arrival in the United States from Switzerland in the nineteenth century, had created a financial empire. They supoorted good causes and established philanthropic foundatioлs.

Guggenheim began to form an art collection of works by Old Masters until, in the mid-1920s, he met Baroness Hilla Rebay von Ehrenweisen. She introduced him to the avant-garde artists of the time— Robert Delaunay, Albert Gleizes, Fernand Léger, Marc Chagall, Wassily Kandinsky.

Converted by Miss Rebay's enthusiasm and expertise, he began to buy steadily until his apartment became a gallery. The collection was then converted into a foundation and a museum that opened on June 1, 1939, as the Solomon R. Guggenheim Collection of Non-Objective Paintings.

In 1943, Frank Lloyd Wright was commissioned by Guggenheim to build what is now a fascinating, unusual building. Opposition to the architect's plans came from the municipal Department of Buildings, whose opinions regarding the building's construction and locale were for many years at odds with Wright's. Sixteen years elapsed between the commission of the present museum and its completion. The late Harry F. Guggenheim, nephew of the founder and former president of the Board of Trustees of the Solomon R. Guggenheim Foundation, said that the building was basically unchanged from the original plan, and that "its composition, its beauty, and its majesty are evident."

The prolonged battles between Wright and the city building authorities were given much attention in the press as Wright strove to override New York's antiquated building code, and apparently succeeded. But disputes also developed between Wright and James Johnson Sweeney, the director; disputes that were only resolved when the architect died six months before the new museum opened. Sweeney resigned nine months later.

From the day it opened on October 21, 1959, the Wright building brought the Guggenheim Museum worldwide recognition, and the sensational landmark became an instant attraction in New York as much for the building as for the art it contains. It occupies an entire block fronting Fifth Avenue and attracts 600,000 visitors a year.

144

Visitors take the elevator to the top landing and then walk down a circular half-mile of sloping ramp until they reach bottom. "A museum," said Frank Lloyd Wright, "is an organic building where all is one great space on a single continuous floor." Progressing downward, the

Pop Art by Roy Lichtenstein.

visitor views works of art seemingly floating in space. The art is set within cubicles or bays along the curved walls.

Each cubicle is about large enough for two seven-foot-wide paintings. Except for the spiderweb glass dome (ninety-five feet above the floor), there are no windows. There are almost no seats along the ramps, which are protected by a waist-high parapet.

Its spiraling ramps punctuated by little doorways serve as entrances to each new floor. One of these leads to a separate gallery housing the superb Justin K. Thannhauser Foundation Collection of modern art treasures, consisting of seventy-five paintings and sculpture. Its strength lies in a group of Impressionist and Neo-Impressionist masterpieces antedating the Museum's original collecting scope, and therefore it serves as a historical background for the museum's collection.

145

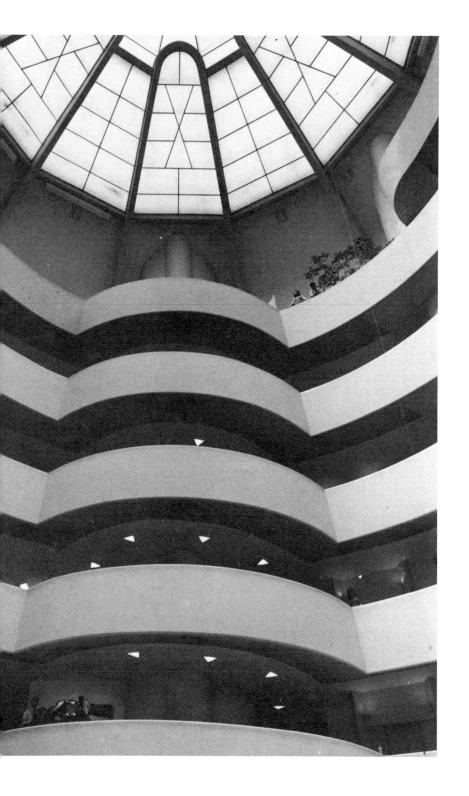

At present the collection contains works from the late nineteenth century to the present, with emphasis on early abstractions. Kandinsky is represented by more than 210 artworks. Paul Klee, Franz Marc, Robert Delaunay, Albert Gleizes, Marc Chagall, Lázló Moholy-Nagy, and Fernand Léger are some of the twentieth-century masters owned by the Guggenheim. The collection has works by sculptors Alexander Calder, Alexander Archipenko, and Constantin Brancusi.

The acquisition program, as Louise Averill Svendsen, the Curator, points out, ". . . has followed a comprehensive pattern oriented toward historical periods to fill existing gaps . . . to enrich the collection with principal examples of masters of our time, plus the works of younger artists from the United States, Europe and Latin America."

To carry out its objectives of promoting, encouraging, and educating in the arts, the museum offers an average of five major exhibitions annually. By far the most successful, in terms of attendance, publicity, and critical acclaim, was the Alexander Calder mobile-stabile sculpture. Its other major shows include exhibits devoted to van Gogh, Francis Bacon, the Abstract Expressionists, Nicolas de Staël, Kandinsky, David Smith, and Roy Lichtenstein.

NATIONAL ACADEMY OF DESIGN

Address: 1083 5th Ave. (at 89th St.), New York, N.Y., 10028.
Phone: 369-4880

Days: Open daily, 1—5. Closed June 1 to September 15.
Admission: $.50—$1.00.

Subway: IRT Lexington Ave. to 86th St. station. Walk west to 5th Ave., north to building.
Bus: Fifth Ave. or Madison Ave. bus to 89th St.
Auto: North on Park Ave. or Madison Ave. Limited street parking.

The National Academy of Design is in the Fifth Avenue town house that was originally built about 1900 for Archer Huntington, founder of the Hispanic Society. This building was given to the academy in 1940. A new building around the corner on 89th Street houses the School of Fine Arts of the National Academy. The style of the new building captures the spirit of the institution. 147

The Academy's exhibition program consists of half a dozen group shows a year, among them the Annual Show of the Allied Artists of America, the Annual of the American Watercolor Society, the Annual of the Audubon Artists, and the annuals of the New York Society of

The dome and tiers inside the Guggenheim.

Women Artists or the National Association of Women Artists. This list, of course, should include the annual exhibition of the National Academy of Design.

The Academy was founded on November 8, 1825, with the intention of forming a group "that would be governed solely by artists for the development in this country of the highest standards in the arts." Members and associates were to be elected on the basis of "their standing as painters, sculptors, architects and workers in the graphic arts." The academy's founder and first president was Samuel Finley Breese Morse, artist, inventor, businessman, educator, and a leading citizen of New York. Of the thirty founding members, eleven are represented in the collections of the Metropolitan Museum of Art, and many famous and important architects, painters, sculptors, printmakers, and illustrators are currently members of the academy.

THE JEWISH MUSEUM
Address: 1109 5th Ave. (at 92nd St.), New York, N.Y., 10028.
Phone: 860-1888

Days: Open Sundays, 11–6; Mondays through Thursdays, 12–5; closed Fridays, Saturdays, and Jewish holidays.
Admission: Adults $1.50; children $.75; members free.

Subway: IRT Lexington Ave. to 96th St. station. Walk west to 5th Ave., south to museum.
Bus: Fifth Ave. or Madison Ave. bus to 92nd St.

Auto: FDR (East River) Drive to 96th St. exit, east to 5th Ave., south 4 blocks. Limited street parking.

Gift Shop: Museum shop offers Jewish ceremonial objects, publications, and unique jewelry.

Membership: Student $10.; benefactor $2,500. Privileges include discounts on books, lounge and library privileges.

The Jewish Museum is the world's largest and most comprehensive repository of Jewish ceremonial art and other historical Judaica in the fine arts. It operates under the auspices of the Jewish Theological Seminary of America, one of the nation's foremost educational institutions. The collections and galleries are in the former home of Felix M. Warburg. This French Renaissance landmark, built in 1908, was presented to the Jewish Theological Seminary by his widow, Mrs. Frieda Schiff Warburg. The adjoining modern wing, completed in 1962, is the Albert A. List building. The board of governors of the museum

149

The National Academy of Design.

is under the chairmanship of Mrs. Albert A. List.

Museum activities are divided loosely into two categories: the permanent collections, which seek to illustrate the continuity between the accomplishments of the past and the present, and the changing exhibition program that seeks to illustrate the temper and spirit of contemporary life as related to Jewish culture.

The changing exhibitions are held on the first floor. On the other two floors are the permanent collections with their four categories: ceremonials used to mark the epochs of a lifetime, ceremonials associated with holidays, religious objects for the synagogue, and objects for the Jewish home. The Harry G. Friedman collection contains Torah crowns, headpieces, breastplates, pointers, candelabra, Passover plates, amulets, Sabbath lamps, mezuzahs (door pieces), tefillin bags, kiddush cups, embroidered linen Torah wrappers, scrolls, and silver

Entrance wall of the Persian Synagogue (with Torah cases).

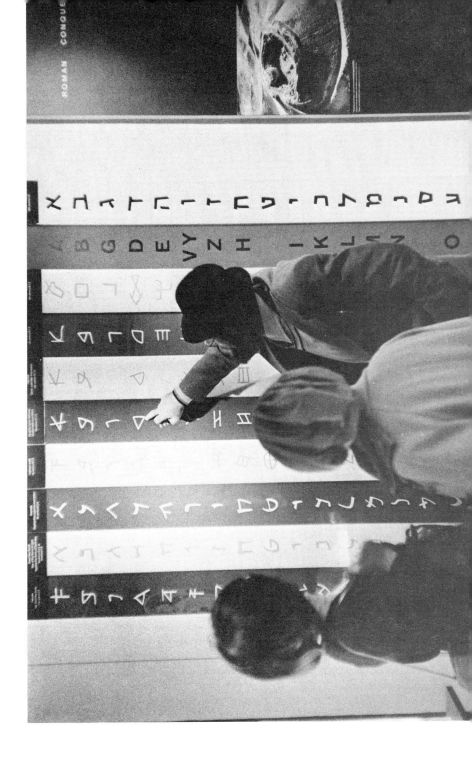

Visitors at the Jewish Museum study an alphabet display.

Cooper-Hewitt Museum of Decorative Arts and Design.

ceremonial objects. The Benguiat Collection contains a Torah ark given to the synagogue of Urbino, Italy in 1551. The ark, like the altar of a Christian church, is the focal point of the service, and contains the Torah, the scroll on which the Five Books of Moses are inscribed.

A group of Italian ceremonial objects demonstrates a combination of finesse and beauty in the Italian decorative arts as applied to traditional Jewish ritual objects. In Europe in the Middle Ages many of these were fashioned for Jews by Christian artisans because Jews were not allowed to belong to the silversmiths' guilds.

The Samuel Friedenberg Collection of medals and plaques commemorate Jewish notables. The entire collection is described in a comprehensive catalogue. There is also an interesting sixteenth-century synagogue wall of faience mosaic from Iran, the only one from Persia in this country. The Philip and Lillian Leff Gallery contains an outstanding and extensive group of turret-form silver spice containers. The museum owns the famous black-box sculpture "Homage to 6 Million" by Louise Nevelson. Recently the museum presented an immensely interesting and moving photographic exhibit called "The Lower East Side: Portal to American Life." It depicted that area of New York from 1870 to 1925, during the great wave of immigration to America. A later photographic show, "Israel—the Reality," was also hugely successful.

COOPER-HEWITT MUSEUM/
SMITHSONIAN INSTITUTION
NATIONAL MUSEUM OF DESIGN

Address: 2 East 91st St., New York, N.Y., 10028.
Phone: 860-6868

Days: Open Tuesdays, 10—9; Wednesdays through Saturdays, 10—5;
Sundays, 12—5. Closed Mondays.
Admission: Free.

Subway: IRT Lexington Ave. to 86th St. station. West to 5th Ave.
Bus: Fifth Ave. or Madison Ave. bus to 91st St.
Auto: North on Park Ave. or Madison Ave. Limited street parking.

The Cooper-Hewitt Museum of Decorative Arts and Design is an affiliate of the Smithsonian Institution and is the only museum in the
United States devoted exclusively to contemporary and historical
decorative arts. Cooper-Hewitt serves the world of the student, scholar, and designer with emphasis upon educational and workshop activities, study, and direct visual and tactile experience. Some museum
collections are shown only on request.

   The museum is in the Andrew Carnegie Mansion, a sixty-four room,
modified Georgian-Eclectic quasi-palace, built between 1899 and 1903
by architects Babb, Cook, and Willard. Founded in 1897 by Peter
Cooper's granddaughters, Sarah and Eleanor Hewitt, the museum is
rich in drawings, prints, wallpapers, glass, porcelain, furniture, em-
broideries, laces, and metalwork that represent a wide range of artistic creation of the past and present. The Textile-Design Collection is
one of the finest in America considering its scope and size.

   The textile collection contains embroidery and prints on cotton,
linen, and velvet dating from the third century, and showing designs
from Turkey, Yemen, Egypt, India, Persia, China, Spain, and Italy.
One embroidered twenty-one-inch panel from late sixteenth-century
Italy shows adoring winged figures and winged cherubs' heads emerging
from foliage, flower sprays, birds, fruits, and ribbons—all serving as an
eleborate border around a small picture of the Nativity that is embroidered in pale silk and shaded in gold. Inside the circle are the kneeling
Mary and Joseph, the Infant, shepherds, and angels.

   In the textile group is an extraordinary English beadwork cabinet,
the size of a lady's jewel box, with about eight tiny drawers. It was
made in 1630. The most delicately minuscule colored-bead arrangements show the family coat of arms on the side doors and, on the top,
a lady and her three attendants standing before a seated king.

   The collection also has intricate examples of cuff flounces in needle-
lace from France (c. 1690) showing flying figures, cupids, Indians, and

153

fish cornucopias. These dramatic examples of elaborate laces, known as Points de France, were developed under the royal patronage of Louis XIV. From the sixteenth century until the Revolution, lace was worn as much by men as by women, as evidenced by their cravats, collars, and cuffs in portraits of this period.

Fabrics are collected for a variety of reasons: pattern, color, structure, patterning techniques, historic value, social interest, or sheer joy and appreciation. The oldest and perhaps the most important items in the entire museum are a bonnet and a pair of mittens, both of silk, from China of about the third century B.C.

The wallpaper study group contains superb, rare English, American and French wallpaper designs, pilaster panels, overdoor panels, and borders. Some of the early examples are of leather tooled with fancy bird and flower designs. The Cooper-Hewitt Museum has seventy-five decorated early American hatboxes.

The drawings and prints are rivaled only by those in museums in Europe. The scope is broad, ranging from early block printing to contemporary American, including impressions of Japanese nineteenth-century woodblock prints. The department houses a delightful and fascinating adjunct of peep-show prints, decoupage, cut-paper work, pinpricked pictures, and shadow puppets.

In the fields of decorative arts and design the library of the Cooper-Hewitt Museum provides the most complete and accessible reference collection in New York. In specialized areas there are seventeenth- and eighteenth-century architecture books, catalogues of world's fairs, auction sales catalogues, and an encyclopedic picture collection.

INTERNATIONAL CENTER OF PHOTOGRAPHY
Address: 1130 5th Ave. (at 94th St.), New York, N.Y., 10028.
Phone: 860-1777; 860-1783 (Groups)

Days: Open Tuesdays, 11—8; Wednesdays through Sundays, 11—5.
Admission: $1.00.

Subway: IRT Lexington Ave. to 96th St. West to 5th Ave.
Bus: Fifth Ave. or Madison Ave. bus to 94th St.
Auto: FDR (East River) Drive to 96th St. exit. West to 5th Ave.

Gift Shop: Photographic books, portfolios, posters.

154   *Membership:* General $25; contributing $1,000.

The International Center of Photography (ICP) is the first and only museum in the city devoted exclusively to photography. It was established by Cornell Capa who made it the most influential institu-

International Center of Photography.

tion in both photo journalism and photographic art in New York.

The museum is housed in a four-story, red brick Federal-Eclectic landmark townhouse that was built by Delano and Aldrich in 1915 for Willard D. Straight, founder of *The New Republic.* The museum conducts seminars, workshops, lectures, photography classes, shows films, maintains darkrooms, publishes a newsletter, circulates exhibitions, and is involved in every aspect of the city's photographic community.

An important feature of ICP is the Photography Hall of Fame, honoring those who have made significant contributions to the art and science of professional photography.

155

Establishment of ICP was one of the primary goals of the International Fund for Concerned Photography, a non-profit, tax-exempt organization founded "to encourage and assist photographers of all ages and nationalities who are vitally concerned with their world and times;

to find and help new talent; to uncover and preserve forgotten photo-graphic archives; and to present such work to the public." The Fund was dedicated to the memory of Werner Bischof, David Seymour and Robert Capa, Cornell's brother.

According to Cornell Capa, ". . . photography provides an undistor-ted image of man's actions and his reverence for life. Such images are both works of art and moments in history; they sharpen human aware-ness and awaken conscience." This humanistic and esthetic philosophy has been basic to the creation of such important thematic exhibitions as "The Concerned Photographer," "Behind the Great Wall of China," and "Jerusalem: City of Mankind." Since the opening of the Interna-tional Center of Photography in October 1974, it has shown the work of over 300 individual photographers, including one-person shows by Cartier-Bresson, Weegee and W. Eugene Smith.

MUSEUM OF THE CITY OF NEW YORK
Address: Fifth Ave. at 103rd St., New York, N.Y., 10029.
Phone: 534-1672

Days: Weekdays, 10—5; Sundays and holidays, 1—5. Closed Mondays, and on Christmas. When a legal holiday falls on a Monday, the mu-seum is open but is closed the following Tuesday.
Admission: Free.

Subway: IRT Lexington Ave. to 103rd St. station. Walk west to 5th Ave.
Bus: Fifth Ave. or Madison Ave. bus to 104th St.
Auto: FDR (East River) Drive to 96th St. exit. West to Madison Ave., north to 103rd St. Limited street parking.

Gift Shop: Exceptionally well-stocked shop to left of lobby entrance sells books on New York, Delft miniatures, toy reproductions of antique autos, souvenirs, posters.

Membership: Annual membership $15.00 up. Members receive invita-tions to special events, discounts, and Calendar of Events.

Special Events: Concerts (for adults) Sundays at 3 from October to May. "Please Touch" demonstrations on Saturdays, October through May. Admission $.50. Puppet shows Saturdays at 1:30. Adults $1.00, children $.50. Also, puppet workshops for children. Call for schedule.

156

Tours: Walking tours of New York City, alternate Sundays at 2:30, April to October. $3.00 fee; museum members, $2.00.

Dioramas of old New York, unique toys, costumes, fire engines, trolley cars, and clipper ships have attracted generations of city children to the Museum of the City of New York. The museum visually re-creates history so as to define our cultural heritage and describe, particularly for children, the story of New York City.

For an adult, the best place to start is on the fifth floor, with the Rockefeller rooms. A teen-ager might begin on the second floor, with the marine collection. Young children would start in the basement, where the water fountain and the fire engines are. The red-paneled Fire-Fighting Gallery has two life-size pumpers and a collection of miniature scale models of fire-fighting equipment, notably the first aerial ladder and a hose carriage. Old prints depict some of New York's early fires. The popular 1858 Currier & Ives print of the American fireman, "The Perfection of Graceful and Vigorous Manhood," is here. Much of this material duplicates the collection in the Fire Department Museum on Duane Street.

"Punch's Progress, Heroes of the Puppet Stage," interprets the evolution of Punch and Judy puppets, particularly those made by the master magician, Harry Houdini. A puppet theatre stands next to this display. From early hand puppets to the current rod puppets used on television, the figures have grown significantly larger. For example, the avant-garde Bread and Puppet Theatre once located in the Bowery, and not represented in this collection, uses puppets that are two stories high. The basement's miscellany is rounded off by a chronology of baseball from 1700 to 1950, with a dozen autographed baseballs and a panorama of Yankee Stadium, Ebbets Field, and the Polo Grounds. Soon they will all belong to history.

By taking the elevator to the fifth floor, one finds two rooms from a John D. Rockefeller house that stood at 4 West 54th Street. Rockefeller bought the house in 1884, about twenty-five years after it was built. Both the dressing room and bedroom were inspired by 1880 designs of the English architect Charles L. Eastlake. Satinwood with rosewood woodwork is inlaid with mother-of-pearl and intricate carvings. The plush elegance of the rooms epitomizes the grandeur of Victorian taste. The Fifty-fourth Street house was demolished in 1938; the site is now occupied by the garden of the Museum of Modern Art. (Another roomful of furniture from the same house is on view in the Brooklyn Museum.)

On the fourth floor are administrative offices, study rooms, a print section, and the theatre and music collections, all of which can be seen

by appointment. The third floor has the most diverse collection of dollhouses and toys available in any museum. Enchanting six-room miniature reproductions of complete scale-model houses, toy theatres, paper dolls, zoos, trolley cars, trains, pewter tea sets, animal farms, teddy bears, penny mechanical banks, iron coal stoves, complete kitchens,

Community-related exhibition on alcoholism.

and hobbyhorses offer children entertainment on a rainy afternoon.

About thirty-five dolls from the Sophia McDonald Collection provide excellent examples, some extremely rare, of almost every type of doll made from the late-eighteenth to the mid-nineteenth century. "Mehitabel Hodges," one of the oldest known imported dolls in America, was brought here from France in 1724.

"The History and Progress of Communications in New York" is dramatically presented by a series of dioramas showing the overland mail service, use of visual signals, Morse laying the submarine cable, the

Ship's figurehead of Andrew Johnson from the frigate "Constitution," 1812.

first stock ticker, telephone, radio, and the effects of the blizzard of '88. In front of each little boxlike theatre that houses a diorama, a ladder enables children to step up to see.

The third floor corridor contains an early nineteenth-century Duncan Phyfe drawing room. All the chairs, card table, sewing table, and other pieces here were made in his workshop from 1795 to 1847, and sold from his warehouse and store at 168 Fulton Street.

Duncan Phyfe's own sideboard is in the museum and was made by the famous cabinetmaker for his own residence at 193 Fulton Street. At his death in 1854 it was inherited by his daughter and remained in the family until it was given to the museum.

The Empire-style sideboard made about 1825 is both monumental and elegant with classic columns, Ionic capitals, exceedingly flamboyant mahogany veneers, gilded leaf, and paw feet. The mirror at the back of the lower section of the piece is an unusual feature that reflected a sarcophagus-shaped cellaret. This sideboard is a rare example of New York cabinetwork.

On the second floor the musuem's marine collection relates the maritime development of the city, from its Dutch trading-post days to the present. One diorama shows the Florentine navigator Giovanni da Verrazano startling the Indians as he sails into New York harbor in 1524. The diorama of the South Street waterfront during the clipper-ship era is so realistic that it is outdone only by the new forced-perspective technique used in a shipbuilding diorama that creates a fantastic illusion of depth, and offers a 360-degree view of Victorian New York. Figureheads, scale models of tugs, cutters, and ferries generate the excitement and adventure of the great harbor. The second floor also has a gallery devoted to Wall Street and a vast collection of silver.

The remaining gallery on the second floor contains six large alcoves of authentic room settings, some with costumed mannequins. There are an 1830 drawing room, from 7 Bowling Green; a 1760 English Colonial interior, from 29 Cherry Street; a 1906 drawing room, from 32 Park Avenue; and a Victorian drawing room, from 1 Pierrepont Street. The periods from 1690 to 1740 are also represented.

A number of fine American portraits hang on the first floor. In the Altman Foundation Gallery is a fascinating display of maps, prints, and views of early New York that trace the city's progress from 1800.

The truly fascinating Davies Gallery on the first floor displays ship models of the "Half Moon" and "Dauphine." Other exhibits relate to the period of Dutch settlement, as well as to the background of European events that led to the age of exploration and colonization. A diorama of Fort Amsterdam gives a 360-degree forced-perspective view of the skyline as it looked in 1660.

In addition to permanent and temporary exhibits, the museum conducts Sunday Walking Tours of every historical section of New York,

A bedroom from the Rockefeller house.

from the Battery to Brooklyn. Under the expert direction of an architectural historian, these popular two-hour excursions offer a unique opportunity to explore New York's history and architecture. Special tours are also conducted by Spanish-speaking guides.

The museum's "Please Touch" exhibits are for children aged six to thirteen. They can handle seventeenth- and eighteenth-century household objects. This is but one of many features the museum offers to thousands of schoolchildren who visit each year.

The Dazian Library, a collection of material on the visual arts of the stage, is open to students, historians, and designers. The museum library has a collection of New York City guidebooks dating from 1807, histories, biographies, and city direcrories. The first directory was compiled in 1786.

162

When the Museum of the City of New York first opened, on July 31, 1923, it was in Gracie Mansion in Carl Schurz Park, at 88th Street and the East River. In January, 1932, the museum moved into its present

Georgian building, which was designed by Joseph H. Freedlander. The average annual attendance is about 220,000. The museum is a non-profit organization operated by an independent Board of Trustees. The city's contribution toward the annual cost of operating the museum is so minimal that the principal funds must come from membership dues, gifts, bequests, and special fund-raising events.

The museum plans a program of reorienting many of its collections of decorative arts as related to material on the political and economic growth of the city. New exhibits will present the history of the city in chronological order; each period will be illustrated with appropriate costumes, furniture, portraits, and household items.

In outlining plans for overall expansion, refurbishing, and restructuring the museum's role in the community, Joseph Veach Noble, the director, says the museum must continue to collect the works of artistic and historic importance, but also must play a positive role in the life of the city today. The museum's new outlook was established with his famous "Drug Scene" and shows a serious effort to help combat drug abuse and drunken driving. Further plans include other community-oriented shows as well as a wing for formal-instruction classrooms.

THE NEW-YORK HISTORICAL SOCIETY

Address: Central Park West at 77th St., New York, N.Y., 10024.
Phone: 873-3400

Days: Museum open daily, except Mondays, 1–5; Saturdays, 10–5. Library open Tuesdays through Saturdays, 10–5; holidays, 1–5. Closed on major holidays.
Admission: Free.

Subway: IND 8th Ave. to 81st St. station. Walk south to museum.
Bus: Eighth Ave. and Central Park West buses to 77th St.
Auto: West Side Highway to 79th St. exit, east to Central Park West.

Gift Shop: Publications of the society, postcards for sale.

Membership: Annual from $10 to $250.

163

Special Events: Free films, concerts for children and adults, special school programs, guided tours for groups. Calendar of Events, printted three times a year and available at Information Desk, lists complete activities.

The New-York Historical Society.

The New-York Historical Society building contains fine portraits, historic prints, rare maps, handmade furniture, toys, and household furnishings—all of which are not only beautiful but also represent the roots from which many New Yorkers grew.

The New-York Historical Society, founded by John Pintard and ten leading citizens, occupied the first City Hall from 1804 until 1809. For about thirty years the society was always either in or close to City Hall. In 1837 it moved uptown to 659 Broadway, into the Stuyvesant Institute, and then to the northeast corner of Washington Square East, where the main building of New York University is now. For the next fifty years, from 1857, the society was at 170 Second Avenue, at 11th Street. After seven moves, it settled on Central Park West in 1908.

164

Early New York City milestones.

The collections of the society should be seen by everyone interested in this city. The examples of paintings, sculpture, and decorative arts that have come to the Society in 175 years of collecting Americana are outstanding. Quality, not quantity, has been the yardstick for acquisition.

One of these outstanding permanent exhibits is devoted to John James Audubon's "Birds of America." A number of the original drawings from that extraordinary volume hang in the gallery. Audubon drew 1,065 life-sized bird portraits representing 489 species found in North America. He published the double Elephant Folio engravings, all hand colored and drawn from nature, after considerable effort to solicit a subscription fund to cover its expense. In 1838, approximately 200 volumes were published, priced at $1,000 each. The New-York Historical Society has four volumes. The gallery was recently refurbished

165

The Peale Family by Charles Willson Peale.

to house this priceless collection, and the prints are rotated frequently.

The American Silver Gallery is particularly rich in the works of early New York silversmiths, such as Benjamin Wynkoop, who worked from 1690; Thauvet Besley (1727), Myer Meyers (1745), Daniel Christian Fueter (1754), William G. Forbes (1773), and Garret Eoff (1806). (The Brooklyn Museum has some samples of the work of Jacob Boelen and Jacobus van der Spiegel, who worked in New York before 1750. Other major collections of American silver are in the Museum of the City of New York and the Metropolitan.)

The period covered here ranges from about 1730 to 1850. Tankards, porringers, canns, salvers, toasting forks, sugar tongs, candle snuffers, nutmeg graters, snuffboxes, winetasters, tea caddies, toddy pots, saltcellars, and some commemorative silver pieces are on display.

Silver was introduced to America with the arrival in 1635 of Richard Storer of England. As the Colonies prospered, the use of silver increased. Quantities were produced for domestic use and in observance of civic and family events.

On the first floor are views of New York from 1679 to 1900. There is a wealth of maps, drawings, and colored lithographs of general views, churches, theatres, hotels, the harbor and waterfront, street scenes, and bridges. An auditorium is in the center of the first floor, and hallways around it display views of the Hudson River.

In the basement of the museum is the Fahnestock carriage collection of Brewster and Company coaches of the 1900s—Stanhope Gig, Park Drag, Tandem Cart, Panel Book Victoria, road coaches, and calèches. They are accompanied by a collection of New York City milestones, resembling fat tombstones, which marked the miles from City Hall to Kingsbridge, a distance of fourteen stones, and were important features of the early highway system. Oftentimes stagecoach inns were located at the milestones. The first group of stones was made in 1769 by George Lindsay.

A Volunteer Firemen's section is devoted to scale models and full-sized ancient equipment. This represents the third major collection of fire-fighting archives in the city. Special emphasis here is on prints and documentation of the conflagration of December 16, 1838, which wiped out a staggering portion of lower Manhattan in the Water Street, Front Street, Coenties Slip area.

On the second floor are the research library and the Library Gallery. The Katherine Prentis Murphy collections display early American wooden and mechanical toys, such as carved wooden horses, beaded doll furniture, toy soldiers, Noah's ark with three hundred animals, squeak toys, pottery banks, and whistles and jackstraws. Noteworthy is a large group of hand-carved animals by Wilhelm Schimmel, an itinerant Pennsylvania woodcarver who made toys in exchange for room and board.

Numerous articles illustrate New York under Dutch rule. An old New York map pinpoints the locations of Indian tribes that inhabited Manhattan. Outstanding in this collection are examples of the Duke of York laws of 1665; a remarkable sepia painting, dated 1679, of a Dutch cottage on Beaver Street; Peter Stuyvesant's Bible of 1637, and William Bradford's cracked tombstone. A copy of the tombstone is now in Trinity Churchyard.

The major exhibition of the Revolutionary and Federal periods is divided into historic sections dating from 1763 to 1800, and covers

Cigar store Indians.

the struggle for the Hudson River, New York as a Federal City, the Presidency, Revolutionary battles, and British occupation and evacuation. One of the many famous portraits of George Washington by Gilbert Stuart is here. It should be noted that many of the exhibits in the New-York Historical Society are rotated frequently and some works described may not be on view.

168

Also on exhibition are New York stoneware jugs, Rockingham pottery, American glass, earthenware, Worcester porcelain, green glazed pottery, Delftware salt-glaze ware, and Whieldon ware. The J. Insley Blair Collection of Old Blue English Staffordshire ware, depicting historical scenes of New York and New England, is one of the finest collections of this china in the country.

The completely furnished eighteenth-century parlor, bedroom, and seventeenth-century dining room reconstructed in this section form part of the Prentis Collection of Colonial New England. The collection also contains a number of printed cotton kerchiefs and textiles that commemorate historical events and personalities. The earliest, immortalizing George Washington, were printed in England and France in the 1800s.

In the third-floor galleries and corridors are folk art paintings of the highest quality, American pewter, lighting devices, household utensils, cigar-store wooden Indians, painted boxes, signs and weathervanes, paintings on glass, old advertisements and posters from the Bella C.

Beekman Family coach, imported from England, 1771.

*Paintings from "The Course of Empire"
series by Thomas Cole.*

Landauer collection. There is a map and print room as well as a collection of Early American military weapons, equipment ranging from flintlocks of Colonial days to weapons of the late nineteenth century. A group of sixty-seven figurines, dressed in costumes from 1610 to 1946, can also be found on this floor.

On the fourth floor is a marble sculpture by Thomas Crawford, who also did the colossal figures surmounting the dome of the United States Capitol. The title of his piece is "The Dying Chief Contemplating the Progress of Civilization."

The fourth-floor galleries are predominantly used for showing the paintings of prominent individuals, including Dutch New York portraits, Colonial New York portraits, presidents and statesmen, prominent men in the history of the Revolution, American artists and authors, late-eighteenth-century and nineteenth-century American landscape and genre painting. There is also a hall gallery devoted to the Reed, Bryan, and Durr Collection of European art.

Martha and George Washington by Rembrandt Peale.

There are a number of extremely fine paintings in these galleries, particularly in the presidential and landscape groups, where there are works by Asher B. Durand, Thomas Sully, Rembrandt Peale, Samuel F. B. Morse, John Trumbull, and Thomas Cole. Some of the painters themselves are the subjects of paintings in the section on artists. The recently acquired self-portrait of landscape painter Thomas Cole, for example, is the only one known to exist. It complements the Society's renowned series of five paintings by Cole called "The Course of Empire," which hang nearby and were painted in 1836.

The American furniture collection of the seventeenth, eighteenth, and nineteenth centuries features, in chronological order, examples of New England, Hudson River Valley, Pennsylvania, and New York City cabinetwork. An unusual wardrobe by Thomas Burling of New York City, about 1790, is one of the very rare labeled pieces. There are some pieces of Victorian furniture carved by John Henry Belter. Any student or scholar of American or New York history would find these paintings and household furnishings an invaluable source of knowledge and pleasure.

For New York City schoolchildren, as well as adults, the Society offers an extensive educational program that includes special school programs, a concert series, motion pictures, filmstrips, publications, guided tours, high-school loan exhibitions, story hours, puppet shows, and folk music. The Society is a privately endowed institution, and receives no financial support from the city. Its annual attendance is now about 160,000.

THE AMERICAN MUSEUM OF NATURAL HISTORY

Address: Central Park West at 79th St., New York, N.Y., 10024.
Phone: 873-4225 or 873-1300

Days: Open weekdays, 10—4:45; Sundays and holidays, 11:00—5:00; Wednesday evenings until 9.
Admission: By contribution.

Subway: IND 8th Ave. local to 81st station.
Bus: (1) 79th St. crosstown bus connects with East Side subways. (2) 8th Ave. or Columbus Ave. bus to 79th St.
Auto: West Side Highway to 79th St. exit, east to Central Park West. Parking lot adjacent to Planetarium on West 81st St. Open Sundays and holidays, 10—6:30; Monday through Friday, 9:30—5:30; Saturday, 9:30—6:30. Fee is $2.75 for private cars, $4.00 for buses. Some street parking.

Restaurant: Cafeteria in lower level of Roosevelt Memorial Building serves hot meals and snacks. No box lunches permitted. Open weekdays, 11:30—4:30; Sundays and holidays, 11:30—4:30; Wednesdays, 6—8.

Gift Shop: Museum Shop offers American Indian handicrafts, jade and coral, Mexican sculpture, Persian pottery, books on conservation, ornithology, botany, geology, genetics, Indian lore, anthropology; stone paperweights, crystal, quartz, onyx eggs, petrified wood; Junior Shop has telescopes, magnets, gyroscopes, shell sets, magnifiers, toys.

172

The American Museum of Natural History.

Special Events: Calendar of Events, published bimonthly September to June mailed free to members within the metropolitan area. Museum lectures, field trips, and tours for adults at nominal cost. Free films and lectures weekdays as announced. Free films for children and family groups on Saturday.

Membership: General membership is $10.00. Benefits include 10 issues of *Natural History Magazine,* 10% book discount, use of Members' Room, plus two bonus gifts. More expensive annual memberships, $20.00 and up, have additional benefits such as admission to Planetarium and Laserium, invitations to special member programs.

Library: For research only, Monday to Friday, 11—4. Closed Saturday, Sunday, and holidays.

Tours: Slide talks, film programs, gallery talks meet at Information Desk, 1st floor, Roosevelt Memorial Building; classes and groups required to register by phone or mail with Department of Education three weeks in advance. Not available weekends or holidays.

Children's Facilities: The Alexander M. White Natural Science Center and Discovery Room for Young People. School study aids available to teachers. Unescorted children under 18 not admitted to museum before 2 P.M. on New York City school days.

The American Museum of Natural History, the largest institution in the world devoted to the natural sciences, is directly across Central Park from that other mammoth institution, the Metropolitan Museum of Art. The American Museum was originally housed in the Arsenal building in Central Park along Fifth Avenue. Its physical plant now occupies three city blocks. The section facing West 77th Street, in Romanesque Revival style with segmented arches and imposing turrets, makes it obvious that this is a museum in the classic sense. This great museum receives over 4,000,000 visitors annually.

The section facing Central Park West was designed by the architect John Russell Pope in 1936 as a memorial to Theodore Roosevelt. The colossal scale of the main entrance is particularly evident from the inside. Pope's Colonnade Court can be seen at the Frick Collection.

The American Museum has approximately thirty-eight exhibition areas, each of which constitutes a small-size museum. The twenty-three acres of floor space include scientific and educational offices, laboratories, libraries, photography departments, restoration workshops, and storage areas, that contain tens of millions of zoological, geological, anthropological, and biological specimens for use by scientists, students, and scholars from all over the world. The museum also maintains field stations on Long Island, in Florida, Arizona, and the Bahamas. Its expeditions are always in progress.

The idea of the museum was conceived by Professor Albert Smith Bickmore, a naturalist who studied at Harvard. In 1865 he sailed for the Spice Islands, and in three years traveled 40,000 miles throughout the East Indies, Asia, and Europe, collecting birds, shells, and other specimens. The museum was formally established in 1869, and the two guiding principles that gave meaning and order to this vast institution are the evolution of life and the interdependence of all living things, including man.

The museum's scientific departments include: Animal Behavior, Anthropology, Astronomy, Entomology, Herpetology, Ichthyology, Invertebrate Paleontology, Living Invertebrates, Mammalogy, Mineralogy, Ornithology, Vertebrate Paleontology, and special activities. The nonscientific departments include Education, Exhibitions, and Graphic Arts, the Library, Scientific Publications, and *Natural History Magazine*. The educational program includes evening lectures, field

175

Dakota Indian Chief.

walks in natural science, museum tours, scientific-society meetings, and programs for young people conducted in the Natural Science Center. These programs highlight the wildlife of the metropolitan region, and present demonstrations of live animals. The American Museum also has courses for teachers in the social and natural sciences, and conducts a nursing education program.

Exhibits of the museum's collections are divided into the following categories: Astronomy, Birds, Invertebrates, Mammals, Man, Man's Environment, Minerals, Prehistoric Life, and Reptiles. The museum distributes a floor plan that shows the location of exhibits on all four floors. As part of its continuing pageant of achievement, renewal and improvement, it was recently announced that the museum would soon open new exhibits such as Peoples of Asia, Peoples of the Pacific, and Hall of Insects. Those just opened include Hall of Reptiles and Amphibians, Hall of Meteorites, Minerals and Gems, and the Childs Frick Wing, over 250,000 extraordinary fossil mammals that is the greatest single collection of its kind.

Komodo dragon of Indonesia.

*A peregrine falcon brings food to
its young on the New Jersey Palisades.*

Biology of Birds shows how birds originated, the kinds of birds that exist, those that are extinct, how birds fly, migrate, court, and breed. Three skeletons of giant flightless birds are shown—the ostrich, moa, and the Diatryma, a huge billed bird, dug up in Wyoming, that lived 50 million years ago.

Oceanic Birds were brought to the museum by the Whitney South Sea expedition (1920 to 1940), which was unique both in its duration and in the geographic area covered. Over 250 kinds of birds previously unknown to science were collected. Thorough study of the material brought back broadened concepts in the fields of evolution and distribution of life. This hall, showing about eighteen bird groups in various oceanic settings, was presented to the museum, together with a unique collection of 280,000 bird specimens acquired over a lifetime by Lord Rothschild, by Mrs. Harry Payne Whitney.

177

Bird of the World presents twelve realistic settings showing the differences in bird life from continent to continent. "North American Birds" in the Frank M. Chapman Memorial Hall shows 160 species of

Environment of the gemsbok group.

birds in settings approximating their original habitat. Upland game birds, common loons, desert birds, marsh birds, whooping cranes, California condors, the bald eagle, and peregrine falcon are all placed in realistic settings. The fascination and beauty of these life-size dioramas are due to the splendid background mural paintings of Fred Scherer, Raymond de Lucia, Matthew Kallmenoff, and Richard Kane, working with George E. Petersen, the Preparation Supervisor.

The Hall of Mexico and Central America presents what archaeology has revealed about the history of Middle America and evokes a feeling for the ancient cultures by chronologically tracing their development.

The Biology of Invertebrates covers the origin and structure of life. Glass models of invertebrates illustrate some universal biological themes by exhibiting animal species lacking backbones. The continuity and adaptability of life, as well as its interdependence, are also shown.

Insects are arranged here with reference to their origin, structure, habits, variations, and the ways in which they benefit and harm man.

Hall of Ocean Life and Biology of Fishes is an immense two-story gallery dramatically set off with a supercolossal blue whale suspended in a midair nose-dive position. The ninety-four-foot, ten-ton replica of a blue female captured in the Antarctic has a steel skeleton and is sculpted in Fiberglas and polyurethane foam. It took two years to complete, and cost $300,000. It is probably the largest museum exhibit in the world. A live whale this size would weigh one hundred tons.

These mammals are the largest creatures ever known. Sometimes they are more than 100 feet long and weigh up to 175 tons. They can swim at 23 miles an hour and look blue in the water, but actually they are black and gray, as seen here.

In the surrounding bays, fifteen dioramas of life in the seas and an exhibit of the phylogeny of fishes details the architecture of fishes, how they adapt to their environment, feeding habits, defense mechanisms, reproduction, and diversity. The dioramas of divers hunting for pearls in the coral reefs and the walrus habitat groups are particularly dramatic.

Discussion and Study Group in the galleries.

The forerunners of modern man.

Early Mammals shows the origin, spread, isolation, and extinction of these Mesonychids, Oxyaenids, and Hyaenodonts. A modern wall display explains how fossils are buried and preserved, then collected, cleaned, prepared, restored, identified, and finally classified by period.

Late Mammals of the Cenozoic Period, the even-toed and odd-toed hoofed mammals, outlines the evolution of the horse, the camel, rhino, and antelope.

The Late Dinosaurs contains the most comprehensive display of Cretaceous dinosaur skeletons in existence. Tyrannosaurus rex, Triceratops, and Trachodonts are grouped in the center island of the gallery. These monsters once existed in the general region of Montana, and were among the last dinosaurs to live on earth. Other examples of dinosaurs to be found here are the horned, armored, aquatic duckbilled, dome-headed dinosaurs, and flying reptiles.

180   Early Dinosaurs is by far the most popular exhibit in the museum. The center island has three great monsters of the Jurassic period: the 67-foot Brontosaurus, the dagger-jawed Allosaurus, and the spiked-tailed Stegosaurus, all of which roamed the Far West about 140 million years ago. At the base of the display are two pairs of Brontosaurus

footprints collected in Texas. Another particularly interesting exhibit is the fossil skeleton of a dinosaur found by a geology class from Columbia University in 1910 in the Palisades near the site of the George Washington Bridge. This is appropriately labeled Fort Lee Phytosaur, Clepsysaurus manhattanensis. The history of fossil fishes is to be found at the far end of the gallery.

Ice Age Mammals are depicted in this gallery, with striking examples of the evolution of the proboscideans, including the long-jawed, shovel-jawed, beak-jawed, and flat-toothed mastodons, and on to the southern hairless mammoths, northern woolly mammoths, and elephants of Africa and India. There are also several giant sloths from the famous La Brea tar pits in Los Angeles (now the site of the Los Angeles County Museum).

The Primates are animals that belong to the same order as man. The distinctive characteristics and relationship of the different groups of primates are shown, including the tiny tree shrews, the lemurs, tarsiers, spider monkeys, howlers, bearded sakis, gorillas, apes, chimpanzees, and man. About 185 of the 5,500 living species of mammals are primates. Charts outline the development of hands, feet, vision, the senses, and reproduction.

In the Hall of the Dinosaurs.

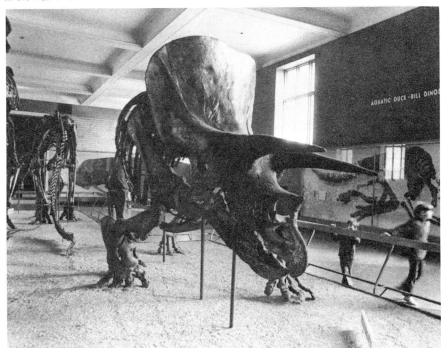

African Mammals are on view in twenty-eight alcoves on two floors of the Carl Akeley Memorial Hall. A balcony offers a fine view of the group of elephants that are mounted in the center of the lower floor. Akeley was a renowned sculptor, taxidermist, conservationist, and inventor who survived incredible adventures. He was once pinned under an elephant, and at another time he strangled a wounded leopard when he ran out of ammunition. He succumbed to fever and exhaustion on his Belgian Congo expedition in 1926 and is buried on the slopes of Mount Mikeno, high in his beloved gorilla country. These beautifully displayed mammals are the results of his expeditions.

Akeley never lived to see the African Plains displays, among the most popular and impressive exhibits in the museum, for these exhibits are startling in their reality. The animals are shown in a complete environment of rocks, bushes, vegetation, insects, trees, water, and background murals of the terrain. One dramatic scene shows hyenas, jackals and vultures attacking a zebra. In another, white rhinos are being stalled off at a water hole by a porcupine. Beautiful impalas graze in the open fields, mandrills inhabit the rain forest, and wart hogs fix their eyes on ostrich eggs hatching under the protection of the frightened parents.

North American Mammals, another group of dramatic habitats, displays game and fur-bearing species—bison, white sheep, coyotes, mountain lions—in environmental settings, including Mount McKinley, the Grand Canyon, and the Great Smokies.

Materials for South Asiatic Mammals were collected in 1922 on expeditions into India, Burma, and Siam by Arthur S. Vernay and Colonel J. C. Faunthrope. In this gallery's realistic settings are the most complete exhibits of larger South Asiatic mammals in existence, including Indian antelopes, gaurs, leopards, sambars, sloth bear, chevrotains, bantings, and other rare animals. A pair of Indian elephants stands in the center of the gallery.

The Hall of Reptiles and Amphibians covers the anatomy, reproduction, feeding, defense, locomotion and sensing of snakes and lizards, frogs and turtles. A particularly fascinating reptile, the Komodo dragon of Indonesia, is the largest existing lizard. It weighs 200 pounds and reaches a length of 10 feet. There are 6,000 different species of living reptiles and about 3,500 species of amphibians. Amphibians date back 350 million years to the Devonian Period; reptiles evolved somewhat later, about 300 million years ago. During the Mesozoic Era they dominated the globe. Today, in an age conspicuously dominated by mammals, reptiles and amphibians nonetheless continue to play an important role in most ecological systems.

The Hall of Northwest Coast Indians contains many totem poles and masks, particularly those of the Kwakiutl Indians. Tribes of woodworkers lived in the coastal region from southern Alaska to the Columbia

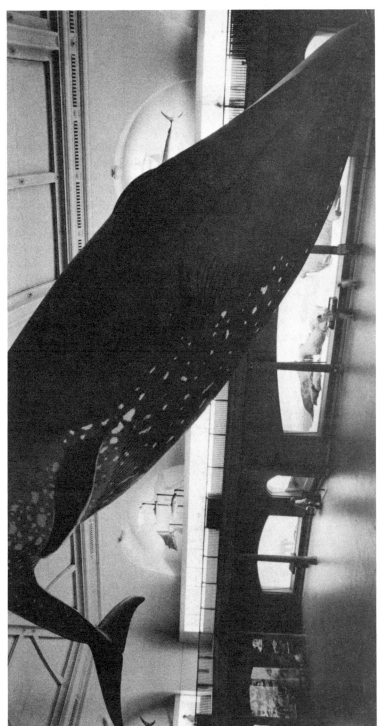

Blue whale in Hall of Ocean Life.

River in Washington and carved cedar into stylized animal and human forms for house and grave posts, masks and tools.

The Eskimo Gallery in the horseshoe around the auditorium depicts the culture of tribes in Canada, Alaska, and Greenland. "Indians of the Northwest Coast" illustrates the domestic and cultural mores of the Kwakiutl Indians of Vancouver, with a scale model showing an entire village. A sixty-four-foot seagoing war canoe of the Haida tribe is displayed in the center of the 77th Street foyer, one of the main entrances of the museum.

Eastern Woodlands and Plains Indians concentrates on the culture of the twenty-five tribes that roamed the plains from the Mississippi to the Rockies and from Texas to Canada until the last quarter of the nineteenth century. The exhibit features six life-sized figures in costumes of dressed skin, heavily decorated with beadwork and the quills of porcupines.

The Biology of Man, a departure from the standard museum exhibits, presents the very latest in visual material that documents life by explaining human cells, endocrine regulation, digestion, growth, and the functions of sensory perception. Heads of Cro-Magnon Man, Peking Man, and other forerunners of *Homo sapiens* are displayed on a platform, showing the successive types that reflect the course of human evolution. An unusual zoological wall chart in tile classifies man and his forebears.

A group of elephants in Akeley Hall.

A 64-foot war canoe carved from a single cedar log by the Haida indians.

The most startling section of the exhibit contains unique plastic specimens of the human fetus in about six stages of growth. This remarkable exhibit is accompanied by (plastic) specimens of lungs, the heart, intestines, and other internal organs. The human circulatory system is graphically presented by means of a life-size plastic sculpture of a woman that also may be lighted to show the functions of the human nervous system.

Man and Nature in the Felix M. Warburg Memorial Hall features landscape settings and exhibits relating human activities and the cycle of life in the soil. The Hall of North American Forests shows the diversity of communities in middle North America, the internal functions of our forests, and how man benefits from them. Life-size dioramas show huge cedar forests, the rain forests near Olympia, Washington, and others. There is a cross section of a giant Sequoia that was 330 feet tall, with a trunk circumference of 90 feet. In 1891, two men took 13 days to cut the tree down. The section contains 1,342 annual rings, which indicates that the growth of the tree began in A.D. 550.

John Lindsley Hall of Earth History features a rotating relief globe of the world more than six feet in diameter, one of the few working

185

Hall of Minerals and Gems.

seismic recorders on public display, and a ten-minute introductory mul-
timedia exposition of the hall's subject matter, which uses eight screens
for simultaneous slide projection accompanied by commentary and
musical background. It is the story of what the earth's core is made of,
what it's covered with; how the rocks, the minerals, the beaches, the
mountains, and life under the sea are formed. A cross section of earth
visibly separates the various layers of geological traps that cause oil and
coal to form beneath the surface of the earth. The geology of New
York is identified in a color-coded relief map.

186

Colossal Olmec head.

The Evelyn Miles Keller Memorial Shell Exhibit shows the six classes of mollusks from all over the world. This interesting seashell collection, in addition to showing shells as objects of aesthetic beauty, illustrates how they have been used by man for food, utensils, ornaments, money, implements, medicine, and even as a source for dye.

Hall of Man in Africa shows how, under different circumstances, different peoples adapted themselves to their environment in ways that made it possible for them to survive; how their society grew in strength and complexity on this basis; and how tribal society achieved stability and developed moral and social characteristics often thought of as being a monopoly of the Western world. To achieve this, the hall is divided into the physical environments that make up Africa: Desert, Forest, Grasslands, and River Valley.

The Hall of Minerals and Gems is the most spectacular exhibit, with its wealth and glitter that is worth nearly $50 million. Exhibits cover such subjects as the properties of minerals, mineral-forming environments, systematic minerology, interaction of minerals and energy, and the esthetics of minerals and gems. The unorthodox hall is curvilinear and multiple-leveled, with ramps and steps leading to individual displays. Among the more unusual and exotic treasures are a 563-carat star sapphire, twelve chunks of iron from outer space, a large garnet crystal unearthed during a New York subway excavation, quartz crystals from the Catskills, a 596-pound topaz from Brazil and an 87.64-carat engraved emerald believed to have been worn 300 years ago by a Hindu prince. Many of the museum's most exquisite minerals and gems were the gift of J. Pierpont Morgan at the turn of the century.

THE AMERICAN MUSEUM-HAYDEN PLANETARIUM
Address: Central Park West at 81st St., New York, N.Y., 10024.
Phone: 873-8828; sky reporter, 873-0404; other, 873-1389

Days: Shows every day of the year. Schedule as follows:
Saturday and Sunday   1, 2, 3, 4, 5 P.M.
Weekdays   2, 3:30 P.M.
Holidays   Call 873-8828 for holiday and special summer schedule.
Laserium: cosmic laser concert: call 724-8700 for schedule.
Admission: Adults, $2.35; children $1.35; Laserium, $3.25.

Subway: IND 8th Ave. to 81st St. station.
Bus: (1) 79th St. crosstown bus connects with East Side subways. (2) 8th Ave. or Columbus Ave. bus to 81st St.
Auto: West Side Highway to 79th St. exit. Parking lot adjacent to Planetarium on West 81st St. Open Sundays and holidays, 10—6:30; Monday through Friday, 9:30—5:30; Saturday, 9:30—6:30. Fee is

$2.75 for private cars, $4.00 for buses. Metered street parking behind museum.

Gift Shop: The Planetarium Shop sells publications on astronomy, space science, star-finders and charts, cards, prints.

Restaurant: See American Museum of Natural History.

Lectures: Courses in the spring and fall for adults and children on astronomy, navigation, and meteorology.

There is a direct entrance from the American Museum of Natural History to the Hayden Planetarium, which occupies its own building facing a large open park on West 81st Street. The building, easily identified by its green dome, is one of ten planetariums in the United States. About 650,000 visitors come each year to visit the planetarium, which was made possible by a gift in 1937 of the philanthropist Charles Hayden. He believed that a planetarium should be a "place of interest and instruction . . . it should give a more lively and sincere appreciation of the magnitude of the universe . . . the belief that there must be a much greater power than man, responsible for the wonderful things occurring in the universe." As S. I. Gale, chief lecturer for twenty-two years, said after his six thousandth lecture on the day he retired, "There are no atheists at the eyepiece of a telescope."

The round building has two floors, both of which exhibit displays of compelling contemporary significance and interest. To the left of the main entrance is the Planetarium Shop, a headquarters for technical books on astronomy, navigation, and meteorology, for celestial globes and paraphernalia for home and classroom use. A catalogue describes courses in astronomy and navigation for adults as well as for young people. On four mornings a week the program of the Planetarium is reserved for school classes.

Directly in the center of the first floor is a lecture theatre called the Guggenheim Space Theatre. A Copernican planetarium, more than forty feet in diameter, shows the relative sizes and speeds of the planets and the satellites by means of globes revolving around a central sun. Corridors around the hall, all dimly illuminated, are lined with exhibits simulating outer space. A "black-light" tunnel of perpetual night, with large luminescent, color-activated murals puts the viewer in the shadowy mountains and craters of the lunar landscape. Other murals vividly detail solar eclipses, the planets, and galactic and spiral nebulae.

189

One remarkable exhibit shows the Ahnighito Meteorite, the largest on display anywhere. This great mass was dug up from the frozen wastelands of Greenland by Admiral Robert E. Peary in 1894. Twelve teams of horses were needed to haul the huge 34-ton meteorite from

A meteorite.

the docks. The Toledo Scale Company built a special platform scale for it. Visitors can stand on the scale and add their own weight to the 68, 085 pounds already registered.

A set of scales on the second floor illustrates a person's weight on other planets. If you weigh 150 pounds on Earth, on Jupiter you would weigh 430 pounds; on Venus, 140 pounds; on Mars, 62 pounds; and on the Moon a mere 26 pounds. The major exhibit on the second floor is the IBM Astronomia, designed and developed by Gordon Ashby. The exhibition, arranged in chronologies of one hundred years, out-

Visual application of the laws of gravitation.

CELESTIAL MECHANICS

CELESTIAL MECHANICS is a branch of astronomy that deals with the problems of mass and motion of celestial bodies through the mathematical application of the laws of gravitation.

lines the major achievements, developments, and theories in the science of astronomy from the year 1400.

The main lecture theatre, on the second floor, houses the huge Zeiss projector that showers the entirely perforated stainless-steel dome with millions of stars to create a perfect sky on a clear night.

The solar system and the miracles of the boundless universe, in perpetual, dramatic flux, are the stars in the show. It is truly a breathtaking experience to see the simulated sky fill with heavenly bodies and to hear the majestic music. For city dwellers this star-studded dome is a wonder that comes to life only in a planetarium or on a trip to the adjacent countryside. The lecture is delivered, live, by one of a staff of nine that operates the panel of forty knobs controlling the projector. The lecturer has over two thousand possible combinations at his command, and is thus virtually in command of the universe.

In the Roerich Museum.

NICHOLAS ROERICH MUSEUM

Address: 319 West 107th St., New York, N.Y., 10025.
Phone: 864-7752

Days: Open every day, except Saturdays, 2—5.

Admission: Free.

Subway: IRT Broadway-242nd St. train to 110th St. station, south 3 blocks.
Bus: Fifth Ave. (Riverside Drive) bus to 107th St.
Auto: West Side Highway to 96th St. exit, then north on Riverside Drive. Ample street parking.

Gift Shop: Postcards, publications for sale.

Special Events: Lectures on art, and music; concert recitals.

Membership: Membership privileges include free attandance at concèrts, bulletins, announcements.

For the past twenty years the Nicholas Roerich Museum has occupied a former town house off Riverside Drive. Three floors of the building are devoted to the work of this artist who became known as the "Master of the Mountain" because of his paintings of Himalayan, Tibetan, and Indian mountain scenes. Anyone seeing his pictures for the first time will be startled by the strange ice-blue, chartreuse, purple, and violet colors. Roerich is represented in the Louvre and the Luxembourg Museum (Paris), the Victoria and Albert Museum (London), National Museum (Stockholm), and the Tretyakov Gallery (Moscow). His landscapes recall the work of Wassily Kandinsky or Franz Marc.
 The principal objective of the museum, an incorporated nonprofit educational institution, is to "disseminate the ideals of art and culture to which the artist dedicated his life." In addition to maintaining Roerich's paintings and publicizing his ideals of peace through culture, the museum exhibits the works of some young artists, offers lectures on art, and presents recitals by concert artists.
 Nicholas Konstantin Roerich was born in St. Petersburg in 1874, and studied art, philosophy, history, law, and archeology. He painted over seven thousand pictures, of which about a hundred are on view here. He was also a mural painter and scenic designer who contributed designs for stage productions, particularly opera, in Russia. Until 1916 he directed the School for Encouraging Fine Arts in Russia. He was also connected with the Moscow Art Theater and the Diaghilev Ballet. In his lifetime he published nearly thirty volumes, besides many essays

193

and articles. As an explorer and scientist he carried out extensive archeological research and excavations in Russia and the Orient.

Roerich lived in Russia, Finland, and England until 1920, when the Chicago Art Institute invited him to visit America on an exhibition tour. He stayed here until 1923, when he organized and conducted a five-year expedition to India, Tibet, Mongolia, and remote areas of Central Asia. The expedition was sponsored by Roerich's Master Institute of United Arts. Roerich eventually made his home in the valley of the Punjab and lived there for eighteen years until his death in 1947.

The original collection of the museum consisted of works brought to America for his exhibition tour and others created whlle the artist was in America, at Monhegan, Maine; Santa Fe, New Mexico; and the Grand Canyon. In the current collection are works produced while he was in Tibet and India.

The Master Institute of United Arts was founded on November 17, 1921, by Nicholas Roerich for the purpose of uniting all the arts under one roof. One unit of the Master Institute was the Roerich Museum, which used to be at 310 Riverside Drive.

As Nicholas Roerich conceived it, the building was to house persons interested in culture and art who followed his doctrines. During the twenties and thirties Roerich's fantastic influence had spread throughout the world. He was revered not only as an artist but also as a mystic. The Roerich Museum and Press, the School of the Master Institute, its living quarters, the International Art Center, and all the other facets of the Institute were intended to be a self-contained utopia of the arts. Roerich's aim was a "synthesis of the arts, the awakening, the nurture and development of the creative spirit," which, at any time, is a noble and worthwhile endeavor.

Roerich was honored in many countries. In 1929 he was nominated for a Nobel Peace Prize, based on his international campaign for better understanding and greater harmony among nations under a pact for international protection, in war or peace, of monuments, institutions, and cultural treasures. The pact was known as the Roerich Pact; its symbol, the banner of peace, utilized three red spheres within a circle. The pact was also intended to draw the attention of mankind to those values that are the common heritage of the civilized world.

GENERAL GRANT NATIONAL MEMORIAL
Address: Riverside Drive at 122nd St., New York, N.Y., 10027
Phone: 666-1640

194

Days: Open daily, 9—4:30; closed Mondays and Tuesdays.
Admission: Free.

Subway: IRT Broadway-242nd St. train to 116th St. station. Walk one

block west to Riverside Drive, north to Tomb.
Bus: Fifth Ave. (Riverside Drive) bus to 122nd St.
Auto: West Side Highway to 125th St. then south on Riverside Drive.

General Grant National Memorial.

Grant's Tomb, one of New York's most durable landmarks and visitor attractions, is among the national memorials supervised by the National Park Service of the United States Department of the Interior, along with the Theodore Roosevelt Birthplace, the Statue of Liberty, Castle Clinton, Federal Hall, and Hamilton Grange.

The tomb of General Ulysses Simpson Grant, resembling a Roman mausoleum, is an imposing, monumental, gray-granite, conical-domed structure with a portico supported by ten fluted Doric columns. The entrance stairs are flanked by two huge American eagles. Over the entrance the inscription says "Let Us Have Peace." The 150-foot high tomb can be seen for miles because it is on a bluff along Riverside Drive, high above the Hudson River.

The entirely air-conditioned interior of the monument is covered with marble, and the sarcophagi of the General and his wife, Julia Dent Grant, both in an open crypt in the center, are also of polished marble. It is a very simple setting, inducing a reverent mood. The crypt is similar to Napoleon's tomb at the Invalides in Paris.

Two exhibit rooms are devoted to pictorial documentation of Ulysses Grant as a civilian and as a battle-seasoned soldier. Allegorical figures between the arches of the rotunda represent the General's life and bronze busts around the crypt show his comrades-in-arms: Sherman, Ord, Sheridan, Thomas, and McPherson.

Grant was one of this country's outstanding Civil War military heroes, having fought in over thirty-five battles. He was later President, from 1868 to 1876. This national memorial is for the purpose of "honoring the memory of the great soldier under whose command the Union Armies brought the Civil War to a victorious conclusion, thus preserving the Union."

INTERCHURCH CENTER
Address: 475 Riverside Drive (at 119th St.), New York, N.Y., 10027.
Phone: 870-2200

Days: Open Mondays through Fridays, 10—5. Closed Saturdays, Sundays, and holidays.
Admission: Free.

Subway: IRT Broadway-242nd St. train to 116th St. station. Walk one block west to Riverside Drive, north to center.
Bus: Fifth Ave. (Riverside Drive) bus to 119th St.
Auto: West Side Highway to 125th St. then south on Riverside Drive.

Restaurant: Cafeteria in basement and lounge open to public.

Special Events: Summer film program; inquire at desk.

Tours: Groups should make reservations in advance for tours. Phone or write to Tour Information, Room 253.

A modern structure faced with Alabama limestone, the Interchurch Center looks toward Riverside Drive and the Hudson River. A piece of rock in the cornerstone is from the agora in Corinth, where "many . . . hearing Paul believed."

The entire city block on which the building stands was donated by John D. Rockefeller, Jr. The center "is a visible symbol of the oneness of many churches in Christ." Its nineteen stories house church-related organizations of the Protestant and Orthodox communions in America. Of particular interest to tourists are the Narthex, the Chapel, the Orthodox Room, and the Treasure Room, all on the street floor.

The Treasure Room, to the right of the entrance, is paneled in English oak. It has floor-to-ceiling sliding aluminum posts for display panels. From September to May art and photography exhibitions with a religious theme are shown in the gallery.

The Narthex (a vestibule or waiting room) to the left separates the Chapel and Orthodox Room. A strange textured tapestry hangs on the wall, and a thousand tiny lucite tubes in the ceiling light the room. The "canopy of stars" is the work of New York sculptor Israel Levitan.

The Chapel demonstrates the fine possibilities of modern design in an ecclesiastical setting. The simplicity of the interior, the selection of white rose bricks, the arrangement of the Chi Rho (ancient Greek symbol for the Christ), and the window of translucent English alabaster create a unified, reverent effect.

The Orthodox Room displays "Byzantine Art in the Service of Christianity" with an impressive array of icons and Eastern Orthodox

197

art objects from the collection of Paul M. Fekula, an active member of the Russian Orthodox Greek Catholic Church of America. His collection, in fifteen glass cases, is said to be one of the finest outside Russia. It features sixteenth-century icons of major holy days of the Church, a bishop's miter, vestments and altar cloths, and ancient books of Orthodox services.

MUSEUM OF THE AMERICAN INDIAN

Address: Broadway at 155th St., New York, N.Y., 10032.
Phone: 283-2420

Days: Open Tuesdays through Sundays, 1–5. Closed Mondays, holidays, and the month of August.
Admission: $1.00; special group rates.

Subway: (1) IRT Broadway-242nd St. train to 157th St. station. (2) IND 8th Ave. Washington Heights train to 155th St. station. Walk two blocks west to Broadway.
Auto: West Side Highway to 158th St. exit. East to Broadway, south to Audubon Terrace. Ample street parking.

Gift Shop: Books on Indians, Indian handicrafts, toys, souvenirs.

Research: Special research facilities in Bronx for scholars.

Tours: School groups welcome, but one adult must be responsible for each 10 children. No guide service.

The Museum of the American Indian is the largest Indian museum in the world. George C. Heye founded the institution, which was opened to the public in 1922. His collections form the nucleus of the museum, whose main purpose is the furthering of a better understanding of the Indians by the collection and preservation of cultural material. Support comes from a modest endowment. The institution receives no city, state, or Federal tax monies. For its members the museum offers identification of specimens, technical advice, and general information. Its publications include bibliographies, ethnological studies, and definitive archeological reports. There is a research branch of the museum in the Bronx, where the bulk of the study specimens are maintained for scholarly research purposes.

198

The public exhibitions at Audubon Terrace are arranged by regions —peoples of the Southeast, the Basin-Plateau region, Indians of the Plains, the Great Lakes Tribes, New England Indians. Exhibits from the

The Wakaruk ceremony
of Southern California tribes.

tribes of each region outline the environment, the tribe's economy, housing, weapons, hunting techniques, foods, religion, social organization, games and entertainments. Exhibits interpret the life of the tribes by displaying the commonplace objects side by side with rare or unique items.

Familiar tribal names are present—Iroquois, Navajo, Algonquin, Hopi. Seminoles are represented with the Creek, Cherokee, and other tribes in a case displaying particularly beautiful Indian dresses, plain pottery, and intricate basketweaving. The Iroquois exhibits are the most extensive to be seen anywhere. One display shows the remarkable

*Shrunken human figures
from the head-hunting
Jivaro Indians of Ecuador.*

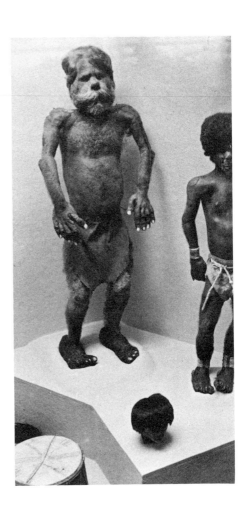

SHE DECORATED HER LEGGINGS AND MOCCASINS

Indian baskets and beadwork.

masks of the Society of False Faces. Masks represent the mythological forest creatures the Indians believed had the power to cure disease. By impersonating the powerful spirit, the man who wore the false face gained the power to cure.

Also on the first floor are some historic wampum belts. "Wampum" meant white string of shell beads. The Dutch gave Long Island the name Sewan Hacky, or "wampum land," because of the quantities of shells found there. These purple and white cylindrical shell beads were used in trading between the Indians and the Dutch, and were made from the lip of the hardshell clam. Near the wampum case hangs an unusual parchment peace treaty made in 1765 between the British and the Delaware, Shawnee, and Mingo tribes. Small, crude animal drawings represent the mark of the tribes.

201

Ethnic material from the Southeast is rare, and the museum display of such specimens is unsurpassed. A section shows peyote paraphernalia and the role played by fetishes and charms. Special exhibitions are held in the gallery to the left of the museum entrance. The gift shop to the right carries a variety of authentic items, Indian basketry, books, Kachina dolls, masks, and small sculpture.

The stairway to the upper floors is hung with a number of decorated elk skins and buffalo robes. The second floor presents the ethnology of the Indians of the Southwest, a major Northwest Coast gallery depicting the California tribes, the Indians of Canada, and the Eskimos. The Northwest Coast people are represented by a tableau depicting the ostentatious display of the potlatch ceremony, examples of copper artwork and many small stone, wood and ivory carvings. There are delicate basketry and featherwork from the California tribes and a unique trio of Diegueno "Death Images." Included here are the beautiful Kachina masks and dolls of the Southwestern tribes.

The third floor contains the Williams Hall of Middle American Archeology. An exhibit of Panamanian Ceramic Art (A.D. 1000–1500) has some superb specimens of blue pottery, and is proof of a highly sophisticated culture in that area. Examples of sculpture, mosaic, and metalwork, especially in gold and silver, are outstanding. Newly assembled exhibits illustrate the arts of northern Mexico, Mayan life, Central American tribes, West Indies, Argentina, Brazil, Chile, Peru. The exhibits emphasize pottery, small sculpture, jewelry, clothing, weapons, musical instruments, masks, and two human bodies shrunken by the Jivaro Indians of Ecuador.

AMERICAN GEOGRAPHICAL SOCIETY

Address: Broadway at 155th St., New York, N.Y., 10032.
Phone: 234-8100

Days: Open Mondays to Wednesdays, 9–12 by appointment only.
Admission: Free.

Subway: (1) IRT Broadway-242nd St. train to 157th St. station. (2) IND 8th Ave. Washington Heights train to 155th St. station. Walk two blocks west to Broadway.
Auto: West Side Highway to 158th St. exit. East to Broadway, south to Audubon Terrace. Ample street parking.

202

Membership: Seven types of membership, ranging from $30.00 annual dues upward. Membership privileges include subscription to the *Geographical Review* and *Focus.*

203

American Geographical Society.

The American Georgraphical Society is a scholaraly research library with a noble history, and its possession of 170,000 bound volumes, hundreds of periodicals, 325,000 maps, 5,000 atlases, and 40,000 photographs gives it an eminent standing. Yet few people realize the existence of this vast storehouse of geographical knowledge.

Unlike the National Geographic Society in Washington, D.C. (1888), with over 4 million members, the American Geographical Society (1852) has only 4,000 members, and does not issue a popular monthly magazine with color photographs. It, however, is the oldest geographical society in the United States.

The American Geographical Society exists for the sole purpose of advancing "geography as a science, as an educational discipline, and as a guide to knowledge." In achieving its objective, the society carries out original investigations in economic and human geography, glaciology, oceanography, and cartography; it issues scientific publications, maintains the largest private geographical library and map collection in the Western Hemisphere, presents lectures, and gives awards for exploration and geographic research. As a tax-free institution, it is open to the public, principally to college students and researchers "who know exactly what they are looking for."

The society is housed in the same Classic Eclectic style as the other museums in Audubon Terrace. The street floor has one exhibition gallery and the World Data Center of Glaciology. The library and card catalogue are on the second floor. The map room on the third floor has maps and charts from all over the world, dating from ancient times to the present. The maps cover everything from topographical structure, political communities, plant-life dispersement, glacial makeup—just about any kind of map imaginable. On the fourth floor the cartographers' skylight studio is busy with reconnaissance maps, small-scale compilations and special maps illustrating the results of research.

THE HISPANIC SOCIETY OF AMERICA

Address: Broadway at 155th St., New York, N.Y., 10032.
Phone: 926-2234

Days: Tuesdays through Saturdays, 10—4:30; Sundays, 1—4. Library open Tuesdays through Fridays, 1—4:30; Saturdays, 10—4:30. Closed Mondays, holidays, and month of August.
Admission: Free.

Subway: (1) IRT Broadway-242nd St. train to 157th St. station. (2) IND 8th Ave. Washington Heights train to 155th St. station; walk two blocks west to Broadway.
Auto: West Side Highway to 158th St. exit. East to Broadway, south to Audubon Terrace. Ample street parking.

Gift Shop: Museum shop sells publications of society, color prints and slides and postcards.

As darkly magnificent, cool, and hushed as the interior of a Spanish grandee's castle, the Hispanic Museum sits in splendor, the ruby-red jewel of Audubon Terrace. In front of the museum the terrace courtyard is dominated by a statue of Spain's national hero, El Cid. The eleventh-century warrior has been re-created as he might have appeared at the siege of Valencia. This piece, and the animal and figure bronzes, stone lions at the museum door, and limestone reliefs of Don Quixote and Boabdil on the courtyard wall were all created by Anna Hyatt Huntington, wife of the museum's founder. She also did the huge bronze of the Cuban independence leader, José Julian Marti at the foot of Central Park.

Archer Milton Huntington made his first trip to the Iberian Peninsula in 1892. From an archaeological camp in Italica, the first Roman colony in Spain, near Seville, he brought home Corinthian capitals, inscribed gravestone fragments, and jewelry. His collection includes sculpture and pottery from Roman times; tiles, metalwork, and textiles from the period of Moorish domination; and Gothic and Renaissance art from the Christian era.

Since childhood, Huntington's thoughts had dwelt on "the foundation of a Hispanic center where source material in documents and examples of the arts of Spain and Portugal might be studied as a basis for original research." In 1904, he established the Hispanic Society. Two years later he donated land near Audubon Terrace for a Spanish church, a site that was known at the turn of the century as Spanish Hill. The Church, Our Lady of Esperanza, has become an important institution where Puerto Rican immigrants can find help learning English, finding work, and adapting to their new environment while preserving the tra-

Main hall of the Hispanic Museum.

ditional faith.

The Indiana limestone facade of the museum building is enhanced by sculptural and architectural detail. The museum's collections consist of prehistoric art through the Visigothic period, Hispano-Moresque, Mudejar, Gothic, Renaissance, baroque, rococo, and neoclassic art, and nineteenth- and twentieth-century paintings.

The library of the Hispanic Society contains about 12,000 books printed before 1701. It also has a collection of maps, globes, incunabula, Bibles, liturgies, chronicles, books on chivalry, codes of law, and some 90,000 other books relating to the art, history and society of Spain, Portugal, and colonial Hispanic America. In the anteroom of the library are hand-carved mahogany choir stalls.

The Hispanic Society of America.

16th-century tomb of the Duchess of Alburquerque.

The main gallery on the street floor is two stories high. The entire room is decorated in the flat red terra-cotta typical of the Spanish Renaissance. Daylight filters into the gallery from an ornamental skylight in the beamed ceiling. Twenty archways surrounding the room separate it from the encircling corridor. Roman sculpture is placed in some of the archways, whose pillars rest on red marble. Each sustaining arch has an escutcheon bearing the arms of a province or city of Spain. Within the arcades are panels from fourteenth- and fifteenth-century Catalan, Valencian, and Leonese retablos, polychrome wood carvings, ivories, samples of gold and silverwork, laces and textiles. One section of the corridor is devoted to the magnificent alabaster and marble tomb of the Duchess of Alburquerque. Inside the gallery hang paintings by Goya and Velázquez.

Spanish tiles and pottery.

Off the main gallery a small room of mosaics leads to the gallery where modern landscapes surround the entire room. The artist, Joaquin Sorolla y Bastida (1863—1923), was honored with a major exhibit here in 1909. His 350 paintings attracted nearly 160,000 visitors in one month. These paintings, commissioned in 1911, depict occupations, activities, and ceremonies of the various Spanish provinces.

The upstairs stairway glitters with Hispano-Moresque ceramic tiles and stone fragments. In the west wing are modern paintings mounted under glass. In the east wing are displays of rugs, gold, velvet brocades. There are Goya prints and watercolors, including examples of his "Caprices." These galleries also display a superb collection of colored engravings of the ritual of the bullfight as seen by artists from the fifteenth century to Picasso's aquatints of 1958. An outstanding bullfight sequence was etched by Goya. There are posters, photographs, books, and programs of bullfighting, architectural studies of bullrings, announcements, displays of weapons, banderillas, and so on.

The balcony that overlooks the main gallery is lined with a gorgeous miscellany of bronze door knockers, Roman glassware, vases, lusterware, huge Gothic tiles, and paintings by El Greco, Goya, and a portrait of Juan de Pareja attributed to Diego Velázquez. A similar painting by Velázquez is owned by the Metropolitan Museum and is reproduced on page 4.

THE AMERICAN NUMISMATIC SOCIETY
Address: Broadway at 155th St., New York, N.Y., 10032.
Phone: 234-3130

Days: Open Tuesdays through Saturdays, 9—4:30; Sundays, 1—4.
Closed Mondays and holidays.
Admission: Free.

Subway: (1) IRT Broadway-242nd St. train to 157th St. station. (2) IND 8th Ave. Washington Heights train to 155th St. Walk two blocks west to Broadway.
Auto: West Side Highway to 158th St. exit. East to Broadway, south to Audubon Terrace. Ample street parking.

210

Library: Open 9—4:30.

Inside the heavy bronze doors of the American Numismatic Society, to the left, are exhibits of the world's coinage. To the right are medals and decorations. On the second floor is the most comprehensive numismatic library in America, with particular emphasis on periodicals and international auction catalogues.

The society was organized on April 16, 1858, and is "devoted to the advancement of numismatic knowledge, especially as it relates to history, art, archeology and economics," by engaging in the collection of coins, medals, tokens, decorations, and paper money. The society offers a vast number of numismatic publications of the highest scholarly quality. It holds summer seminars in numismatics to provide students with an understanding of how this science applies to other fields of know-

American Numismatic Society (rear left).

ledge. Some grants-in-aid, as well as achievement awards, are given. At various times the society has struck its own commemorative medals. Governed and managed by a council of fifteen members, the society has four classes of membership.

The only museum in the world devoted entirely to numismatics, its major exhibition space illustrates the development of coinage since the first coins were introduced some 2,600 years ago. The history of coins is shown in specially designed display cases that contain enlarged photographs, maps, and explanatory texts. These displays rotate periodically.

The museum's wealth of coins from the ancient Greek, Roman, and Byzantine periods derives from the extraordinary collection of over 87,000 pieces bequeathed by Edward T. Newell, president of the society from 1916 to his death in 1941. Other private gifts have further enriched the collections, while a relatively small proportion of the coins were acquired by purchase. Also represented are Italian Renaissance and medieval German coins.

The latest period in coinage history is represented by a numismatic genealogy of England, America, and the new nations of Israel, Libya, Indonesia, Burma, and Pakistan. In the East Gallery a case contains an extremely rare series of large United States copper cents struck from 1793—1857, a gift of George A. Clapp; some Lincoln medals and slave identification tags.

The West Gallery displays medals and medallions. There are Indian peace medals, exposition medals, United States decorations, British Orders of Knighthood, and medals commemorating individuals of note. The plate-sized Waterloo Medallion was designed by the distinguished Italian coin engraver Benedetto Pistrucci. Chief engineer at the London mint, he was commissioned in 1817 to execute a medallion commemorating Napoleon's defeat at Waterloo. It took him thirty years to complete the dies for his elaborate plan.

THE AMERICAN ACADEMY OF ARTS AND LETTERS
Address: Broadway at 155th St., New York, N.Y., 10032.
Phone: 368-5900

212 *Days:* Open daily, 1—4. Closed Mondays and some holidays.
Admission: Free.

Subway: (1) IRT Broadway-242nd St. train to 157th St. station and Broadway. (2) IND 8th Ave. Washington Heights train to 155th St.

The American Academy of
Arts and Letters.

station. Walk two blocks west to Broadway.

Auto: West Side Highway to 158th St. exit. East to Broadway, south
to Audubon Terrace. Ample street parking.

The American Academy of Arts and Letters and its parent body, the
National Institute of Arts and Letters, are the two highest honor so-
cieties of the creative arts in this country. The National Institute,
founded in 1898, consists of 250 Americans who are writers, poets,
painters, sculptors, composers, or architects. The American Academy,
established in 1904, is made up of 50 institute members chosen for

Original manuscripts of Glenway Wescott.

special distinction. Both organizations are chartered by an Act of Congress.

Among well-known Academy members are Pearl S. Buck, Thomas Hart Benton, Aaron Copland, John Dos Passos, Lillian Hellman, Edward Hopper, Jacques Lipchitz, Walter Lippmann, Georgia O'Keeffe, Carl Sandburg, John Steinbeck, Norman Mailer, and Andrew Wyeth.

Each year the institute and academy honor distinguished accomplishment in the fields of arts and letters. Older artists may be cited for their life's work, while a very few young men and women are given awards and grants to assist them in the pursuit of their careers. New members and award winners are also honored by an exhibition of their work.

An annual art exhibition of paintings, graphics, sculpture, and architecture is shown in the art gallery on the north side of Audubon Terrace; the annual literary exhibition is held in the enormous gallery on the south side of Audubon Terrace. There are original manuscripts, notebooks, first editions, and musical scores that may be followed by means of earphones. The vast library collection of first editions and original manuscripts of academy members is available for reference on request and by appointment.

MORRIS–JUMEL MANSION
Address: West 160th St. (Edgecombe Ave.), New York, N.Y., 10032.
Phone: 923-8008

214

Days: Open daily, except Monday, 10—4.
Admission: $.50.

Subway: (1) IND 8th Ave. Washington Heights train to 163rd St. station. Use 161st St. exit. Walk one block east. (2) IRT Broadway-242nd St. train to 157th St. station. Walk north to 160th St., east one block.

Auto: (1) FDR (East River) Drive to 125th St., west on 125th St. to St. Nicholas Ave., north to 160th St., east one block. (2) West Side Highway to 158th St. exit. North to 160th St., then east. Ample street parking.

Restaurant: Picnic parties welcome in rear garden.

The Morris—Jumel Mansion is on Washington Heights, bordering Sugar Hill. This quietly residential, tree-lined section of north Harlem owes its name to its elevation, the highest in Manhattan, and to the fact that it was once an exclusive part of town. From the grounds you can see the Bronx, Queens, and lower Manhattan.

The majestic house, perched atop a layer of glacial rock, is named after its two notable tenants, Lieutenant-Colonel Roger Morris and Stephen Jumel. Morris, an aide-de-camp to the British General Edward Braddock during the French and Indian War, was a friend of George Washington. When he returned from that war, Morris married the wealthy Mary Philipse, whose name had been linked romantically with Washington. Morris built the Georgian-Colonial mansion in 1765 as a summer home. In 1775 Morris, a tory, fled to England.

During the Revolution the house quartered both American and British forces. George Washington made Jumel Mansion his headquarters in 1776, when the Revolutionary Army was retreating after the disastrous defeat on Long Island. It had become a tavern by the time Washington paid a nostalgic visit to the house after the war.

Stephen Jumel, a wealthy French wine merchant living on Whitehall Street, bought the property in 1810 for $10,000. He and his socially ambitious wife restored the house in the most magnificent style of the nineteenth century. They entertained so lavishly that "lordly as a Jumel banquet" became a popular phrase of the day. In 1832 Jumel died, and his widow became one of the richest women in America.

Some time before her husband's death Madame Jumel had met Aaron Burr. After Jumel died, Burr apparently decided to restore his solvency by marrying the wealthy widow. His suit was successful and on July 1, 1833, they were wed. Burr was then seventy-seven years old. In Madame Jumel, Burr found more than a match for his own temper and will. A brief and stormy married life was followed by a separation that lasted until Burr's death three years after the marriage. Madame Jumel lived to be ninety-three. She died in 1865 and was buried in Trinity Church cemetery at Broadway and 155th Street.

Today the entrance to the grounds, from cobblestoned Jumel Terrace, leads to the side of the building. The mansion faces south. Four

215

Morris—Jumel Mansion.

impressive columns, two stories high, frame the entrance. An unusual balcony projects over the front door. The interior tastefully combines the best of Georgian, Federal, and French Empire styles. All the window draperies were woven according to period patterns and donated by Franco Scalamandre.

The small parlor to the left of the front door was the scene of Madame Jumel's marriage to Burr. In the Georgian dining room on the right the table is set. Of particular interest are the wall moldings, semi-elliptical archways, and the wide staircase to the upper floors.

On the second story a children's nursery, originally a dressing room, adjoins Madame Jumel's bedroom. The original bed and two chairs, covered in gold damask, were owned by Napoleon. A mannequin standing in the center of the room wears a copy of one of Madame Jumel's silk dresses. Aaron Burr's room, across the hall, contains his trunk and his desk-table.

In the living room.

To the rear of the house is the office of the curator, Mrs. J. Frank Wood, whose knowledge of antiques, art, and history has proven so valuable in acquiring authentic furnishings for this splendid house. She will lead small groups touring the house, explain its history, and point out its secret passageways.

The rear rooms over the drawing room were Washington's private quarters where he slept, planned maneuvers, and wrote his reports to Congress. Handwoven blankets confiscated from a British tent lie on a replica of his camp bed.

The third floor serves as a repository for a collection of Staffordshire ware, spinning wheels, and equipment for making wax candles.

The city acquired the property and opened the museum in 1907, under the custodianship of the Washington Headquarters Association of the Daughters of the American Revolution. A bench-lined walk circles the property, and leads past a small garden in the back of the house.

THE CLOISTERS

Address: Fort Tryon Park, New York, N.Y., 10040.
Phone: 923-3700

Days: Open Tuesday through Saturday, 10—4:45; Sundays, 1—4:45. (May to September, Sundays, 12—4:45.) Closed Mondays.
Admission: By contribution.

Subway: IND 8th Ave. Washington Heights train to 190th St.-Overlook Terrace (elevator exit). Connects with bus to Cloisters.
Auto: Henry Hudson Pkwy. to first exit past George Washington Bridge, marked "The Cloisters, Fort Tryon." Free parking on premises, limited to three hours.

Gift Shop: Information Desk sells museum publications, etc.

Special Events: Concerts of recorded medieval music Sundays and Tuesdays at 3:30. Live concerts on selected weekends.

Membership: Membership program is included in Metropolitan Museum of Art membership.

218

Tours: Tours every Wednesday at 3. Free guidance for classes from New York City public or private schools. School groups in chartered buses must have permit to enter park.

The Cloisters.

219

The 12th-century
Bury St. Edmunds Cross.

Going to the Cloisters on the peak of Fort Tryon Park is the next best thing to being in a medieval monastery in France. Its medieval herb garden, rampart walks, Belgian cobblestoned courts, view of the Hudson and of the New Jersey Palisades beyond, vividly re-create, in the twentieth century, the spirit of medieval Europe.

The Cloisters, a branch of the Metropolitan Museum of Art, includes parts of the cloisters of five French monasteries, a Romanesque chapel, an original chapter house, Gothic chapels, and exhibition galleries, all chronologically arranged and constructed to incorporate the original structural elements. Within the setting are examples of sculpture, painting, stained glass, retables, tapestries, metalwork, and furniture that are ideally seen on a weekday morning. When the galleries are empty, the supreme simplicity and lack of clutter emphasize the architectural forms and the serene atmosphere. Both the buildings and works of art represent various artistic styles of two periods in the Middle Ages—the

In the Gothic Chapel.

Romanesque, as exemplified by works from monasteries, and the Gothic, as exemplified by relics from churches.

The Cloisters collection was started by George Grey Barnard, a sculptor. He spent many years in France seeking examples of medieval art in barns, farmhouses, and cellars near abandoned churches and monasteries. In 1914 he put the collection on display in a building on nearby Fort Washington Avenue. The Metropolitan Museum bought the collection in 1925 with funds provided by John D. Rockefeller, Jr. When Fort Tryon Park, an area of sixty-two acres, was given to the city by Rockefeller in 1930, part was set aside for the museum. The gift was in accordance with an agreement between the philanthropist and the city, whereby the eastern ends of 64th and 68th Streets were closed and conveyed to the Rockefeller Institute for Medical Research. Land along the Palisades across the Hudson was also acquired by Rockefeller to ensure the view from the ramparts of the Cloisters.

221

222

*Listening to music
in the Cuxa Cloister.*

Visitors interested in proceeding through the Cloisters in chronological order should start with the Romanesque Hall and continue to the Fuentiduena Chapel, St. Guilhem Cloister, Langon Chapel, the West Terrace, Chapter House, Cuxa Cloister, Nine Heroes Tapestry Room, Early Gothic Hall, and thence to the ground floor. From here proceed to the Gothic Chapel, Bonnefont Cloister, Trie Cloister, Glass Gallery, and then to the Treasury. The stairway here leads to the Boppart Room, the Unicorn Tapestries, the Burgos Tapestries, the Spanish Room, Late Gothic Hall, and then out through the Froville Arcade, or main entrance hall.

A cloister is an unroofed space enclosed by a vaulted passageway consisting of colonnades or arcades opening on the court. Cloisters served both as sheltered access to other buildings and as a recreational and social area for monasteries.

The central and largest cloister here is that of St. Michel de Cuxa. It is an enclosed rectangular garden, open to the sky and surrounded

223

*A silver-gilt and enamel shrine made in Paris about 1340,
now on display in the Treasury of the Cloisters.*

by pink marble arches and columns that date from before 1188. Concerts of recorded medieval music are held here on Sundays. During the fall three apple trees in the center of the cloister bear dozens of delicious apples. An unusually grotesque face set in the marble wall fountain of the arcade came from the monsatery of Notre-Dame du Vilar. The other cloisters are those of St. Guilhem-le-Désert (1206), identified by the potted plants in the center of the court and a modern overhead glass skylight. The Bonnefont en Comminges, founded in 1136, and the Trie Cloisters are popular both because of the herb garden and their position overlooking the Hudson River.

The Gothic Chapel contains a notable alabaster sculpture from the tomb effigy of Jean d'Alluye, who died about 1248. A life-size figure

*"The Unicorn in Captivity," seventh in the
great series of Unicorn Tapestries.*

represents the young man, fully armed, lying with hands joined on his breast in an attitude of prayer. His feet rest against a marble lion, symbol of courage. In the center of the chapel are three stained-glass windows, of which the middle panel is original. In the two new panels modern glassmaking techniques have not been able to duplicate the original off-white tone of the metallic ores used in the Middle Ages. Twelfth-century windows are characterized by rich, dark colors, single figures, and scrollwork; by the beginnings of the thirteenth century, figures were used singly and also in groups.

The Early Gothic Hall contains a number of painted and gilded stone and wood sculptures of bishops, kings and Virgins in thirteenth-century Gothic style. The Virgin and Child at the end of the gallery, one of the finest statues from the Ile-de-France, is in an extraordinarily fine state of preservation.

The most notable feature of the Romanesque Hall is the entrance doorway from the Abbey of Moutiers Saint Jean, with life-size figures of King Clovis and his son King Clotaire on each side. Throughout the history of ecclisiastical architecture the entrance door to the cathedral has possessed a special importance. In medieval texts the church door is referred to as the Gate of Heaven, the Portal of Glory, the Triumphal Gate. The three portals incorporated in the Romanesque Hall exemplify the long evolution of these sculptured portals.

The Hall of the Unicorn Tapestries contains a set of six hand-woven fifteenth-century textiles that are among the most prized of our inheritances from the Middle Ages. The tapestries were given to the museum by John D. Rockefeller, Jr., in 1935. Depicting the Hunt of the Unicorn, they are thought to portray an allegory of the life of Christ, who is supposed to be represented by the fabulous Unicorn, symbol of purity. Other authorities hold that the Hunt is an allegory of secular courtship and love. The tapestries are remarkable for their beautiful color and design and the intensity and vitality of their pictorial realism. It is believed that all but one were woven for Anne of Brittany, in celebration of her marriage to Louis XII on January 8, 1499.

The Treasury contains some of the earliest and most precious objects that have survived from the Middle Ages: the Chalice of Antioch, reliquary statuettes, Limoges enamels, bronzes, the Monkey Cup, Book of Hours of Jeanne d'Evreux, and the recently acquired silver-gilt and enamel shrine made by Parisian goldsmiths about 1340 and believed to have been the personal possession of Queen Elizabeth of Hungary.

A view of the Bonnefont Cloister.

DYCKMAN HOUSE

Address: 4881 Broadway (204th St.), New York, N.Y., 10034.
Phone: 942-8560

Days: Daily 11—5. Closed Mondays. Children under 16 not admitted
 unless accompanied by an adult.
Admission: Free.

Subway: (1) IND 8th Ave. Washington Heights train to 207th St. Leave
 train by south exit, walk one block south. (2) IRT Broadway-242nd
 St. train to 207th St. station; walk west up the hill to Broadway,
 then one block south.
Auto: Henry Hudson Pkwy. to Dyckman St. exit. East to Broadway,
 then north to 204th St. Ample street parking; meters on Broadway.

Dyckman House.

Dyckman House, set on a slight hill, is surrounded by supermarkets, apartment houses, and gas stations. It is a civic miracle that the original eighteenth-century farmhouse has survived the inroads of twentieth-century progress to become today the only Dutch Colonial farmhouse remaining in Manhattan.

William Dyckman inherited the estate from his grandfather, who built the first house here in 1748. During the Revolution it was burned by the British and rebuilt in its present form in 1783. In 1915, two descendants of Dyckman purchased the property, restored the house and grounds, and presented them to the city.

All the Dutch and English Colonial furnishings, clothes, china, and ornaments are authentic period pieces. The interior is relatively modest, and represents the ordinary style of living in New York at that time. The kitchen, with its caldrons, pothooks, irons, skillets, and ovens is the most interesting of the five rooms.

A large Indian village once flourished in the vicinity of present-day Inwood Park, a short distance away, and Indians remained in the vicinity well into the nineteenth century. In fact, a walk four blocks north and then four blocks east brings you to Indian Road and West 215th Street. Continuing across the open field of Inwood Park to a spot near the cliffs, you will find a large boulder marking the site of the principal Manhattan Indian village of Shorakkopoch. Here Peter Minuit purchased Manhattan Island from the Indians in 1626 for trinkets and beads worth then about 60 guilders ($24.00).

VAN CORTLANDT HOUSE MUSEUM

Address: Van Cortlandt Park, Broadway near 242nd St., New York, N.Y., 10471.
Phone: 546-3323

Days: Open Tuesdays through Saturdays, 10—5; Sundays, 2—5. Closed Mondays and the month of February.
Admission: $.50 on Sunday, Tuesday, Wednesday, and Thursday. Other days free.

Subway: IRT Broadway-242nd St. train to 242nd St. station.
Auto: (1) From FDR (East River) Drive north to Willis Ave. Bridge. Major Deegan Expressway to 238th St. exit. Continue west to Broadway. Right turn onto Broadway. House visible from outside park, on Broadway, near 246th St. (2) From Henry Hudson Pkway., exit at 246th St. Turn right to Broadway. Ample parking.

Like other important men of his era, Frederick Van Cortlandt built his manor in 1748 with his own labor force—carpenters, masons, and blacksmiths. The elegant Georgian-Colonial mansion was a country estate where flax was woven and spun, stock raised, and crops planted. In the 1740s the inhabited section of New York City extended to Canal Street. North of Canal were farms and forests.

The mansion was built of rough stone with brick trimming. Satyr-like carved faces are set as keystones above the windows. Carved-face keystones of this genre also appeared later in New York tenements of the period 1890 to 1910. Many can be seen on the Lower East Side, but these particular early faces are unique in Colonial architecture. Since all the faces are different, it is possible they were carved on the spot by an enterprising stonemason, rather than imported from Europe. The windows under the keystones once had shutters, but they have all been removed, as have the Dutch half-doors.

The house is surrounded by a high wrought-iron fence. Once you are inside, it is apparent that the house has an English atmosphere with Dutch accents. The exhibition room, for example, contains a fine collection of Delftware. This room was originally a dining room.

The east parlor, to the right of the entrance, has a Georgian mantel, a handsome secretary of Massachusetts origin that contains an unusual Whieldon tea set; a spinet that was made in London in 1771, and a Chippendale mirror that is dated 1760. The dining room, formerly the west parlor, was occupied by General George Washington in 1783 when the area from Vault Hill (behind the house) to Kingsbridge was the scene of almost constant skirmishing.

The kitchen, below ground level, has a huge fireplace, caldrons, kettle, long-handled peels, or oven shovels for drawing out hot bread pans, and curious waffle irons. The southeast bedroom, upstairs, is where Washington slept. The room has a typical canopied bed and a cherry writing desk. There is also a seventeenth-century Dutch bedroom with a bed completely encased in wood to ward off the cold air. A walnut wardrobe (Dutch *kas*), elaborately painted in grisaille, held linens. The nursery on the third floor contains an Early American dollhouse. In the spinning room next door are fifteen-inch-wide floorboards that were handmade and are held together by wooden pegs.

231

Van Cortlandt Mansion.

WAVE HILL CENTER

Address: West 249th St. and Independence Ave., Bronx, N.Y., 10471.
Phone: 549-2055

Days: Daily 10—4:30, house and grounds.
Admission: Free Mondays through Saturdays; Sundays, $1.00.

Subway: IRT 7th Ave. Broadway line to 231st St. station, then No. 10 or No. 100 City Line bus at northeast corner 231st St. and Broadway, or phone 881-1000 for mid-Manhattan/Riverdale express bus schedule; IND 8th Ave. A train to 207th St. station, then No. 100 City Line bus at northeast corner 211th St. and Broadway. Leave bus at 252nd St., walk across parkway bridge and proceed two blocks on 252nd St. to Independence Avenue. Turn left to Wave Hill gate at 249th St.

Auto: Henry Hudson Parkway to 250th St. exit, left on 252nd St. to Independence Ave., then left to Wave Hill gate at 249th St.

Programs: Lectures, courses, workshops, concerts, calendar.

Special Events: Environmental studies for school children.

Membership: From $10 to $500.

Wave Hill is about 260 blocks north of the Battery at the top end of Van Cortlandt Park in Riverdale near the Westchester County line. It is peaceful and serene with a magnificent view of the Hudson River and the Palisades. There are 28 acres surrounded by gardens, lawns and woods. Wave Hill manor was built for William Lewis Morris before 1830. It was later owned by William Appleton and then by George W. Perkins, a financier and conservationist who added gardens, stables and greenhouses to the beautiful estate.

Teddy Roosevelt, Mark Twain and Arturo Toscanini once lived there as well as the United Kingdom Ambassador to the United Nations. In 1960 Perkins' daughter, Mrs. Edward Woolsey Freeman gave the property to the City of New York. In 1966 Wave Hill was designated a historic landmark by the New York City Landmarks Preservation Commission.

Wave Hill functions mostly as an active public educational-cultural center for the study of environmental sciences, particularly those related to the city. It has classes for teachers and school children, urban research programs, art exhibitions, concerts, film programs, performing arts events, and other activities including a nature trail, sculpture garden and adult classes in everything from batik dyeing to photography and stargazing.

The main attraction of Wave Hill is as a representative of a private estate that no longer exists in New York City. Turning a private estate into a modern public facility is a complex venture. Wave Hill preserved the best of each period of its past. The fieldstone facade and central Georgian portion were carefully preserved. The 1890 oval northern wing, with intricately carved Victorian teakwood paneling, is now used for an audio-visual room. The servant wing and upper bedrooms were modified for offices.

The Armor Hall was designed in 1927 by James Dwight Baum for Bashford Dean as a Gothic chapel for his unique collection of armor. This is now a concert-lecture hall. Its medieval architectural character was kept intact as new heating and insulation, windows, fire exits and theatrical lighting were installed. The Learning Center, below the Armor Hall, serves visiting school groups.

Glyndor, a Georgian Revival mansion that is Wave Hill's second major building, was adapted for office and research uses. Three greenhouses built in 1905, the potting shed and the Palm House were reconstructed on the existing stone foundations. The Palm House and the other greenhouses now bloom with a changing series of flowering exhibitions and permanent horticultural collection of cacti, succulents and tropical plants. They are surrounded by cultivated gardens—the rose garden, the English-style wild garden and the aquatic garden with an herb border. Also preserved was the classic facade of the carriage house that is now a garage.

Wave Hill Center.

HAMILTON GRANGE NATIONAL MEMORIAL

Address: 287 Convent Ave., New York, N.Y., 10031.
Phone: 283-5154

Days: Open Mondays through Fridays, 9—4:30; closed weekends.
Admission: Free.

Subway: IND 8th Ave. to 145th St. station.
Bus: Broadway bus to 145th St.
Auto: North on Amsterdam Ave. Ample parking.

Hamilton Grange is on the fringe of Harlem Heights in an historic landmark district. The two-story frame house is sandwiched between a church and an apartment house and is two blocks from the City College campus. There are many fine townhouses along Convent Avenue. Hamilton Grange, which was moved from a nearby location, is in a neighborhood that was once a quiet agricultural community.

Alexander Hamilton was born in 1755 in the West Indies and came to New York in 1772. He made his first patriotic speech at a political rally here in defense of the Boston Tea Party.

When the American Revolution began, Hamilton won a position as Washington's aide-de-camp and, at age 26, served at Yorktown in the last major battle of the Revolution. In the following years, Hamilton helped draft the Constitution, wrote the influential *Federalist Papers* and later became the first Secretary of the Treasury.

Hamilton Grange National Memorial.

In November 1798, Hamilton and his wife, daughter of General Philip Schuyler, built the new Federal-style house that was designed by John McComb, the architect of New York's City Hall. Completed in 1802, the Grange was high on a knoll with a majestic view of both the Hudson and Harlem Rivers.

Hamilton's oldest son, Philip, was killed in a duel that resulted from a political quarrel. It is ironic that two years later, on the same field in Weehawken, New Jersey, Aaron Burr and Alexander Hamilton climaxed years of political and personal animosity with a duel. Despite the fact that Hamilton helped to outlaw duels in New York, he felt compelled to accept Burr's challenge. On the morning of July 11, 1804, he discharged his weapon into the air to avoid killing his antagonist but was himself fatally wounded by Burr. Hamilton's dream of a happy old age at the Grange was cut short only two years after the house was completed.

THE HALL OF FAME FOR GREAT AMERICANS

Address: 181st St. and University Avenue, Bronx, N.Y. 10453.
Phone: 367-7300

Days: Open daily, during campus hours only.
Admission: Free.

Subway: IRT Broadway or Lexington Ave. Jerome-Woodlawn train to Burnside Ave. station.
Auto: FDR (East River) Drive via Willis Ave. Bridge to Bronx. Left onto Major Deegan Expressway, north to Fordham Road exit. Continue on Fordham Road to University Avenue. Right to 181st St. Right again, up hill to stone posts marking Bronx Community College campus. Enter gate. Hall of Fame on right directly past parking lot. Free parking.

The Hall of Fame for Great Americans owned by New York University is on the uptown campus of Bronx Community College. Designed by Stanford White and financed as a gift to the university by Mrs. Finley J. Shepard, the Hall of Fame consists of an open-air colonnade, 630 feet long. It was dedicated in 1901. The Cloisters at Fort Tryon Park can be seen in the distance. Within the colonnade are the silent bronze heads facing each other, row after row. All eyes stare unnervingly at some point above the visitor's head . . . all the determined chins thrust forward.

235

To become eligible for nomination one must have been dead at least twenty-five years and also have contributed to the history, culture, or development of the United States. In a recent year there were 225 nominations submitted to the Hall of Fame Committee. Selections are made every five years. Elections are held by a College of Electors chosen by the university, and the electors represent all states of the Union and a wide variety of professions.

At present the Hall of Fame honors ninety-seven Americans, including Eli Howe, Alexander Graham Bell, Robert Fulton, Thomas A. Edison, Tom Paine, Benjamin Franklin, George Washington, Henry Clay, Abraham Lincoln, and so on.

An official handbook published by New York University relates story of founding, brief biographies of famous men. It can be purchased only at NYU bookstore, 18 Washington Place.

The Hall of Fame.

The Edgar Allan Poe Cottage.

EDGAR ALLAN POE COTTAGE

Address: Grand Concourse at East 193rd St., Bronx, N.Y., 10468.
Phone: 881-8900

Days: Open Wednesdays through Fridays, 1–5; Saturdays, 10–4; Sundays, 1–5. Closes at 3:00 in winter. Closed holidays.
Admission: $.50.

Subway: IND 6th Ave. "D" train to Fordham Road station. Walk one block north on Grand Concourse to Poe Park.
Auto: FDR (East River) Drive north to Willis Ave. Bridge, Major Deegan Expressway. At Fordham Road exit, turn right. Continue past Grand Concourse one block, then go left at Valentine Ave. to Poe Park. Metered street parking.

Poe Cottage, the home of Edgar Allan Poe from 1846 to 1849, is a small country house with a single story and an attic. It was built by John Wheeler about 1812 as a farmhouse. The city acquired the cottage in 1912 and moved it from Kingsbridge Road to Poe Park.

    The cottage is sparsely furnished, and only the three rooms on the lower floor are open to the public. They comprise a small hand-carved four-poster bed and dresser, a writing desk, rocker, hooked rugs, Franklin stove, cupboard, two wall clocks, a table and two kitchen chairs, and a large cabinet with Staffordshire platters and tureens.

237

Poe's young wife, Virginia, died in this house, where he wrote "The Literati of New York City" for *Godey's Lady's Book* and his famous poems "Annabel Lee," "Ulalume," and "Eureka." After his wife's death in 1847, Poe fell in love successively with several women, and was once engaged to Sarah Helen Whitman, as well as to his boyhood sweetheart Elmira Shelton. Poe died on October 1, 1849.

Today the Poe Cottage has a caretaker, an authoritative guide, and a curator involved in an expanding restoration program. The house sits quietly in a little-frequented corner of a city park, as much overlooked by the passerby as it must have been during his lifetime.

VALENTINE—VARIAN HOUSE

Address: 3266 Bainbridge Ave. (East 208th St.), Bronx, N.Y., 10467.
Phone: 881-8900

Days: Saturdays, 10—4; Sundays, 1—5.
Admission: Adults $1.00.

Subway: IND "D" 6th Ave. to 205th St.
Bus: Concourse line to Van Cortlandt East.
Auto: Bronx River Pkwy. to Gun Hill Road exit. West to Bainbridge Ave. Left to 208th St.

The Valentine-Varian House is a well-preserved Colonial fieldstone farmhouse that is the headquarters of The Museum of Bronx History. The wide pine floorboards were originally set in place in the 1750s. One room shows the exposed inner wall structure revealing the original hand-hewn chestnut laths held together by a mortar of mud and cow hair.

On February 2, 1758, Isaac Valentine bought the property. During the Revolutionary War the house was occupied by British and Hessian troops, but escaped war damage. In 1791, 260 acres and the house were sold to Isaac Varian for $7,500. One of his sons, also named Isaac, was Mayor of New York from 1839 to 1841.

In 1965, William C. Beller, owner of the house, donated it to the Bronx County Historical Society, and it was moved across the street to its present site. The museum contains modest exhibits illustrating Bronx history from the time of the Indians to the present.

NEW YORK BOTANICAL GARDEN

Address: Bronx Park, Bronx, N.Y., 10460.
Phone: 220-8700

The Valentine—Varian House.

Days: Daily, including holidays, 10–7 (May through September); 10–5 (October through April). Museum and conservatories, Tuesdays through Sundays, 10–4.
Admission: Free. Parking on premises, $2.00. Conservatory admission, adults $1.50; children $.75.

Subway: (1) IND 6th Ave. "D" train to Bedford Park Blvd. station. Use south exit and walk east eight blocks. (2) IRT 7th Ave. No. 4 Bronx express, or Lexington Ave. East Bronx express to Bedford Park Blvd. and 200th St. and walk east one block.

Railroad: From Grand Central Station take Conrail Central Harlem Division to Botanical Garden station. Main entrance opposite station.
Auto: Main roads approaching garden are marked with New York Botanical Garden signs. Follow: (1) Bronx River Pkwy. to Fordham Road to the gardens. (2) Hutchinson River Pkwy. to Pelham Pkwy. (3) New England Thruway to Pelham Pkwy. (4) Henry Hudson Pkwy. to Mosholu Pkwy. (5) Grand Concourse to Bedford Park

239

Blvd. Main entrance is on Southern Blvd. near Fordham University. Cars can enter garden daily and Sunday. $2.00 entrance fee. Parking permitted througout garden. Family membership includes unlimited free parking.

Restaurant: Snuff Mill Cafeteria has hot food, snacks, sandwiches. Outdoor terrace. Picnic tables near restaurant. Snuff Mill open all year from 9—4.

Gift Shop: Sales counter in museum offers publications; special horticultural and botanical books, gardening tools, bulbs, seeds.

Special Events: Seasonal displays throughout the year. Some of the major attractions are the Pot Plant Show (January), Easter Show, Rose Day, Chrysanthemum Show (November), and the Christmas Show.

Membership: Privileges include subscription to *The Garden Magazine,* invitations to flower shows, tours, lectures, reduced rates for courses, annual distribution of plants without charge.

Library: Major reference and research center for botanists, on third floor of museum, contains 70,000 volumes, 300,000 pamphlets. Open to public for reference, not lending. Research Laboratory building not open to public.

Lectures and Tours: Public-education program with two-year certificated courses in gardening, landscape gardening, and botany. Free lecture series and day and evening courses for adults.

Children: Special children's courses include a late spring-summer gardencraft course in which the children plant and tend their own plants and take home their produce in the fall.

". . . I will look upon thy face again, my own romantic Bronx. And it will be a face more pleasant than the face of men. . . ." This legend by the poet Joseph Rodman Drake appears on a bronze plaque fastened on a boulder that stands beneath a footbridge by the old Snuff Mill.

The gorge of the rapid Bronx River, complete with its ten-foot waterfall, glacial rock, hemlock forest, and towering trees has probably changed little since the poet wrote those words. The stream runs through the middle of the Botanical Garden.

Since the gorge is one of the most attractive features of the garden, it is natural to find along the bank a terraced restaurant overlooking

241

The Enid Haupt Conservatory.

The old Snuff Mill.

the river, footpath, and waterfall. The building was once the Lorillard Snuff Mill, built here in 1840. Snuff was ground and tobacco packed in this factory building.

Another attractive feature of the garden is that it is possible to drive directly into it. Following the Circuit Drive, you can see fields of daffodils and lilacs, magnolias and roses, the Snuff Mill, the museum, and the conservatory. There are 230 acres of garden.

Near the main entrance is the museum, housed in New York City civic architecture of the 1890s. The museum has occasional exhibits. But the main area is devoted to a large museum plant shop that sells potted plants and related items. The museum owns a series of excellent English colored lithographs depicting the cultivation of rice in China. Horticultural exhibits usually show plant families, plant evolution, tree leaves, flower families, seed distribution, cycad evolution, and flower structure. All the exhibits are arranged in clear and simple order.

The second floor contains hundreds and hundreds of ceiling-high steel lockers packed with legal-size file folders containing dried plants.

242

Giant plants in the greenhouse.

243

This extraordinary herbarium of three million plants seems to include every plant of North and South America, and on the third floor is a herbarium of local plants. The vast botanical and horticultural library, which ranks among the three best in the Western Hemisphere, has just been installed in a brand new six-story building called the Harriet Barnes Pratt Library Wing. The library receives twelve hundred current periodicals on botany. The librarians welcome members and will permit them to examine the botanical specimens in the herbarium. Across the drive from the museum is the modern research laboratory. Visitors are not permitted to enter.

The gorge of the Bronx River.

The magnificent glass-domed rotunda of the great greenhouse is visible from the main entrance. The Enid A. Haupt Conservatory was restored in 1978 at a cost of $5,000,000. As the visitor enters the conservatories he encounters a heavy, subtropical, unmistakably jungle atmosphere. An immense sugar palm tree shoots straight up into the rotunda (ninety feet high). There are tropical trees from Africa, Brazil, Australia. In the hushed quiet of this tropical foliage one can easily hear the low drone of the IRT subway.

To the left of the palm house are winding paths leading to eleven other greenhouses, which contain, among other specimens, ground ivy, tropical flowering and foliage plants, hanging baskets, lime bushes; fig, grapefruit, apple, and plum trees; strange screw pines, bromeliads, cissus and fern plants, and, in a ninety-nine degree hothouse, ageless cactus plants in all shades of green. In the courtyard in front of the greenhouses are the water-lily ponds.

The garden, incorporated in 1891, was patterned after the Royal Botanic Gardens at Kew, England. Its purposes, according to the Act of Incorporation, are the collection and culture of plants, the advancement of botanical science, and the entertainment, recreation, and instruction of the people.

NEW YORK ZOOLOGICAL PARK (BRONX ZOO)
Address: 185th St. and Southern Blvd., Bronx, N.Y., 10460.
Phone: 220-5100

Days: Opens at 10 daily. Closes at 4:30 in winter, 5:30 in summer.
Admission: Free Tuesdays, Wednesdays, and Thursdays. Fridays, Saturdays, Sundays, and Mondays $1.50 adults; $.75 children; under 5 free. Monday through Friday free for organized groups.

Entrances: Main—Pelham Pkwy. Others—Fordham, Crotona, Boston Road, Buffalo, Bronxdale.
Subway: (1) IRT 7th Ave. No. 2 express to Pelham Parkway; follow pedestrian signs to zoo. (2) IRT Lexington Ave. No. 5 express to East Tremont Ave.; walk north to Zoo. (3) IND "D" express to Fordham Road; change to Bx 12 bus traveling east on Fordham Road; from stop at Southern Boulevard, walk to Rainey Gate entrance.
Bus: Bx 12, 20, and 31 all stop near Zoo entrances.
Auto: (1) Triborough Bridge and Bruckner Expressway east to Bronx River Parkway north. Take the parkway exit marked "Bronx Zoo." (2) West Side Highway to the Cross Bronx Expressway. Drive east to Bronx River Parkway north. Take the parkway exit marked "Bronx Zoo." (3) Bronx-Whitestone Bridge and Hutchinson River Parkway north to Cross Bronx Expressway. Drive west to Bronx

245

River Parkway north. Take the parkway exit marked "Bronx Zoo."
Parking: (1) Fountain Circle: Main entrance off Pelham Pkwy.
   (2) Bronxdale: Alongside Bronx River Pkwy.
   (3) Crotona: At 182nd St. and Southern Blvd.
   (4) Buffalo: Bronx Park South and Boston Road (closed in winter-
   time).
   Parking: $2.00; Tuesday, Wednesday, Thursday $2.50.

Restaurants: (1) Cafeteria: hot and cold dishes, complete meals.
   (2) Zoo Terrace Buffet: salads, sandwiches, snacks.
   (3) Flamingo Terrace: sandwiches, snacks.
   (4) African Terrace: sandwiches, snacks.
   (5) Lake Terrace: picnic parties, snacks.
   (6) Carretinas: soda, ice cream, snacks.

Gift Shop: Souvenirs, books, pennants, toys at Safari Shop. Souvenirs
   also at World of Birds Gift Shop.

Membership: Annual, $25.00. Special privileges plus *Animal Kingdom.*
   Membership dues in the Zoological Society are used to help save rare
   wild animals from extinction; encourage zoological field research;
   improve the Bronx Zoo and the New York Aquarium.

Tours: Wild Asia on Bengali express and Safari Train tours, May—
   August, daily except Sundays and Mondays, start near sea-lion pool.
   Adults $1.00; children $.50, skyfari cable cars, $.50.

Children's Facilities: Children's Zoo open Easter to mid-November,
   10:30 to half hour before zoo closes. Children 1—14, $.25. Persons
   over 14 years, $.25. Adults must be accompanied by children.
   Camel, donkey cart, and pony rides $.50. Tractor trains used at
   1939 New York World's Fair carry children and adults from Boston
   Road gate to main exhibits, $.30 each way. Bronxdale parking field
   to main exhibits and return, $.30 each way.

The New York Zoological Park is the largest zoo in America. It houses
some of the rarest specimens seen anywhere, some almost extinct, some
common, their counterparts still roaming the wilds of Africa and Asia.
Some are in cages, some in fenced-in plots.
   The Aquatic Bird House, near the Fordham entrance, groups its in-
246 habitants by their natural environments: Birds of the Treetops, River-
banks, Tropical Lagoons, Jungle Streams, the Shore, Sea Cliffs, Marsh,
Indian Pond, African Pond, and Swamp.
   The Shore Birds setting looks much like Fire Island, Staten Island,
or Jones Beach, with black terns, wood sandpipers, and other beach

Exploring Wild Asia by monorail.

An American bison ruminates.

birds common to the New York area. The exhibit is completed by re-corded sounds of wind and waves. A map on the wall opposite the ex-hibit shows birds around New York City. The Lila Acheson Wallace World of Birds consists of 200 species.

Outside the Aquatic Bird House are a number of fenced-in bird sanc-tuaries. The Birdwalk is a huge cage the size of a basketball court; it houses a variety of gulls, ducks, pigeons, herons, partridges, cape teals, pelicans, pochards, and swamp hens.

Near the main entrance is the National Collection of Heads and Horns building, "in memory of the vanishing Big Game of the World."

248

A lion in the African Plains area.

Some of the rare wild animal heads were donated by Theodore Roosevelt. The exhibit may be temporarily closed.

The Monkey House is a perennially popular attraction. Across the grass mall are the sea-lion pool, lion house, and zebras. This area is usually crowded with children on their way to the Children's Zoo, the animal rides, and the elephant, rhino, and hippo enclosures.

The Reptile House, in the center of the zoo, is the most visited exhibit. In the nearby hall of small mammals and the Red Light Room, which simulates nighttime, are the dog-faced bat, yellow-throated marten, rusty-spotted genet, fennecs, and Hoffman's two-toed sloth.

The World of Darkness nature theater in a circular building turns day into night, in a unique zoo exhibit. The hall is pitch black during our daylight hours so that visitors will see each creature in his nocturnal activities. Foxes, porcupines, aardvarks, and skunks climb and dart about, and two hundred enormous bats swoop back and forth.

A camel gives rides to children.

Asiatic elephants seen from Wild Asia monorail.

Near the Great Apes Building are the wild sheep, ostriches, and giant Galápagos tortoises, which are now almost extinct.

Toward the Crotona entrance are the black bucks, antelopes, wild swine, and giraffes. Near the Boston Road entrance are the llamas, yaks, wisents, guanacos, and the extraordinary African Plains area, a moated enclosure much like the real plains of Africa, where antelope, lions and their cubs, deer, and birds of the wild all live together in an impressive display.

The bison range occupies a three-acre "prairie" that simulates the bison's natural habitat. This open exhibit re-creates a realistic environment that permits the animals to be seen in a setting as much as possible like their natural habitat.

The New York Zoological Society plays an active role in ecological 251 and conservation programs by providing scientific evaluation and substantive background for legislation to protect wild beasts, migratory birds, Alaskan fur seals, American bison, and numerous other creatures on their way to extinction.

BARTOW—PELL MANSION MUSEUM AND GARDENS

Address: Shore Road, Pelham Bay Park, Bronx, N.Y., 10464.
Phone: 885-1461

Days: Open Tuesday, Friday, and Sunday, 1—5.
Admission: $.50. Children free when accompanied by adult.

Subway: IRT Lexington Ave. (Pelham Bay Park) to last stop. Bus to Split Rock Golf Club, Memorial Day to Labor Day.
Auto. FDR (East River) Drive, Willis Ave. Bridge, to Bruckner Blvd., Hutchinson River Pkwy. to Orchard Beach exit. At Orchard Beach traffic circle follow north along Shore Road. Mansion is across from the Split Rock golf course, its entrance marked by a gate and a small plaque.

The Bartow-Pell Mansion in Pelham Bay Park easily ranks as one of the most beautiful spots in all New York. It is so untouched by the crowds usually found in the city's public places that one fears to publicize its beauty.

The landscaped grounds, the immaculately manicured gardens, the beautiful flower beds, the wide vista of Long Island Sound, the stately architecture, the serene terrace with its wrought-iron chairs and tables capture the ambiance of a European chateau more than anything on view in New York. It is a miniature Versailles, Schönbrunn, and Villa Borghese all wrapped into one. Life as it must have been in a Bronx with quiet woods, dirt footpaths, flowing streams, singing birds, and open meadows is re-created here.

On November 14, 1654, Thomas Pell obtained 9,000 acres of land from the Sewanoe Indians. Pell, an Englishman, swore allegiance to the Dutch of New Amsterdam and ruled as lord of the manor at Pelham. Undoubtedly he was pleased when the English captured the Dutch colony. On October 6, 1666, Pell was granted a royal patent from the Duke of York.

The original manor house is said to have burned to the ground. In 1836, Robert Bartow, descendant of the original Pell and Bartow families, acquired the property. The present mansion was built some time between 1836 and 1842. Its architect is unknown. The windows and the classic recesses on the garden side of the stone house indicate Italian inspiration. The conventional front may indicate Georgian influence, while the interior detail is definitely Greek Revival.

252   In the entry hall a beautiful elliptical stairway indicates the extremely sophisticated taste of the builder, and the double drawing room and dining room, separated by two sliding doors, exemplify Greek Revival at its best. These rooms, though larger, are similar to the parlor-floor rooms in the Old Merchant's House in lower Manhattan. Here the pil-

Bartow—Pell Mansion.

asters are Corinthian, and the pediments over the windows and doors are decorated with carved eagles and winged cherubs.

The sitting room, library, hall dining room, and the bedrooms on the upper floors are all superbly furnished with canopied sleigh beds, pillar-and-scroll mantel clocks, Sheraton convex mirrors, and Aubusson carpets. The rooms reflect the good advice and guidance of authorities on the period. Some of the furnishings are on loan from the city's museums.

Credit for the restoration of the mansion and the care of its lovely Sunken Garden and grounds can be attributed to the 400 members of the International Garden Club and to Mrs. Charles Frederick Hoffman, who founded the club in 1914. The mansion has been the club's headquarters since that time. For two summers while he was mayor, Fiorello H. La Guardia lived here.

The Sunken Garden behind the house is surrounded by a high wall of native stone. A series of steps leads from the terrace down to the garden, where there is a pool surrounded by formal beds of tulips and roses. Three gates of hand-wrought iron lead from the garden to the woods beyond, to the waters of Long Island Sound, and to a walk, bordered by rhododendron and ivy, that slopes to a small cemetery where the descendents of Thomas Pell are buried.

An Empire bedroom.

TRANSIT AUTHORITY MUSEUM
Address: Boerum Place and Schermerhorn St., Brooklyn, N.Y., 11201.
Phone: 330-3060

Days: Daily, 10—4.
Admission: Adults, $.50; children, $.25. Groups must reserve in advance.

Subway: IND to Hoyt-Schermerhorn station; IRT to Boro Hall station; BMT to Court St. station.
Auto: Brooklyn Bridge, then continue straight ahead 3 blocks to subway entrance at corner of Boerum and Schermerhorn St.

Gift Shop: Subway guidebooks, T-shirts, tote bags, postcards of subway mosaics, posters.

Lectures & Tours: Nostalgia train, adults, $3, children, $1.50. Does not run in winter.

The purpose of the New York City Transit Authority Museum is to give the public an idea of what the transit system is all about, to show what the trains and operating parts look like, how the train actually works, where they go, a history of where they came from, and a projection of what public transportation will be like in the future.

The Transit Authority hopes that this broad educational program will help reduce vandalism and that the public will have more respect for the system on which their whole economic existence may depend.

The Museum is underground in an abandoned subway spur of the Court Street station that was built about 35 years ago. The station is in the heart of downtown Brooklyn and, symbolically, is situated under the Board of Education building.

On each side of the station tracks, vintage subway cars are on display as well as turnstiles, collection boxes, belly stoves and transit memorabilia. There is a room-size, three-dimensional model showing the track layout for the entire subway system. The exhibit includes a tour of the station's signal tower. Visitors learn how switches are controlled and can follow the switching of the tracks and the light-signaling systems.

A popular exhibit focuses on the beautiful mosaics from various IRT and BMT stations. This anonymous art decorates the stations at Fulton Street, Astor Place, Chambers Street, Grand Central and many other stations. Many of these works are still visible but some have been covered with new tiles. These terra cotta mosaics picture bridges, beavers, steamboats, locomotives and were meant to be visual aids for immigrants who couldn't read English, but many were simply decora-

255

tions on the subway platforms. Many of these tiles are reproduced on postcards and are on sale in the museum.

The folklore of public transportation—including subways, buses and trolley cars—dates back to America's first street railway, when horse-drawn cars on wooden rails began service in 1832. Horsecars were the only public transportation in New York until elevated lines were introduced in the 1860s. Cable-operated street cars first ran in the 1880s and were then electrified in the 1890s. Early photos of public transportation make up a large part of the exhibits in the Transit Authority Museum. One unique display is hundreds of scale models of trolley cars that were hand-built by George T. F. Rahilly, a Fort Lauderdale orthopedic surgeon who lived in New York and photographed and collected pictures of thousands of different trolley cars during his childhood.

New York's first subway officially opened October 27, 1904 and the development of modern routing and signaling devices made it possible to operate subway trains safely and efficiently. Today's subway cars are all steel, with plexiglass seats, fluorescent lighting, air conditioning, public address systems and many safety devices. The New York City

New York City subway train pulling into the 14th Street station.

subway system covers 263 miles through four boroughs. (Staten Island has its own railroad.) It is the busiest subway in the world and in 1970 the number of passengers peaked with 2,081,810,464. There are 460 subway stations. The record for traveling the whole system, according to the *Guinness Book of World Records* is 21 hours, 8½ minutes set on October 8, 1973 by Mayer Wiesen and Charles Emerson.

During the season the Transit Authority Museum operates a three-car Nostaligia Special, a train of 1913 BMT subway cars that rattles its way to the Jamaica Wildlife Sanctuary in the Rockaways. The train leaves from the 57th Street and 6th Avenue IND station, first going to the Transit Museum and then continuing on its nostalgic journey. It operates twice weekly and is meant to encourage remembrances of the past for old-time New Yorkers as well as introduce youngsters to the the joys of a subway with a ride to the scenic Gateway National Park. The four-hour journey winds up at Rockaways Playland before returning to Manhattan.

THE LONG ISLAND HISTORICAL SOCIETY
Address: 128 Pierrepont St., Brooklyn, N.Y., 11201.
Phone: 624-0890

Days: Open Tuesdays through Saturdays, 9–5. Closed Sundays, Mondays, national holidays, and month of August.
Admission: Free.

Subway: IRT Broadway-7th Ave. to Borough Hall or Clark St. station.
Auto: FDR (East River) Drive south to Brooklyn Bridge, Fulton St. exit. Left at Fulton, right at Montague, right again at Clinton to Pierrepont. Metered street parking.

Membership: The society welcomes as members those who wish to do research in local or family history and wish to further its purposes. Privileges include personal access to library materials, receipt of publications, and *The Journal of Long Island History.*

The Long Island Historical Society is in Brooklyn Heights at the western tip of Long Island. The society, founded in 1863, is a private historical library serving its members as an archive for material related to Long Island. Although the public is allowed access to the building, one must be a fully qualified, elected member in order to use the precious historical records and collections.

The library on the second floor has a twenty-foot balcony, supported by spindly-looking wooden posts, that surrounds almost the entire floor. It looks like a picturesque version of a Civil War era bookstore. The library floor is the only section open to the general public.

257

258

Long Island Historical Society.

There is usually an exhibit of relics from the society's collections on display.

A wide selection of periodicals covers regional, state, and local history with such titles as *New York Folklore, Nassau County Historical Society Journal, Newsletter from the Society for the Preservation of Long Island Antiques, New York Genealogical and Biographical Record, Long Island Forum,* etc.

The society welcomes books of any kind published about or in Brooklyn and Long Island: church and club histories; diaries, letters, directories; family records, genealogies; legal documents; property maps; early business account books; early broadsides, and sheet music. It is also interested in medals, guns, and swords owned by natives of the area; newspaper clippings; portrait paintings, drawings, lithographs, and photographs of people, places, objects, and events related to Long Island. The society also has on file microfilms of Federal census records of Long Island from 1790 to 1880.

THE BROOKLYN CHILDREN'S MUSEUM
Address: 145 Brooklyn Ave., Brooklyn, N.Y., 11213.
Phone: 735-4432; 735-4400 (Office)

Days: Open every day except Tuesdays, 1—5.
Admission: Free.

Subway: (1) IRT 7th Ave. New Lots train to Kingston Ave. Walk 1 block west to Brooklyn Ave., 6 blocks north to Museum. (2) IRT Lexington Ave. express to Nevins St. Change to IRT 7th Ave. New Lots train. Follow above instructions. (3) IND "A" express to Kingston-Throop Aves. Walk 1 block west to Brooklyn Ave., 6 blocks south to Museum.
Bus: B47, B45, B44, B65, B25.
Auto: (1) Via Brooklyn Bridge. Straight off bridge onto Adams St. (becomes Boerum Place). South about 8 blocks to Atlantic Ave. Left on Atlantic Ave. Follow above instructions. (2) Via Manhattan Bridge. Enter bridge from Canal St. Follow Flatbush Ave. and its Extension from bridge to Grand Army Plaza. Turn right off Plaza onto Eastern Pkwy. Follow above instructions.

Gift Shop: Books, seashells, sharks' teeth, arrowheads, cats' eyes, starfish, ethnological, technological, natural history items.   259

Special Events: Calendar of Events for $1.00 annual subscription lists out-of-school activities, film programs, Saturday programs, pet shows, music events, and neighborhood programs.

Membership: From $5—$100.

Workshops: Photography, art, music, science, geology.

The design of the Booklyn Children's Museum, both inside and outside, represents the most revolutionary concepts of museum architecture. It breaks sharply with traditional Corinthian columned facades and dusty exhibition halls to provide a truly inspirational environment for children.

The "plant" itself appears to be buried underground and is invisible from Brower Park above. The park space contains a grandstand amphitheatre with bleacher seats. In the center of the park is a huge highway sign that says, "Brooklyn Children's Museum." In the subterranean bowels of the park is something that resembles a magical space-age factory with exposed timbers, steel girders, purple pipes, yellow ex-

Mayor Edward I. Koch
at Brooklyn Children's Museum.

*A few of the many activities available
at Brooklyn Children's Museum.*

haust ducts and multi-colored neon lights. It has a raw, bare appearance and is the brilliant work of architects Hugh Hardy, Malcolm Holzman and Norman Pfeiffer.

The entrance ramp is a huge corrugated galvanized sewer culvert, much like an amusement park Tunnel of Fun that rotates to tip its occupants. This culvert doesn't turn, but slants downward, so that its base, which contains a huge water trough, runs downstream. The trough inside the tunnel runs about 120 feet and at various levels has water wheels, turbines, steam controls, sluiceways, and water gates that show how a river canal works. All of the apparatus is operated by children who go down the ramp like a descending escalator.

261

Surrounding the tunnel in the Museum space is an enormous Buckminster Fuller-type molecular maze that children can climb up into like a jungle gym. This "curved space labyrinth" and the tunnel are the core of the museum. Molecules designed by Peter J. Pearce are made of dozens of sections of clear unbreakable plastic.

Catwalks and ladders link multi-level platforms (or depots) that contain separate exhibits such as a working windmill, a ripple tank, steam engine, a hydraulic and an air-pressure lift mechanism. A huge gas tank serves as an auditorium. These devices focus attention on self-identification, fire/light, water, air, earth, and cultural links.

The museum can be described as a giant play room, whose avant-garde architecture displays unorthodox materials in unusual shapes and spaces that combine to function as a teaching environment. It is both the newest and the oldest children's museum in the country. Opened to the public on December 16, 1889, its purpose has remained the same: to help children better understand the world they live in by active participation. The museum concentrates on the natural, physical and social sciences, as well as in cultural history. The environment unifies all the museum's exhibition resources within one giant space. Children can explore the laws that govern nature and the many ways in which humans have interacted with nature to produce culture. The museum has more than 40,000 authentic objects of ethnological, technological and natural history, ranging from African masks to seashells and minerals as well as technical artifacts that are the learning tools of this unique museum.

PROSPECT PARK ZOO AND LEFFERTS FARMYARD

Address: Flatbush Ave. near Empire Blvd., Brooklyn, N.Y., 11225.
Phone: 965-6587

Days: Open daily, 8—dusk. Buildings open, 11—5.
Admission: Free.

Subway: BMT Brighton Beach to Prospect Park station.
Auto: Bowery to Manhattan Bridge, continue on Flatbush Ave. to Grand Army Plaza, then Flatbush Ave. to Prospect Park Zoo. Ample street parking.

Restaurant: Restaurant with outdoor café at left of entrance has light lunch, snacks. Picnic tables at right of entrance stairways.

262

Children's Facilities: Pony cart rides $.15.

Note: Some sections of the zoo may be under restoration.

At the Prospect Park Zoo spacious moated enclosures, about the width of a two-lane highway, for the Chapman zebras, Tibetan yak, elephants, and elks, provide an excellent perspective for animal-watching. Various kinds of bears amble about large boulder-strewn slopes. The generous space allotted to these animals compensates for the rather modest selection of hoofed stock and wild beasts.

Characteristic of this zoo are the droves of tagged preteens from day camps, private and public schools, YMCA's and community centers from all over Brooklyn who are shepherded from cage to cage by their counselors or teachers, who point out and try above the din to explain about the kinkajou, black leopards, the ocelot, and the civet cat.

A sea-lion pool is at the center of the zoo. All the sea-lions were stoned to death by vandals but the Parks Department hopes to replace the animals as soon as funds are available. The animal houses and the moated enclosures extend around the pool and to either side. Within reasonable walking distance from the zoo are the Lefferts Homestead, Brooklyn Botanic Garden, and the Brooklyn Museum.

Riding the pony carts at Lefferts Farmyard.

THE LEFFERTS HOMESTEAD

Address: Flatbush Ave. near Empire Blvd., Brooklyn, N.Y., 11225.
Phone: 965-6587

Days: Wednesday, Friday, Saturday, and Sunday, 1—5, except 2nd Saturday of month from November to May inclusive.
Admission: Free.

Subway: BMT Brighton Beach train to Prospect Park station.
Auto: Bowery to Manhattan Bridge, continue on Flatbush Ave. to Grand Army Plaza. Homestead is several yards past main Prospect Park Zoo entrance. Ample street parking.

The Lefferts Homestead was at one time the most northerly dwelling in Flatbush. On August 23, 1776, the family abandoned the house to escape the anticipated invasion of Kings County by the British. During the Battle of Long Island that followed, the house was destroyed.

When the Lefferts family returned, they salvaged the lumber and hardware, and in 1777 erected the present homestead. Judge John Lefferts had inherited the home from his father, Peter, the son of Pieterse Lefferts who arrived in the New Netherlands colony in 1660 from northern Holland with his parents. Pieterse Lefferts settled in Flatbush in 1675.

The Lefferts Homestead is a notable example of Dutch Colonial style. Like the Dyckman House in upper Manhattan, it has a steeply pitched gambrel roof, accentuated by three dormers and a deep overhang supported by slender columns. The paneled front door with its small paned-glass side windows, hall wall moldings, fine archway, and banister are of particular interest.

Downstairs are the library, dining room, tea room, and a back parlor containing a pre-Revolutionary sword, a Dutch table of 1661 vintage, and the familiar Gilbert Stuart portrait of Washington. In the tea room are a Hepplewhite sofa, a Pembroke table, mahogany grandfather clock, a family Bible under glass, dated July 29, 1637, and two colored lithographs of early New York.

The library and dining room contain a flax wheel, a Hepplewhite dropleaf table, a Queen Anne lowboy, a Chippendale highboy; rush-seated side chairs and a wing chair from a house in Kent.

On the upper floor the southwest bedroom has a quilting frame, hackle for combing flax, and an early Franklin stove. A sleigh bed and several Dutch Bibles are in the northwest bedroom. Other bedrooms have dolls and "playthings of early America." In the hall cupboard are some pieces of china used by Nathan Hale's brother Enoch. The upper floor may be closed because of budget cuts.

Descendants of the family presented the Homestead to the city in

264

The Lefferts Homestead.

1918. It was moved to Prospect Park from its original location on Flatbush Avenue.

BROOKLYN BOTANIC GARDEN AND ARBORETUM
Address: 1000 Washington Ave., Brooklyn, N.Y., 11225.
Phone: 622-4433

Days: Grounds open daily, 8—6; and from 10 on Saturdays, Sundays, and holidays. Greenhouses open daily, 10—4; Saturdays, Sundays, and holidays, 11—4.
Admission: Free. Ryoanji Rock Garden, $.25; greenhouses, $.10 on Saturdays, Sundays, and holidays.

Subway: (1) IRT Lexington Ave. to Atlantic Ave., cross platform to 7th Ave. train to Eastern Pkwy.-Brooklyn Museum station. (2) IRT 7th Ave. New Lots Ave. or Flatbush Ave. train to Eastern Pkwy.-Brooklyn Museum station.
Auto: Bowery to Manhattan Bridge, continue on Flatbush Ave. to Grand Army Plaza, left at Eastern Pkwy. Right onto Washington Ave. and Gardens. Street parking. Parking lot at Brooklyn Museum.

Gift Shop: Exceptional garden shop with wide variety, plants, bulbs, seeds, tools.

Bloom Periods:

March 15—30	Crocus
April 1—15	Forsythia, Magnolias
April	Daffodils
April 1—May 10	Cherries, Crabapples
April—June	Rock Garden
May 1—15	Azaleas, Lilacs, Wisteria
May 15—30	Peonies
May—June	Iris
June—November	Roses
July—September	Lotus, Water Lilies
July—November	Annuals
September—November	Chrysanthemums
Spring—Fall	Wildflowers

266

Membership: $15 to $1,000 annually. Members receive announcements of popular classes, handbooks, "plant dividends."

Library: 50,000 volumes on horticultural subjects.

Children: Children's Garden for children over 9 to cultivate vegetables and flowers.

The Botanic Garden, on fifty acres, is almost in the center of Brooklyn. It contains a magnificent selection of familiar and exotic flora set in myriad small gardens, including the Herb Garden, Ryoanji Rock Garden, Fragrance Garden, Japanese Garden, Wildflower, Cherry Esplanade, Children's Shakespeare Garden. The grounds are well kept, and guards patrol the walks on motor scooters.

The garden is surrounded by the 526-acre complex of Prospect Park, which also includes the Brooklyn Public Library, Soldiers and Sailors Memorial Arch at Grand Army Plaza, Lefferts Homestead, the zoo, picnic grounds, horseback-riding trails, tennis courts, baseball diamonds, a lake, and the famous parade grounds.

Picnicking or bringing food into the Garden is strictly forbidden, which may account for the absence of gum wrappers, half-chewed

The main greenhouse at the Brooklyn Botanic Garden.

A view of the Japanese Garden.

bologna sandwiches, beer cans, and broken glass that have become a sadly familiar feature of the city's public facilities.

The conservatories, to the left of the Washington Avenue entrance, have a charming Victorian atmosphere. The main greenhouse houses a tropical forest of sugar cane, pineapple, bamboo, New Zealand flax, and cassia-bark trees from China, a variety that produces eighty-five percent of the cinnamon used in the United States. There are also the soursop, banana, avocado, Chinese fan palm, and the Panama-hat plant, a native of Peru. The trumpet tree is characterized by a completely hollow trunk and branches that, in Brazil, are inhabited by ants. The sapodilla tree is the main source of chicle. Fruits of this species are a tropical delicacy. The brown fruit, about the size of an apple, is actually a berry.

Another greenhouse contains ferns, which are found in almost every part of the world, and range in size from a few inches to the eighty-foot tree ferns of the tropics.

268

The Botanic Garden's famous collection of miniature Japanese bonsai trees is housed in a special hothouse. They range in age from two years to about one hundred years, and from a couple of inches to no more than two feet in height. One three-inch trident maple is more than eighty years old. A dwarf oak is well over one hundred. By severe pruning of roots and branches, and training by wire, interesting shapes and dwarf sizes can be sustained for decades. The Botanic Garden offers a course for those interested in learning the art of the bonsai tree.

The cycad greenhouse simulates great forests of 100 million years ago. The garden how has nine types of cycads growing. These trees form the link between ferns and cone-bearing forms. Many species have

A Japanese bonsai tree.

A replica of the Ryoanji Temple Stone Garden.

a thick, unbranched columnar trunk that bears a crown of large, leathery pinnate leaves.

Charts in the greenhouse show major plant groups as they appeared on earth, with algae, fungi, liverworts, and mosses appearing about a billion years ago; ferns and horsetails about 300 million years ago; cycads about 200 million years ago; other conifers (pine, fir, spruce) about 100 million years ago; and flowers and grasses a mere 55 million years ago. Cycads are the most primitive living seed plants. Some cycad seeds are rich in starch, and are used as food by natives of the tropics. Cycads are commonly used for altar decorations at Eastertime.

The Garden of Fragrance to the right of the conservatories is designed for the blind, and has garlic, marjoram, lavender, peppermint, spearmint, Roman wormwood, and a variety of plants to which one's nostrils and fingers are sensitive. Signs describing the plants are in braille. The only other garden like this in the United States is in Los Angeles.

There are three types of gardens in Japan: hill-and-pond style, tea garden, and the flat style. The flat style is typified here by the Ryoanji Temple Stone Garden. Tea gardens are small, simple, unimposing gardens attached to teahouses, and may be identified by stepping-stones, paved paths, stone water basins, and stone lanterns.

The Botanic Japanese Garden is in the hill-and-pond style, intended for boating, viewing, or strolling. Architectural features are the pavilions, lanterns, and shrines. The Japanese have refined this style by the use of "borrowed scenery": gardens were so placed that the features of the terrain served as panoramic backdrops to the overall effect.

On entering the garden from the "pavilion," one looks across a lagoon to an imposing torii, which forms a decorative gateway, or portal, in Japan, where it is commonly found at the entrance to Shinto temples. The torii consists of two upright wooden posts connected at the top by two horizontal crosspieces. Torii are frequently reproduced on Japanese travel posters.

Directly behind the torii is the Religious Shrine, typical of the traditional Shinto shrines in Japan. This one is dedicated to "Inari," the God of Harvest, and Protector of Plants. In Japan such shrines are seen along the streets and in or near private estates. Woods used in this shrine are white cedar, ash, redwood, and cypress, and the shrine is held together by wooden pegs.

Behind the Japanese Garden are the crabapples and the Cherry Esplanade, probably one of the most beautiful scenes in New York at cherry-blossom time. Beyond the esplanade are the Armistice Maples,

The Rose Garden.

271

planted on November 11, 1918. They have become huge shade trees. The walks around the esplanade have benches.

The Cranford Rose Garden is particularly noted for its hybrid tea roses of infinite variety, with such evocative names as Captain Fain Bold, First Love, Gracious Lady, Rochefort, Suntan, Oklahoma, and Opera.

At the southern end of the Botanic Garden is the Ryoanji Temple Stone Garden, a replica of the five-hundred-year-old original in Kyoto. The garden has no trees or bushes, and is about the size of a tennis court. It is paved with finely crushed stone, arranged in straight and slightly curving rows, like new plantings on a farm or like ripples from a stone thrown into a quiet lake. Among the rows are arranged groups of rocks. This beautiful and most unusual garden is a marvelous pool of peace and calm in our great city and should not be missed.

BROOKLYN MUSEUM

Address: Eastern Pkwy. at Washington Ave., Brooklyn, N.Y., 11225.
Phone: 638-5000

Days: Wednesdays through Saturdays, 10—5; Sundays and holidays, 1—5. Closed Mondays and Tuesdays.
Admission: By contribution.

Subway: (1) IRT Lexington Ave. to Atlantic Ave. station. Cross platform to 7th Ave. train to Eastern Pkwy.-Brooklyn Museum station. (2) IRT 7th Ave. New Lots or Flatbush Ave. train to Eastern Pkwy.-Brooklyn Museum station.
Auto: Bowery to Manhattan Bridge to Flatbush Ave. Continue on Flatbush Ave. to Grand Army Plaza. Follow Eastern Pkwy. signs around traffic circle. Continue on Eastern Pkwy. to Museum, on right. Metered parking in front of building. Public parking lot at rear of building. Fee, $.50.
Restaurant: Museum cafeteria, first floor rear, has hot lunches, snacks, tea. Open Wednesdays to Saturdays, 10—4:30. Sundays and holidays, 11—4:30. Hot dogs by Nathan's Famous.

Gallery Shop: Exceptional collection of handicrafts for sale. See description below. Museum publications are also available.

272   *Membership:* $15.00 up. Membership privileges include lecture course, discounts at Gallery Shop, etc. Junior memberships free.

Library and Research: Art reference library, closed July and August. Open Wednesdays to Fridays, 1—5.

Lectures: Background Hour lectures for school classes, call museum.

Children's Facilities: Children's concerts, art classes, excursions; junior members' programs include clubs, subscription to *Junior Bulletin,* etc. Junior Aide program enlists young volunteers.

If you were sitting on the back of a burro climbing the Andes of Peru, and you passed a large group of men and women, you might well ask where they came from. The answer could be: "The Brooklyn Museum." If you were out driving in Connecticut on a Sunday afternoon and flipped the radio dial to a concert, you might well wonder where the music came from. The announcer might answer just at that time: "The Brooklyn Museum." And if you took a Staten Island bus and encountered a group of teen-agers on their way to dig for Colonial artifacts,

The Brooklyn Museum.

Modern American painting and sculpture.

you wouldn't have to ask where they were from; you would already know. These are just a few examples of the many activities the Brooklyn Museum is engaged in.

The diverse activities, programs, and services of the Brooklyn Museum include visits to historic houses and museums, seminars on art, museum treasure hunts for young members, dance programs, films, children's art classes, an art reference library, Community Committee's "Annual Fence Show," a Fashion and Design Laboratory, a Conservation Laboratory (where paintings are cleaned by ultrasonic apparatus), and a vast art training program. The Museum Art School has a separate entrance, at the right wing of the building, and offers courses in paint-

274

A raven mask from the South Seas.

ing, drawing, sculpture, and ceramics. It also provides a number of scholarships.

The original building was designed by the famous architectural firm of McKim, Mead & White. Since its construction in 1897, a number of revisions have been made, of course. A monumental front staircase once led to the present third floor, and without the stairs the first-floor entrance looks somewhat out of proportion to the rest of the facade. The museum, along with the Botanic Garden, Lefferts Homestead, the public library, and Prospect Park Zoo, completes Brooklyn's major cultural center.

The museum is conceived as a place for enjoyment, recreation, and education, not as an institution where art is kept remote from the common man. The museum's success as one of the major cultural forces in New York is measured, not by attendance, but by an "individual's recollection of what was seen, what was thought, and what was felt."

There are five floors of exhibition space. The first floor is the special exhibition area. Its galleries are devoted to the arts of the primitive peoples of Africa, pre-Columbian Central and South America, North American Indians, Oceania, South Seas, and the Ainu. There is an outside garden devoted to sandstone and brownstone "tenement sculpture" of the 1890—1910 period, collected by the Anonymous Arts Recovery Society. The society is composed of enterprising art scholars who have made great efforts to recover keystone sculpture and reliefs from the hands of demolition crews. Carved ornaments of this type still adorn many Lower East Side tenements. Gargoyles, limestone flowers and beasts, columns and pediments in the garden are all from demolished buildings. They are good examples of the art of stonemasonry. The first floor also contains the cafeteria and Gallery Shop.

The Gallery Shop sells folk art from over sixty countries. It is the only museum shop with an exhibition program featuring original arts and crafts of high quality sold at reasonable prices. For $.10 you can buy tiny handmade toys from Japan, or for $30 you can buy a silver necklace from Pakistan. Some of the other handicrafts are exotic bud vases from Israel, traditional toys from Japan, miniature Chinese wood carvings, ceramic bulls from Peru, costume dolls from Italy, Polish painted roosters, Zuni ceramic owls from New Mexico, paper puppet cutouts from Greece, shell animals, palm buttons, jumping jacks, glass dragons, feather birds, and toy friction bugs. The Gallery Shop most appropriately leads into the gallery of primitive arts.

The entrance room has thirty-two glass cases, each of which contains a weapon (spear, machete, hatchet, bow) and a piece of woven textile. The two objects in each case represent what is attributed to the men and what to the women of a tribe. The tribes are those of the Pacific Islands, Africa, and the Americas. Each exhibit clearly reveals the specific qualities, materials, and techniques of each culture and the direct relation of arts and crafts to daily life. Each culture has produced objects that are useful and beautiful. The Brooklyn Museum was among the first institutions in the United States to collect the native arts of Africa, Oceania, and Indian America. Even before the turn of the century, museum expeditions were sent to all parts of the world to document and assemble the sculpture, ornaments, costumes, and crafts of the cultures exhibited here.

To the right are the crafts of the Pacific Islands, with ceremonial shields, boomerangs, drums covered with lizard skins, face masks, and a variety of betel-nut crushers. The "Art of Africa" display has spears, ceremonial masks in the form of hideous creatures, antelope, buffalo,

Enrico Giordano teaching drawing.

secret-society and initiation masks, fetishes, male and female figures, ceremonial shields of bamboo and mahogany, and wooden doors with allegorical motifs.

Dominating the Hall of the Americas are five magnificent ceiling-high totem poles. Carvings of mythological animals and figures represent the ancestral crests of the families that owned the houses in front of which the totems were placed. Four huge cases in the Great Hall of the museum present a comprehensive picture of the colorful arts of Indian peoples from the Arctic to the Argentine. With the last vestiges of Indian life in the Americas disappearing, this collection constitutes a unique source of information. One section displays the art of the ancient and modern Eskimo, including spirit masks, carved ivory, kayaks, and outerwear made from the skins of seal and caribou.

In the area devoted to the Northwest Coast tribes, mythical and ceremonial objects include grotesque manlike figures that are particularly fearsome. An electrically operated straw-covered raven mask clicks its beak up and down in the darkened case. A thunderbird mask represents a mythical creature whose flapping wings made thunder while his flashing eyes made lightning. On exhibit also are unique examples of Central Andean weaving, painted cloth, tapestry pouches, fringed robes, silver, pottery, feather caps, burial urns, jewelry, and effigy jars.

The Nathan Sturges Jarvis Collection on the Plains Indians contains some of the oldest and historically most important pieces in existence: bone chest ornaments, carved pipes, decorated buckskin shirts and robes, feather war bonnets, moccasins, snowshoes, and implements of war. This material, unique because of its age and documentation, was collected by Dr. Jarvis while he was an army surgeon at Fort Snelling, Minnesota, between 1833 and 1836. Specimens comparable to this collection that are in other museums are generally without documentation.

The second floor houses the William A. Putnam Memorial Print Room, Edward C. Blum Design Laboratory, American and European print collections, and the arts of the East: China, Japan, India, Thailand, Persia.

The collections of the Edward C. Blum Design Laboratory have traveled all over the world, as well as to design schools throughout the country. Much has been shown on both films and television. In one year the laboratory staged fifteen public exhibitions.

The William A. Putnam Memorial Print Room (open by appointment) has 20,000 prints and drawings from the late fourteenth century to those of the most contemporary artists, with particular emphasis on German Expressionists. From this collection come the exhibitions on this floor. Individual monographs on contemporary Americans are compiled, prepared, and published here.

*"Holy Wisdom," a limestone lunette from Egypt
of the Coptic period, 5th century A.D.*

Also sharing the floor are the exhibits of "Arts of Islam and the Indian East." Various types of glazed, lustered, and painted ceramics are shown. Indian miniature painting (Rajput) and Islamic rugs are also here. In the center of the gallery is a Jain Rest Home, with carved pillars and door and walls all covered with Golconda cotton panels. The home, about six by eight feet, was a room attached to temples for the convenience of worshipers. This room is not always on exhibit.

A large part of the second-floor gallery is devoted to Oriental arts of the Han, T'ang, Chou, Yin, Ming, and Ch'ing dynasties. Many centuries of civilization and religious transition are represented. The Oriental collections indicate a more complicated social organization and a wider range and subtlety of form and subject than the collections on the first floor.

The third floor contains Coptic arts, Egyptian, Greek, and Roman art, art of the Near East, the Lecture Hall, the Auditorium, and the Wil-

279

George Washington by Gilbert Stuart, 1796.

bour Library of Egyptology, which ranks among the finest in the world. Some Coptic art may not be on view.

The Hagop Kevorkian Gallery of the Ancient Middle East consists of twelve Assyrian reliefs of gypseous alabaster taken from the royal city of Kalhu. In the wing to the left are works of Ramessid, Roman, Ptolemaic, and Late periods of Egypt. At the very end of the gallery is the portrait of an Egyptian official. It is of the late Ptolemaic period, and ranks among the best portraits from the Nile Valley before Roman domination.

The section on predynastic and early dynastic Egypt contains early Egyptian sculpture. The pottery figures date from 4000 B.C., and include female figures with birdlike heads, with arms outstretched, possibly engaged in ritual dances. A rare representation in black granite of a female sphinx made circa 1900 B.C. is considered one of the great examples of Egyptian Middle Kingdom sculpture.

The gallery surrounding the auditorium has works of Coptic Egypt, an era when Christianity was replacing paganism. The Copts tended to draw on classical mythology for art subjects. Architectural reliefs and elaborately woven fabrics were major accomplishments of the period. The auditorium may be closed for special exhibits.

The fourth floor holds American and European costume collections, Tiffany vases and lamps, Art Nouveau glass, and twenty-seven completely furnished Early American interiors, of the period 1715 through today, from New England, the South, New York, and New Jersey.

In the central gallery the Jan Martense Schenck House, a clapboard farmhouse with Dutch doors built in 1675, has been reconstructed beam by beam. The house is an example of seventeenth-century Brooklyn architecture, and was formerly at 2133 East 63rd Street. The only surviving inhabited Dutch cottage of that era in Brooklyn is the Pieter Claesen Wycoff House, at Claredon Road and East 59th Street. Built in 1637, it is now in a sadly dilapidated conditon. It is the oldest occupied frame house in the United States.

In contrast with this Dutch house is the jet-age contemporary room setting and the Art Deco Worgelt Study created for a Park Avenue apartment in 1928. The remainder of the fourth floor is devoted to room settings from American homes of the Victorian, Colonial, and early Republican periods. The parlors, bedrooms, dining rooms, and

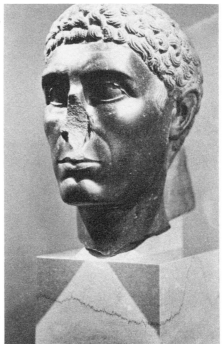

281

An Egyptian official
of the Ptolemaic period
about 60 B.C.

kitchens are carefully detailed, as in the James Perry Plantation, built in 1806 near Summerville, North Carolina.

Representing the Victorian era is a sitting room from the John D. Rockefeller four-story brownstone that stood on West 54th Street in Manhattan. This is a vivid example of home decoration around 1884, when tastes ran to exotic Moorish tiles, gold-brocaded walls, ebony and oak panels, decorated ceilings, plush velvet, and candelabra.

The fifth floor and mezzanine house collections of American and European paintings, sculpture, watercolors, medieval, and Renaissance art. More than a thousand paintings at the Brooklyn Museum, which were inaccessible to the public, have just made their appearance for the first time in a novel method of display. The Open Study Storage Gallery is open weekdays by appointment and offers its panorama of paintings on a series of rotating and sliding panels, a method of display that is used by large commercial galleries.

The Department of Painting and Sculpture usually presents an exhibition from one major private collection each year. There have been exhibitions of the Nelson Rockefeller, Louis E. Stern, Hirshhorn Foundation, and the Herbert A. Goldstone collections. This special exhibition program exists primarily to create, develop, and reward aesthetic perception.

The American Collection traces American painting from the Colonial period. The museum has built a comprehensive collectin of Colonial portraits. The Federal period is identified with Benjamin West, the first American to go abroad to study art, and around whom a school developed. Thomas Sully, Charles Wilson Peale, Ralph Earle, and Gilbert Stuart were his best-known disciples. Stuart's portrait of Washington is a prime example of the excellence of early portraiture.

The Hudson River School of painting is represented by a number of pastoral scenes depicting the wonders of our national landscape in a romantic glorification of nature. Other sections of the American Collection are devoted to paintings by "The Eight," Social Realists, prewar and postwar Abstract Expressionists and Impressionists. The fifth-floor mezzanine displays a sizable collection of watercolors by John Singer Sargent, Winslow Homer, and other American and European artists.

283

A sculpture in the Frieda Schiff
Warburg Garden of works collected by
the Anonymous Arts Recovery Society.

NEW YORK AQUARIUM AND OSBORNE LABORATORIES

Address: West 8th St. and Surf Ave., Brooklyn, N.Y., 11224.
Phone: 266-8500

Days: Open daily, 10–5.
Admission: Adults $2.00, children 2–12, $.75. Special group rates must be prearranged. Children under 2 free.

Subway: IND 6th Ave. "D" train to West 8th St., Coney Island.
Bus: B36 Nostrand Ave.; B68 Prospect Park.
Auto: Brooklyn-Battery Tunnel to Gowanus Pkwy., Shore Pkwy. to Ocean Pkwy. exit, then to Surf Ave. and Aquarium. Two-hour metered parking on Surf Ave. Aquarium parking lot fees: weekdays $1.00; Saturday and Sunday, $2.00.

Restaurant: Outdoor café-restaurant has light lunches, snacks, and view of beach. Picnic tables near small snack bar.

Gifts: Shop near whale tank has large stock of aquatic toys and marine souvenirs. Good selection of hobby supplies, books. Guide to Aquarium is excellent.

On entering the aquarium you immediately face the underwater tanks of the beluga whales. These whales may reach 17 feet at full growth

"Touch-it Tank."

Humboldt penguins.

and weigh more than 4,000 pounds. They are not completely white until they are five years old. The whale tank can also be viewed from above, on the terrace.

At the tank of electric eels a demonstration is given that shows the ability of the eels to produce sufficient electricity to light bulbs, sound buzzers, flash strobe lights, and shoot from 375 to 550 volts into a voltmeter. These eels, which have no teeth, scales or spines, and cannot even see very well, reach a length of nine feet.

Beluga whale.

The morays are closely related to eels, and are feared by fishermen and divers who encounter them in the crevices of coral reefs and find them savagely aggressive.

Among the other fish displayed are the hogfish, which has a nose shaded red and which, from the front, looks like a hog; the piranha, a fearsome South American species noted for its viciousness; the venomous stonefish, and the zebra fish, a member of the scorpion fish family, with thirteen spines, all believed to be venomous.

In the world's oceans there are more varieties of creatures than all the kinds of mammals, birds, and reptiles of the earth combined. The aquarium has many curious sea animals on display, including the sea anemone, with beautiful white tentacles that wave gracefully in the water; the Pacific sea cucumber, related to starfishes, which feeds on sand and mud and lives in that part of the ocean where weirdly lighted, ghostly creatures haunt the depths; one of the most graceful sights is that of the schooling fish—striped bass, herring, mackerel, dogfish, and Nova Scotia alewhite—which swim counterclockwise in unison around and around almost hypnotically while the sunlight streams down into the tank.

Outdoors there are penguin and seal pools, a unique "touch-it tank," and shows by performing dolphins.

The setting for the New York Aquarium is a strip of beach with a boardwalk separating it from the Atlantic Ocean. The aquarium has been on this site since 1942. Previously it was in the Castle Clinton structure in Battery Park, Manhattan. The present building on twelve-acre Seaside Park plans to build additional wings. Attendance at the aquarium is about 500,000 annually.

INTERNATIONAL SYNAGOGUE

Address: John F. Kennedy International Airport, Jamaica, N.Y., 11430.
Phone: 656-5044

Days: Open daily, 9—5. Closed Saturdays.
Admission: Free.

Subway: IND "E" or "F" train to Kew Gardens, then Q10 bus to Airport.
Auto: Long Island Expressway to Van Wyck Expressway to JFK Airport to the International Arrivals Building. Continue driving toward airport exit following signs to chapel.

Restaurant: Restaurants in airport buildings.

Library: Ferkauf Library by appointment only.

Aircraft landing at JFK, where this synagogue museum is located, can identify the building from above because there is a large Star of David on the roof. The Synagogue and Museum is sponsored by the New York Board of Rabbis and is situated in the airport's Tri-Faith Plaza, adjacent to the lagoon and the fountains in front of the International Arrivals Building.

The interior space of the Synagogue is distinguished by a 40-foot-high twin stone sculptural interpretation of the "Tablets of the Law" (the Ten Commandments) adjoining the Holy Ark in the sanctuary. The work is by the distinguished sculptor Chaim Gross, and is the gift of Mr. and Mrs. Joseph Meyerhoff of Baltimore. The Chapel is patterned after the first synagogue built in America, the Spanish and Portugese Mill Street Synagogue, which was completed in 1730.

The Synagogue houses the Ferkauf Library, which includes literature of many languages, and the Ferkauf Museum with rare religious items donated by more than 85 Jewish communities all over the world. The religious museum includes a Torah that was buried in a Berlin cemetery during the Nazi era, a Torah scroll used by two generations of Jewish immigrants at Ellis Island, silver breastplates from the collection of the Central Synagogue of Moscow, Kiddish cups and seder plates on loan from the collection of Sol Rozman, and a 200-year-old shofar or ram's horn used by the so-called "black Jews" of Cochin, India.

There are also many other items in the museum—Chanukah menorahs, mezuzahs, dreidels, bronze and wood gragers, hand-woven Kalleh bags, alms boxes, spice containers in the shape of windmills, birds and fish, and an intricately carved ivory circumcision set.

The International Synagogue also holds exhibits from time to time

*Holy Menorah
inside International
Synagogue Museum.*

and in the past has shown "1000 Years of Jewish Life and Faith in Czechoslovakia," "Jewish Life in Hungary During the Past 1000 Years," "The Holocaust and Resistance," a show of captured Nazi photographs, and a Judaic stamp exhibit.

Included in the Tri-Faith Plaza at Kennedy Airport is the Protestant Chapel called The Ecumenical Christian Shrine of Aviation and Our Lady of the Skies, a Roman Catholic Church.

QUEENS BOTANICAL GARDEN
Address: 43-50 Main St. at Dahlia Ave., Flushing, N.Y., 11355.
Phone: 886-3800

Days: Wednesdays through Sundays, 9 to dusk.
Admission: Free.

Subway: IRT Flushing line from Times Square.
Bus: Q44 to Elder Ave.
Auto: Queens-Midtown Tunnel to Long Island Expressway. Main St., Flushing exit north to Dahlia Ave. Ample street parking.

288 *Membership:* $15.00 to $100.00 annual membership. Members receive publications.

Lectures: Variety of lectures on horticultural subjects. Inquire in Administration Building.

The Queens Botanical Garden is the most recent addition to the botanic gardens of New York City. Because it is conveniently located in the heart of Flushing, the garden, the historic Quaker Meeting House, the Bowne House, and the Kingsland Homestead may easily be encompassed in one excursion. The garden is still in the early stages of development. Many young trees and plantings are in evidence, as well as a new administration building, completed in 1963, that appears spacious, well lighted, and cheerful. It expresses the outlook of the Botanical Society in providing expanded facilities for the Queens community. Plans for the future include more greenhouses and a fragrance garden.

Some of the features of the garden are: spring flowering bulbs (narcissus and tulip); the Perkins Memorial Garden, which contains thousands of popular varieties of roses; an ericaceous garden (woody plants, shrubs, and small trees); an aster collection with twenty varieties; cold frames that protect the plants over the winter; soil-testing facilities; turf trails that demonstrate characteristics of grasses, and an arboretum of one hundred fifty evergreen trees.

To serve its community and interested visitors, the Garden Society offers a wide and interesting variety of practical lectures and demonstrations devoted to designing home gardens, flower arranging, lawnmaking, pruning, care of house plants, attracting birds to a garden, fertilizers and weed killers. A nominal fee is charged for the lectures.

Perkins Memorial Garden at the Queens Botanical Garden.

Quaker Meeting House.

QUAKER MEETING HOUSE
Address: 137-16 Northern Blvd., Flushing, N.Y., 11354.
Phone: 762-9743

Days: Sundays 2—5. Visitors welcome at worship, Sunday at 11. When closed, out-of-town visitors may call 657-0959 or 897-8350.
Admission: Free.

Subway: IRT Flushing line from Times Square or Grand Central to Main St. station.
Auto: Queens-Midtown Tunnel to Long Island Expressway. Main St., Flushing exit north. Right at Northern Blvd. to Meeting House. Metered street parking.

Lectures: Free guided tour of building.

290   It is unlikely that anyone would pass by the historic Quaker Meeting House in the busy shopping center of Flushing without noticing the building. There is nothing quite like it anywhere in the city.

    The Meeting House was built in 1694 on land given by John Bowne, and is one of America's oldest places of worship. It has been in continuous use, except for a period during the Revolution. British soldiers seized the property and used it variously as a prison, a hospital, and for storage of hay.

This rare specimen of Colonial architecture stands behind a low stone wall. The two-story, rectangular wooden building is distinguished for its four-sided hip roof, wooden shutters, and small-paned windows. There is an open porch across the entire front of the lower story. The porch roof is supported by slender square wooden posts. The doors from the porch swing open by means of a weight on ropes and a system of pulleys. Original handmade iron door hinges, latches, and locks are still in evidence. The doors open directly into the meeting room, which has plain white plaster walls, no decorative cornices, tinted glass, or glowing fabrics. The room has simple, open-back wooden benches covered with fiber matting. All the benches face the center of the room. The overhead beams are held up by wooden posts. The corners are anchored with "ship's knees," the Colonial version of today's ell-shaped brackets.

Although the building's historical significance is assured simply by its being such a well-preserved monument of its era, it is also a memorial to the early citizens of the Flushing area who refused to persecute the Quaker settlers as ordered by the governor of their colony.

BOWNE HOUSE
Address: Bowne St. at 37th Ave., Flushing, N.Y., 11354.
Phone: 359-0528

Days: Tuesday, Saturday, and Sunday, 2:30—4:30.
Admission: Free.

Subway: IRT Flushing line from Times Square or Grand Central to Main St. station.
Auto: Queens—Midtown Tunnel to Long Island Expressway. Main St. Flushing exit north. Right turn at Northern Blvd. Right turn at Bowne St. to 37th Ave. Ample street parking.

The Bowne House is on a quiet side street in Flushing among the pleasant two-family houses typical of this area. Numerous oak trees shade the wide street.

The oldest part of this two-story saltbox was erected in 1661 by John Bowne on land purchased from the Indians ten years earlier. In addition to being one of the oldest buildings extant in New York, it is also considered a shrine to religious freedom.

Bowne House.

The earliest section of the house is the kitchen, which has its original, pegged floors. The semicircular oven in the great fireplace could bake as many as forty pies at one time. On the mantel is a rare pewter plate with a Dutch inscription, dated 1656. There are also a rare "betty lamp" and a rushlight. A cupboard holds a set of leather drinking tankards with figures embossed in the leather.

In this kitchen John Bowne expounded his Quaker philosophy, in violation of Governor Peter Stuyvesant's edict of 1657 that the religion of the Dutch Reformed Church was to be the only religion. It was forbidden for anyone in the colony to entertain a Quaker or attend a Quaker meeting. Bowne permitted illegal meetings in this house and was arrested, imprisoned and subsequently banished to Ireland. It was his courageous commitment and determination that eventually brought freedom of assembly for the Quakers.

George Fox, founder of the Quaker faith, preached outside the house on June 7, 1672. Etchings inside the building show the Fox oaks, marking the site where he spoke. A plaque in the garden commemorates the Flushing Remonstrance, an appeal dated December 27, 1657, petitioning the governor for liberty of conscience for the Quakers.

KINGSLAND HOUSE
Address: 143-35 37th Ave., Flushing, N.Y., 11354.
Phone: 939-0647

Days: Tuesdays, Saturdays, Sundays, 2:30—4:30; Wednesdays, Thursdays, Fridays, 11—2 P.M.
Admission: Donation, $.50.

292

Subway: IRT Flushing train to Main St. station.
Auto: Long Island Expressway to Main St. exit, Main Street to Northern Blvd., right to Parsons Blvd., then to 37th Ave.

Membership: Individual, $5; Life $100.

The Kingsland House, visible from the rear of the Bowne House, is situated in Weeping Beech Park next to the oldest weeping beech tree in America. The huge farmhouse looks a little awkward in its new location because the front porch is about 20 feet from the iron fence of the park. The house probably would have looked better if the front had been placed facing 37th Street or Parsons Boulevard and had been set more in the center of the park lot.

The architecture is a mixture of the Dutch and English style once common to New York City and Long Island. The gambrel roof, the quadrant windows, central chimney and general appearance are typically English while the split-front doors and the building's proportions reflect the Dutch influence.

The Kingsland Homestead was built in 1774 by Charles Doughty and his wife, Sarah Dusenbury. Doughty was a wealthy Quaker farmer who was reputed to be the first person to free a slave in Queens. The name "Kingsland" was derived from the last name of Captain Joseph King, an English sea captain who married Charles Doughty's daughter and inherited the house her father built.

Captain King's daughter, Mary King, married Lindley Murray of the "Murray Hill" family. Several generations of the Murray family lived in the Kingsland House until it was sold to a developer.

The early American farmhouse was originally located at 155th Street and Northern Boulevard. In 1968 when Kingsland was threatened with demolition for a shopping center, local community groups, the City Planning Commission, the Landmarks Preservation Commission and the Parks Department arranged to move the old building and deliver it a dozen blocks away to the park. It has been further restored with private funds. In its present location on the Flushing Freedom Mile, the Kingsland House site embodies the rich historical heritage of Flushing and Queens County.

The Kingsland Preservation Committee and the Queens Historical Society oversee the building and its broad program of lectures, workshops, exhibitions of local history and decorative arts, walking tours, and preservation projects.

Kingsland Homestead.

HALL OF SCIENCE

Address: 111th St. and 48th Ave., Queens, N.Y., 11368.
Phone: 699-9400

Days: Open Wednesdays through Fridays, 10–4; Saturdays, 10–5; Sundays, 11–5.

Admission: Voluntary contribution.

Subway: IRT Flushing line to 111th St. station.
Bus: B58 Maspeth-Flushing route to 108th St.
Auto: Long Island Expressway to exit 111th St.

Restaurant: Snack bar and picnic tables in museum.

Gift Shop: Many inexpensive souvenirs.

Special Services: Various clubs meet at museum; teacher programs; facilities for the handicapped.

This museum is located in Flushing Meadows where the 1939 and 1963 World Fairs were held. The parklike setting appears vastly neglected and presents an unfinished appearance. The museum complex includes a Space Park of imposing full-scale models of U.S. rockets and spacecraft. On view are a 52-foot propulsion section of the Saturn V rocket, a Gemini capsule attached to a Titan II booster surrounded by the Apollo Command and Service Module and the Lunar Excursion Module (LEM), and Mariner II, the world's first successful Venus probe. It is a unique display.

The museum structure, about 80 feet high, was finished in 1964 and is an unusual design. It has wavy, honeycombed serpentine concrete walls punctuated by inset panels of royal blue glass. The two lower floors contain exhibits, and the remainder of the interior space is hollow.

The clear, simple exhibits are implemented with buttons to push, knobs to pull, levers to switch, as well as ear and eye pieces to absorb the information. The Hall of Science is geared to young students interested in astronomy, amateur radio, photography, printing, space science, the metric system, the weather and other science-related subjects that have particular significance to everyday life in the city. Exhibits are supplemented by lectures and workshops in science, physics, chemistry, and electronics.

Technology of New York City is particularly interesting. Models and renderings of many city structures, a working scale-model of the water and sewage disposal system, a cross-section of the track and ties and

294

Hall of Science.

signal system from the subway, a traffic-counting computer, a 28-foot scale model of the Williamsburg Bridge and the original sections of bridge cable from three bridges are included. Priceless original drawings of the Brooklyn Bridge signed by William Roebling are among the highlights of the exhibit.

THE QUEENS MUSEUM
Address: New York City Building, Flushing Meadow—Corona Park, Flushing, N.Y., 11368.
Phone: 592-2405

Days: Tuesdays through Saturdays, 10—5; Sundays, 1—5. Closed Mondays.
Admission: Free.

Subway: IRT Flushing line to 111th St. station.
Bus: B58 Maspeth-Flushing route to 108th St.
Auto: Long Island Expressway to exit for 111th St.

Gift Shop: Books, catalogues, postcards relating to Queens.

Special Events: Films, guided art tours, concerts, workshops, art and craft classes.

Membership: Students, $5; benefactors, $1000.

The home of the Queens Museum is in the New York City Building directly in front of the unisphere in Flushing Meadow-Corona Park. It is one of the last remaining structures of the 1939 World's Fair. From 1946 to 1950, the United Nations General Assembly met in the City Building and cast the historic vote that created the state of Israel in November 1947. It was used again for the 1964 World's Fair. The Queens Museum shares the space with a public ice skating rink.

The Museum's goal is to bring great art into Queens through an ambitious program of rotating shows by providing exhibition space for Queens artists and craftspeople (both professional and novice) and by sponsoring workshops, films, lectures and other cultural events and exhibits. Some of these extend beyond a Queens orientation such as "West African Art," "Medieval Crafts," "Peruvian Ceramics," "Chinese Painting and Calligraphy," "Antarctica," and "Ritual Masks." One of its most successful shows was "The Tulip and the Rose," which is the official seal of Queens, that was an exhibition of Queens history.

The most ambitious permanent display at the Museum is the panorama of New York City, a huge model done on a scale of one inch to 100 feet that shows every street, building, railroad, bridge, river, park, and highway in the metropolitan area in three-dimensional form. The model is 180 feet long and 100 feet wide and took two years to build at a cost of $653,000. Made for the 1964 World's Fair by Lester Associates Incorporated, it is a remarkable achievement of miniature modelmaking.

The Museum's record of intense community service and its spirited plans for the future reveal a strong commitment to further de-

The Queens Museum.

velop and enliven the cultural life in Queens and in New York City. As an example, under the astute leadership of Janet Schneider, the Museum is enthusiastically committed to an innovative expansion program that includes "Parkarts." Parkarts is an association of organizations that is currently operating a public facility within the Flushing Meadow—Corona Park to improve the services to the public. The organization is made up of the Queens Museum, the Hall of Science, the Queens Botanical Garden Society, the Queens Cultural Association, the Queens Festival Theatre, the United States Tennis Association, and the Queens Council for the Arts. Parkarts in this spectacular, spacious setting combines some of the most fruitful and diverse cultural activities in New York.

KING MANSION
Address: 153rd St. and Jamaica Ave., Jamaica, N.Y.
Phone: 523-1653

Days: Thursdays, 1—4.
Admission: $.50. Children under 14 not admitted without an adult.

Subway: Eighth Ave. Queens "E" train to Parsons Blvd. station. Walk two blocks to King Park at 89th Ave. and 153rd St.
Auto: Queens—Midtown Tunnel to Long Island Expressway. To Parsons Blvd. exit to Jamaica Ave.; turn right to 153rd St. Metered street parking.

The King Mansion stands at the edge of a pleasant neighborhood park that has an old-time circular, domed, open bandstand in the center.
Rufus King bought the estate on November 20, 1805, for $12,000; it consisted of ninety acres, extending north to the present Grand Central Parkway and east to Grace Episcopal Church. The church is on Jamaica Avenue today, just two blocks away. Its graveyard contains some extraordinary gravestones that look almost new but are as old as 1738 (such as that of Elbert Willett). The quality of the primitive angels' heads, skeletons, skull and crossbones places these early markers in the category of Early American folk art. Rufus King and dozens of his descendants are buried in the Grace Episcopal churchyard.
The Kings were one of America's leading families. Rufus King was a "carpetbagger" from Maine. Graduating from Harvard in 1777, he served as a delegate to the Continental Congress in the late 1780s, was a minister to England under Washington, Adams, and Jefferson, and became one of the first two United States senators from New York in 1789.

King mansion.

For the short time that King himself lived in the mansion, he enjoyed the life of a gentleman farmer, continuing his correspondence from his library with the influential and prominent men of the day and entertaining in his beautiful dining room. King and his wife, Mary Alsop, reared five brilliant children: John Alsop King, governor of New York in 1856; Charles, editor of the New York *American* in 1823 and president of Columbia College; James Gore, president of the Erie Railroad and congressman from New Jersey; Edward, founder of the Cincinnati Law School; and Frederic Gore, a distinguished physician.

The mansion's barnlike appearance can be attributed to its gambrel roof. The eight-room house has three sections; the oldest, in the rear, dating from 1700, is now a storage depot for the wheelbarrows, shovels, and rakes of the city's Parks Department. At various times the house has been an inn, a farmhouse, and a parsonage for Grace Episcopal's ministers (1710–1755).

Around the turn of the century the building was acquired by the city. Because over the years it has been decorated piecemeal by volunteer workers, the furnishings have fluctuated from a time of total neglect to that of an overzealous modern decor. At one low point ugly radiators were installed. The floors in many of the rooms suffered from repeated coats of heavy-duty paint, as did the delicate wall moldings, woodwork, and even some of the furnishings. The wallpapers reflected contemporary bargain-basement prices rather than the taste of the Sheraton or Empire periods. Since then the mansion has been restored.

STATEN ISLAND INSTITUTE OF ARTS AND SCIENCES
Address: 75 Stuyvesant Place, Staten Island, N.Y., 10301.
Phone: 727-1135

Days: Daily 10—5; Sundays, 1—5. Closed Mondays and major holidays.
Admission: Free.

Subway: IRT 7th Ave. or IRT Lexington Ave. to South Ferry station; then take Staten Island Ferry to St. George.
Taxi: From St. George ferry, about five minutes' cab ride.
Auto: Drive south to Battery and Staten Island Ferry. Alternate driving route via Brooklyn—Battery Tunnel, Belt Pkwy. to Verrazano—Narrows Bridge (Rt. 278). Principal attraction of bridge for Manhattan-based Staten Island-bound motorists is avoiding the long lines at ferry. Leave Rt. 278 at Hylan Blvd. exit, continue to Bay St., past New York ferries to Richmond Terr., left at Hamilton Pl., left again at Stuyvesant Pl. Metered street parking. Those coming off ferry in St. George take scenic walk 3 blocks along Richmond Terr. and turn left at Wall St.

Special Events: Sunday concerts, nature programs, film series, lectures and demonstrations in arts and crafts.

Membership: $10.00 annually, includes subscription to monthly bulletin, art rental gallery privileges, etc.

Gift Shop: Sales counter near lobby entrance for hobby supplies, toys, books.

This two-story neo-Georgian brick building has a pleasant entrance with a semi-circle of benches grouped around the front door. It is a modest museum that serves the community with exhibitions that relate specifically to Staten Island.

The impending move to much larger quarters at the handsome Greek Revival buildings and grounds at Sailors' Snug Harbor will enable the Staten Island Museum to display its permanent collections in an appropriate setting. The museum has gradually and judiciously accumulated significant holdings in practically every area of the fine arts.

299

The paintings in the collections form the nucleus of an attractive group of historical portraits of Staten Islanders that give a remarkable impression of life there in the last century. Some impressive landscapes have captured the appearance of the Island in what has been called its "Golden Era" prior to the turn of the century. Chief among the landscapes is "Looking Eastward from Todt Hill" by Jasper F. Cropsey who was born in Rossville and ranks among Staten Island's most distinguished native artists.

Its collections of prints, drawings, maps and photographs illuminate the role of Staten Island in the life of New York Harbor. The John J. Crooke collection (1860–1875) is the largest single picture source illustrating the appearance of the island during the Civil War.

A major project of the Staten Island Museum is the High Rock Nature Conservation Center, a seventy-acre, hilly oak and hickory woodland of nature trails where Audubon buffs and conservationists can enjoy the sight of sweet gum, cherry birch, and swamp azalea. Booklets are available for self-guided walks. The entrance to High Rock is on Nevada Avenue, four blocks north of Richmond Road.

Staten Island Institute.

STATEN ISLAND ZOO IN BARRETT PARK

Address: 614 Broadway, Staten Island, N.Y., 10310.
Phone: 442-3100

Days: Open daily, 10–5. Closed holidays.
Admission: Adults, $.75; children, $.50; children's zoo, free.

Subway: IRT 7th Ave. or IRT Lexington Ave. to South Ferry station. Take Staten Island Ferry to St. George.
Bus: From St. George take bus No. 107 to Broadway.
Auto: (1) From St. George turn right on Richmond Terrace, left at Broadway to zoo. (2) From Verrazano Bridge take Clove Road exit to zoo at Broadway. Free parking lot at zoo.

Restaurant: Vending machines for soda, ice cream.

Gift Shop: Sales counter has candy, toys, hobby supplies, Zoological Society publications.

Library: Small reference library open to public and students.

Lectures: Staff members available only to organized groups (school-children, Boy Scouts, etc.) for tours and lectures; call 442-3174.

Publication: Staten Island Zoological Society monthly *News Bulletin.*

This special zoo is set in an eight-acre park delightfully shaded by tall pin oaks, Norway maples, and sweet gum trees. The zoo has separate bird and mammal wings, a reptile wing of international repute, and an aquarium.

The aquarium has a fine collection of American alligators and many kinds of frogs and toads: green tree and leopard frogs, Colombian horned and bull frogs, North American tiger salamanders, and Blomberg toads.

The famous collection of reptiles includes blood pythons, boa constrictors, and one of the largest collections of rattlesnakes ever assembled anywhere—the Panamint, the Mojave, Sonora sidewinder, mottled rock, ridge-nosed, black-tailed, timber, tiger, diamond back, and midget faded. There are also the West African green mamba and the puff adder, which are among the deadliest in the world.

The bird collection includes woodpeckers, robins, concave-casqued hornbills, birds from India, Burma, Java, and the Himalayas; shiny cowbirds from Argentina; a king vulture, a crowned hawk-eagle, and a golden eagle. Many of the bird enclosures simulate the natural habitats of the birds.

301

Children's Farm-Zoo.

The Children's Zoo has a country barn, windmill, and waterwheel. It re-creates a farmlike atmosphere with chickens, ducks, geese, goats, sheep, and a pretty pony, all within arm's length of the youngsters.

FORT WADSWORTH MILITARY MUSEUM

Address: School Road and Bay St., Staten Island, N.Y., 10305.
Phone: 447-5100 ext. 731

Days: Saturdays 10–4; Mondays, Thursdays, Fridays, Sundays, 1–4;
closed Tuesdays, Wednesdays and holidays; groups accommodated.
Admission: Free.

Subway: IRT 7th Ave. or IRT Lexington Ave. to South Ferry, then
take Staten Island Ferry to St. George.
Bus: From St. George take bus No. 2 to School Road.
Auto: (1) From St. George left along Bay St. to Fort. (2) From Verrazano Bridge, exit at Hylan Blvd., then to Bay St., right to Fort. Free
parking lot.

This may be a small museum, but it will have a particular appeal to
children who are fascinated by military history. Here are to be found
the rampart cannons, rifles, uniforms, medals, flags, and other paraphernalia that document a dozen or more wars from the Dutch-Colonial
period to Vietnam, including some rare Axis flags of World War II.

*View of Battery Weed and Verrazano—Narrows Bridge
from the Fort Wadsworth Military Museum.*

Relics of World War II.

This museum, established in 1966 by Maj. General T. R. Yancey, is situated in three bays of the quadrangle in Fort Tompkins barracks built in 1847. Built on a hilltop, Fort Wadsworth affords a spectacular view of the Narrows, the Lower Bay, and the Verrazano Bridge. The abandoned Battery Weed is directly below Fort Tompkins barracks.

These fortifications have been held successively by Dutch, British, and Americans since 1663. As a military museum this certainly ranks along with those at West Point and Fort Ticonderoga, New York.

BILLIOU—STILLWELL—PERINE HOUSE

Address: 1476 Richmond Road, Staten Island, N.Y., 10304.
Phone: 987-7379

Days: Saturdays and Sundays, 2—5, April to October.
Admission: Adults $.25. No school tours.

304 *Subway:* IRT 7th Ave. or IRT Lexington Ave. to South Ferry, then take Staten Island Ferry to St. George.
Bus: From St. George bus No. 113 or No. 117 to Norden St.
Auto: (1) From St. George left along Bay St., right to Victory Blvd., left at St. Paul's. Continue as road name changes to Van Duzer, then

to Richmond Road. Continue to No. 1476. (2) From Verrazano Bridge, Richmond Road exit to house. Ample street parking.

The Billiou—Stillwell—Perine House closely resembles a European farmhouse of the seventeenth century. It was built by Pierre Billiou in 1663 on property he acquired under a Dutch patent granted two years earlier. Billiou headed the first permanent settlement on Staten Island.

The rear section of the house was the original parlor-kitchen. It has a remarkable fireplace without sides that is surmounted by a great chimney supported by a framework and two columns just below the ceiling beams. This construction was typical of the Low Countries, and gives the room its Old World charm. The walls on this side of the farmhouse are composed of French or Belgian stone about 18 inches thick. Their soundproofing quality would be the envy of dwellers in contemporary thin-walled apartment houses.

In 1677, Captain Thomas Stillwell, a sheriff, a magistrate, and militia captain received an English patent for the Billiou property. Stillwell had married Billiou's daughter in 1670. It is believed that Billiou trans-

Perine House.

A welcoming hearth.

ferred the property to his son-in-law for safekeeping when he lost favor with the British.

The portion of the house facing Richmond Road was put up separately by Stillwell in 1680. The Staten Island historian Loring McMillen believes that the Stillwell portion of the house may be an old house from Oude Dorp at South Beach that was abandoned in 1679, or the house may have belonged to Thomas Stillwell, who moved and reassembled it, piece by piece, on the Billiou site. That the Stillwell side was added later is evidenced by the smaller, English-style fireplace, different casement windows, and the rafters and beams that indicate former use.

The front and back buildings are so arranged that two families could occupy the property and be independent of each other. In fact, until recently there was no doorway to connect the two houses.

In 1760, 1790, and 1830 additions were made to the house by the Perine family. The property was acquired in 1915 by the Staten Island Historical Society. The Federated Garden Clubs of New York undertook the planning and development of the formal garden at the side of the house.

JACQUES MARCHAIS CENTER OF TIBETAN ART
Address: 338 Lighthouse Ave., Staten Island, N.Y. 10306.
Phone: 987-3478

Days: Saturdays and Sundays, 1–5 (April through November). Phone ahead for summer hours. Closed October 31st to April 1st.
Admission: $1.00.

Subway: IRT 7th Ave. or IRT Lexington Ave. to South Ferry, then take Staten Island Ferry to St. George.
Bus: From St. George take bus No.113 to Lighthouse Ave. Walk up hill.
Auto: (1) From St. George left along Bay St., right to Victory Blvd., left at St. Paul's. Continue as road name changes to Van Duzer, then Richmond Road. Turn right at two stone posts marking beginning of Lighthouse Ave. Continue up hill to No. 338 on right. (2) From Verrazano Bridge take Richmond Road exit. Follow road to Lighthouse Ave. as above. Ample street parking.

Library: Large collection of Orientalia open to public.

The Jacques Marchais Center of Tibetan Art is on top of Lighthouse Hill, the highest point along the eastern seaboard. The museum overlooks the woodlands and lakes of rural Staten Island. On a clear day you can see the entire lower bay of New York in the distance.

The altar in Jacques Marchais Center.

The garden at Jacques Marchais.

Virtually unknown to many natives of both Manhattan and Staten Island, this museum is unique in its tranquil setting and its collections of Tibetan religious art and volumes related to the teachings of Buddha. The entrance, on a shady country street, is marked by a tiny sign that simply says "Tibetan Art." Usually, small children are discouraged from entering because the gardens are built on steep cliffs and are carefully landscaped.

In the gardens, set along niches in the walls or at the stairs, are stone sculptures of squirrels, rabbits, snakes, lizards, frogs, sacred monkeys, and elephants. There are a lotus pool, charming birdhouses, a wishing well, leaf-hidden life-size Buddhas, and cast-iron garden benches with floral and leaf designs.

The Center was built by Jacques Marchais, the professional name of Mrs. Harry Klauber, for ten years a dealer in Oriental art. Mrs. Klauber died in 1948. The museum contains her collection of Oriental Buddhist art. The board of trustees operates the museum as a memorial to Mrs. Klauber, as provided under the will of Mr. Klauber, who died eight months after his wife.

The one-acre, hilltop museum has three main sections: the library, the lamasery altar, and the landscaped grounds. The library, containing all of Mrs. Klauber's books, is furnished with massive, elaborately carved, red-lacquered Chinese furniture. The books are all in English and are intended to serve as a library on the Orient for students. There are no original manuscripts, but there are many books about Tibet, Buddhism, Asian art, and on perfumes, gems, and colors as applied to Tibetan art, as well as a complete set of source books on where to find the "Sacred Books of the East."

The skylit main building has the shape of a Tibetan temple, with an authentic lamasery altar of granite blocks in three tiers. On the shelves are scores of gold, silver, and bronze idols of various Buddhist sects of Tibet and India, China, and Japan. Usually a volunteer guide describes the religious objects, and introduces the visitor to the melodious nara gong, shaped like a huge brass soup pot.

The altar is intended to re-create a Tibetan altar as closely as possible. It is ornate and crowded with hand prayer wheels, incense burners, vases, masks used in religious plays, one-note, metallic-sounding horns used to call the monks into the temple, offering bowls, intricately carved and gilded wooden statuettes of Buddhist deities, and votive altar tablets. Many of the Buddha images bear white scarves, brought here as a mark of reverence by the monks who live in a Buddhist monastery nearby in New Jersey. Many interesting wall banners, or tankas, made by lamas depict stories of various teachers and deities. Opposite the altar wall squats a heroic-sized Chinese Buddha dating from about 1700.

The Jacques Marchais Center is a replica of a Tibetan temple for meditation and inspiration. Images in the museum were fashioned according to regulations in the sacred books.

The Tibetan collection also displays calligraphic wooden blocks; robes; heavy silver skull bowls studded with turquoise and coral, which are used for offerings; Tibetan butter containers from which the lamas replenish their lamps; aprons of carved human bones used by priests in necromantic rites, and hundreds of other objects of Buddhist art.

309

*A view of
the hilltop museum.*

Staten Island Historical Society.

THE RICHMONDTOWN RESTORATION
Address: 302 Center St., Arthur Kill and Richmond Roads, Richmondtown, Staten Island, N.Y., 10306.
Phone: 351-1611; Education Dept., 351-9414.

Days: Tuesdays through Saturdays, 10—5; Sundays, 2—5. Closed Mondays. For school tours contact Education Dept.
Admission: Museum, $.50; restorations, $1.50.

Subway: IRT 7th Ave. or IRT Lexington Ave. to South Ferry, then take Staten Island Ferry to St. George.
Bus: From St. George take bus No. 113 to Richmondtown.
Auto: (1) From St. George left along Bay St. to Vanderbilt Ave. Right to Richmond Road. Follow road to its end. (2) From Verrazano Bridge: Richmond Road exit, follow road to its end. Ample free parking in lot.

Gift Shop: Country store in museum has candy, homemade jellies, small souvenirs, and publications for sale.

310   *Museum Memberships:* From $10.00 annual membership to $1,000.000 as patron member. Members receive quarterly publication.

Library: Books, documents, and photographs about Staten Island. Closed to public except by appointment.

The Richmondtown Restoration is a project New Yorkers can be proud of. It incorporates in a small village some of the finest examples of historical architecture and artifacts on public view in New York. The Restoration expresses the courage and determination of a community to preserve its heritage.

Richmondtown is a community-sponsored project. The City of New York has promised to match all privately donated funds, but since large foundations do not want to allocate funds without assuming some control of the project no donation large enough to ensure the finish of the project has yet come in. Many in the project are volunteers.

When all the elements are complete, the Restoration will contain the following units: Schoolhouse, General Store, Historical Museum, Blacksmith Shop, Wagon Sheds, Law Office, Town Jail, Court Houses, Town Houses, Country Houses, Cottages, Farms, Barns, Mill House, Town Bridge, Cooper's Shop, Basketmaker's Shop, Tavern, Churchyard—about forty buildings that will show the evolution of an American village through the seventeenth, eighteenth, and nineteenth centuries.

The earliest mention of the village was in 1700, when the settlement was referred to as "Cocklestown," because of the oyster and clam shells, or cockles, that were found nearby. After the Revolution, Richmondtown was its accepted name. Growth of the village was dependent on its function as the county seat. When Staten Island became part of the city in 1898, Richmondtown was abandoned as the county seat, and lost its primary incentive for growth. Building was at a standstill

Voorlezer House.

311

from then on; and since there had been little change in the topography of the area since the seventeenth century, historians found it an ideal site for restoration.

An outstanding building in the village is the Voorlezer House, the oldest known elementary-school building in the United States. It was built for the Dutch Church congregation before 1696. "Voorlezer" derives from the Dutch for "fore-reader," a title given to laymen who taught school and read church services. The Voorlezer also lived in the building.

This quaint, two-story clapboard Dutch-Colonial is higher in front than in back, which gives the roof and the building a lopsided look. The foundation walls are two feet thick, and the timbers in the building are of solid oak. The floorboards are white pine, sixteen inches wide.

In the downstairs room with its large open fireplace, services were held. Upstairs were a bedchamber and probably the schoolroom. Of special note are the broad, uneven ax marks left in the garret by the primitive housebuilders. Although the schoolhouse is furnished with present-day copies of eighteenth-century furnishings, the Voorlezer House is nevertheless a distinguished National Historical landmark.

The Samuel Grosset House (Treasure House) was erected on its present site near the Mill Pond and St. Andrew's Church in 1700. Grosset, a tanner, later sold the land with tan vats, yards, curing pits, hides and leather to another tanner. After the Revolutionary War,

Third County Courthouse.

$7,000 in gold was found hidden in the walls of the house, and it is believed the building may have been used as a paymaster's office.

St. Andrew's Church, founded in 1708, and its historic graveyard are separated from the Restoration by Mill Pond stream. The oldest gravestone is in memory of Sibbel Arnol, who died in 1742 at the age of four. Her father was rector of St. Andrew's from 1740—1745.

The Guyon—Lake—Tysen House was built about 1740 by Joseph Guyon. His name is etched over the dining-room door. In the 1800s the Lake family came into possession of the property, and intermarried with the Tysens. The kitchen is considered the earliest portion of the building, and may have formed Guyon's entire house. It has double Dutch doors.

Stephen's General Store, established in 1837, displays a complete post office with pigeonholes, two potbelly stoves, pottery from Bennington, Vermont, and upstate New York, captain's chairs, decorated tinware for flour, sugar, and tea. The shelves carry patent medicines, tobacco tins, innumerable small household items, rolling pins, ladles, and coffee grinders. From the ceiling hang birdcages, oil lamps, baskets, ice skates, huge tin pitchers, ancient scales—all creating a comfortable country-store atmosphere.

The Newspaper Office offers a glimpse of a small-town printing office with a hand-operated typesetter and printing press. One wall is full of cowhide-bound books.

A typical farmhouse carpenter's shop, containing authentic tools, dates from 1830. The imposing Greek Revival building at the Center Street intersection is the Third County Courthouse, dating from 1837.

Reenactment of a Civil War battle.

Revolutionary soldiers.

Dunne's Saw Mill on the peaceful Mill Pond has been the setting for a simulated Civil War battle. The sawmill is authentic of the period (1800) and even has stacks of cut boards and wood chips to create a realistic workaday atmosphere.

The Cooper's Shop and Home by the Mill Pond were built in 1790. A cooper made barrels and wooden utensils.

The Staten Island Historical Society Museum is the keystone of the Restoration. It occpies the County Clerk and Surrogate's Office built in 1848. Many of the cast-iron doors remain. Prints, drawings, broadsides, and colored lithographs show early scenes of Staten Island. There is a modest group of post-office patriotic Civil War covers and other post-office canceled letters from 1818 to 1900. The Elliott Burgher Commemorative Pitcher Collection contains luster, Staffordshire, and Liverpool ware dating from 1785 to 1835, and depicting the landing of the Pilgrims, Cornwallis' surrender, the opening of the Erie Canal, and the Battle of Waterloo.

314   The lower floor also has household effects, coffee grinders, utensils, baking dishes, old sewing machines, pewterware, rare Victorian laundry equipment for washing, wringing, scrubbing, and mangling clothes and, for the finishing touches, the Edward Menden Collection of hand pressing irons used for collars, cuffs, and ruffles. There are also tin candle

makers, spinning wheels, looms, butter churners, blacksmith equipment, and a comprehensive collection of hardware and tools for barrelmakers, wagonmakers, and shoemakers, ranging from clamps, gauges, saws, drills, chisels, braces, mallets—all of which have a vague connection with some of the handyman tools we use today.

The upper floor of the museum has an interesting group of photographs showing historic houses of Staten Island as they were in the late 1800s and early 1900s. Some of the Richmondtown Restoration buildings are in this group. Some have disappeared entirely. Some of the photos are by Alice Austin, a famous Staten Island photographer.

In a glass case is a copy of Milton's *Paradise Lost* printed in Dutch in 1691. There is also a group of relics of the Revolution recovered from the British camps in Richmondtown—handmade buttons, belt buckles, and copper pennies. An antique doctor's kit contains an instrument used for bleeding, old hacksaws, and a case of small pills, all the same size and color.

A toy room displays tin soldiers, dollhouses, puzzles, penny banks, china dolls, trains, and miniature furniture of the 1880s.

315

*Mill Pond
and Cooper's Shop.*

CONFERENCE HOUSE

Address: South end of Hylan Blvd., Staten Island, N.Y., 10307.
Phone: 984-2086

Days: Open daily, 1–6; October 1st to April 1st, 1–4. Closed Mondays.
Admission: $.25. Free Tuesday and Thursday. Chidren free if accompanied by a parent or teacher. School groups call first.

Subway: IRT 7th Ave. or IRT Lexington Ave. to South Ferry, then take Staten Island Ferry to St. George.
Bus: From St. George take bus No. 103 to Craig Ave.
Train: From St. George ferry dock on Staten Island take rapid transit to Tottenville. From Bentley St. turn right onto Craig St., and right again at Hylan Blvd.
Auto: (1) From St. George turn left onto Bay St.; then right at Canal St. Note that street name changes to Tompkins Blvd., then Hylan Blvd. Follow Hylan Blvd. to its end. (2) From Verrazano Bridge take Hylan Blvd. exit south. Follow Hylan Blvd. to its end. Ample street parking.

Food: Ice-cream and soda vendors are stationed at end of Hylan Blvd. most weekend afternoons.

Membership: Conference House Association invites members, $5.00 annual dues maintain building and provide resident caretaker.

The Conference House at the tip of Staten Island gives the impression that almost nothing in and about the house has changed since the building was built in the late 1680s. This section of the island is still beautifully rural. Present-day reality intrudes only in the Sunday congregation of families and couples sprawled in camp chairs and on blankets on the wide lawn that slopes gently down to the sandy shore of the Raritan River. From time to time white sails drift by. There is perhaps no better way to enjoy history.

Inside Conference House is an 1850 lithograph showing the house from across the river. Its legend says that on this location the scenery, fishing, bathing, springs, and "salubriety" stand unrivaled; this is the most beautiful and romantic spot in New York.

Considering that the house was built before 1687, it is remarkable how well preserved its architectural features are. Except for the removal of a high porch, the exterior has changed little. Interior rooms have the original wide-board floors and exposed-beam ceilings.

316

The right parlor on the first floor is sparsely furnished. It contains some chairs and an inlaid tilt-top table given to John Adams by Lafayette. It is in the dining room on the left that the historic conference

Conference House.

giving the house its name was held. A set of iron kettles and cooking pots hang in the huge cellar fireplace. The exposed rough stones are particularly attractive, and show what pioneer builders could do with raw materials. There is also a thirty-foot vault that may have been used as a dungeon.

In the bedroom upstairs are many chairs and cribs. A small cubicle contains dozens of Indian arrowheads collected around the property. In this small room Christopher Billopp is supposed to have killed one of his slave girls in a fit of violence.

Thomas Billopp, a captain in the British Navy who built the house, came to America in 1674. He received a grant from the Honorable Thomas Dongan, Governor-General of all his Royal Highness' territory in America, for the Manor of Bentley in 1687. Bentley was the post-office address until 1861, when it was changed to Tottenville. Billopp roamed the seas, and died in England in 1725.

His second daughter, Anne, married Thomas Farmer. Their third son, Thomas Farmer, Jr., born in 1711, inherited the manor from his grandfather. Under the provisions of the will he changed his name to Thomas Billopp. His gravestone is in the underground vault in the cellar.

His oldest son, Colonel Christopher Billopp, born in 1737, lived in the house until the close of the Revolution. Then he, along with other

317

British sympathizers, moved to St. John, New Brunswick, and the Billopp mansion was confiscated.

Lord Howe took possession of Staten Island for the British on July 4, 1776. He soon requested a meeting with a delegation from the colonists to discuss possible peace terms to end the war. On September 11, 1776, a committee consisting of Benjamin Franklin, John Adams, and Edward Rutledge met with Lord Howe at the Billopp Mansion. The delegates for the colonists declined every proposal that would compromise the Declaration of Independence that had been signed only weeks earlier. When peace did come, it is significant that the terms followed those outlined by the colonists at this first, historic peace conference.

Since the Revolution a number of different owners have lived in Conference House. As early as 1846 a historian suggested that the building be preserved. In October, 1918, the Gillespie Powder plant across the river exploded and broke all the windows in the Billopp Mansion. The tenants then moved out, and thus for the only time in its long history the mansion was uninhabited for the next two years. It was during this time that "much was damaged by some of the savages of civilization." Finally, in 1926, a real-estate corporation purchased the estate and generously gave the house and grounds to the city with the stipulation that they be preserved as a museum and park.

A battery of useful pots.

A perfect view of the Raritan River.

Landmarks Checklist

The public and private structures and districts described here represent a selected sampling of the landmarks in New York City that are an indication of the rich architectural and historic treasures the Landmarks Preservation Commission is working to recognize and preserve.

The Commission was established in 1965 at a time when Pennsylvania Station had just been demolished and the city was considering an expressway in lower Manhattan that would have destroyed the cast iron loft buildings in Soho.

Preservationists, property owners and local citizens urged the municipal government to call a moratorium on landmark destruction.

Since 1965 the Commission has saved or preserved more than 500 buildings as official landmarks and thousands more have protection as part of the more than 30 historic districts. The districts discussed here are the largest in the city and each features a diverse collection of architectural artifacts.

The work of the Commission consists of designating, monitoring and preserving those structures, historic districts, scenic and interior landmarks with historic, architectural or aesthetic qualities that should be protected by law for the people of New York City.

Historic and architectural documentation of each subject is prepared by the staff of the Landmarks Commission and designation is usually made after a public hearing.

Gloria S. McDarrah

MANHATTAN

ABIGAIL ADAMS SMITH HOUSE
421 East 61st Street

This Federal-style stone stable, built in 1799, has been converted into a museum and headquarters for the Colonial Dames of America. The stable was to form part of the country estate of Abigail Adams, daughter of President John Adams, and her husband Col. William S. Smith, but work was never completed on the mansion and other out buildings (see page 95).

AMERICAN MUSEUM OF NATURAL HISTORY
Central Park West & 79th Street

The major portion of the museum fronting on 77th Street was designed in Romanesque Revival by Cady, Berg & See and erected from 1889 to 1908. There are now nearly twenty interconnected units including the Theodore Roosevelt Memorial, an impressive classical main entrance to the museum on Central Park West (see page 172).

APPELLATE DIVISION OF THE SUPREME COURT OF THE STATE OF NEW YORK
Madison Avenue at East 25th Street

321

This small marble courthouse is Classic Eclectic in design, but also shows the influence of Andrea Palladio, the Italian Renaissance architect. The three-story building, begun in 1896 under the direction of architect James Brown Lord, expresses the best of the classical tradition, with its Corinthian columned porch and fine sculpture.

THE ARSENAL

830 Fifth Avenue, Central Park at 64th Street

Built to "house and protect the arms of the state," this five-story utilitarian building with crenellated octagonal towers is reminiscent of an early English manorial
fortress. Designed by architect Martin E. Thompson, it was begun in 1847 and
completed in 1851. The ground floor is faced with granite, and the floors above
are of orange-colored brick with limestone trim. The building is now used by the
city Department of Parks as its headquarters.

BAYARD-CONDICT BUILDING
65-69 Bleecker Street

Built in 1897, this is the only building in New York designed by Louis H. Sullivan,
the first American to work in a non-historic, modern architectural style. The first
modern skyscraper in New York, its vertical design is an expression of Sullivan's
theory of the skyscraper as a "proud and soaring thing." It is distinguished by its
terra cotta facade ornamented with leafy forms.

BIALYSTOKER SYNAGOGUE
7-13 Willett Street

This severely plain building of the late Federal Period was built in 1826 of cut
stone. This Synagogue is a fine expression of masonry construction in the vernacular tradition. The Bialystoker Synagogue was once the home of the Willett Street
Methodist Episcopal Church.

BLACKWELL HOUSE
Roosevelt Island (opposite East 65th St.)

This simple well-proportioned house, built for James Blackwell around 1796 is
the sole surviving building on Roosevelt Island which dates from the period when
the island was still privately held property. The Blackwell family owned and
farmed the island from the late seventeenth century until 1828 when it was sold
to the City of New York. In Dutch times the island was known as Varckens
Eylandt, which means Hog Island.

BOND STREET SAVINGS BANK
330 The Bowery

This is an especially interesting cast-iron building, designed by Henry Engelbert
in the elaborate style of the French Second Empire. The wealth of ornamental
detail makes this building an unusually fine example of this important type of
construction. Upon completion in 1874 it was known as the Bond Street Bank
and later became the German Exchange Bank. In 1963 it became the Bouwerie
Lane Theatre.

BOWERY SAVINGS BANK
130 The Bowery

The Chicago World's Fair in 1893 brought to this country a new classicism. This
bank built in 1894 was one of the first to herald the new style. McKim, Mead
& White, the architects, frequently used sculpture where possible. In this building,
the central clock in the pediment is flanked by reclining classical figures and
domesticated lions.

BROOKLYN BRIDGE
City Hall Park, Manhattan to Cadman Plaza, Brooklyn

This beautiful suspension bridge was the first to span the East River. Under the
direction of architects John A. Roebling and Washington A. Roebling, this great
structure was begun in 1867 and completed in 1883. Its majestic stone towers
with buttresses and pointed Gothic arches represents a milestone in American

engineering. It has an overall length of 6,016 feet and the bridge is 133 feet above mean high water.

JAMES A. BURDEN HOUSE
7 East 91st Street

This house with its great ballroom windows, is the finest Beaux-Arts town house in the city. It was built in 1902 for steel manufacturer James A. Burden, Jr. This superb mansion was designed by Warren & Wetmore who also did Grand Central Terminal and the Biltmore Hotel.

CARNEGIE HALL
57th Street at Seventh Avenue

This building with its fifteen-story tower has an intrinsic character and integrity of design which evoke considerable praise. It was completed in 1891 by architect William B. Tuthill. The reddish-brown Roman bricks combined with bandcourses, arches, pilasters and other terra cotta decorations, produces a beautiful color which has mellowed with age. Inside the hall, musical history has been made since the building was opened with a five-day festival at which Tchaikovsky conducted several of his own works.

ANDREW CARNEGIE MANSION
2 East 91st Street

The firm of Babb, Cook and Willard designed this house in 1899. Carnegie wanted a "modest, plain and roomy house." The house and its gardens are one of the grandest residential complexes in New York. Its architecture, reminiscent of an English Georgian country seat, is influenced by styles from France and Italy. The area in which the house is located, known as Carnegie Hill, was once part of the village of Nieuw Haarlem established by the Dutch in 1658. Carnegie was one of the richest men in the world and gave sixty million dollars to the New York Public Library (see page 153).

MRS. AMORY S. CARHART HOUSE
3 East 95th Street

The building was built between 1913 and 1921 as a New York version of a Louis XVI Parisian house for Mrs. Carhart who never occupied the house. This dignified residence is one of the finest examples of this style in New York. The composition and proportions of this elegant four-story house are well organized and express the consummate skill of architect Horace Trumbauer, noted designer of many fine town houses including the Duke Mansion.. Mrs. Carhart died in 1919 and the house was eventually purchased by the Lycée Francais.

CASTLE CLINTON
The Battery

This stone fort, built in 1807 by architect John McComb, Jr. is one of the original harbor forts which guarded New York. Its handsome doorway and imposing curved walls are notable features. The structure has served as a place of amusement, Castle Garden, an opera hall, and as an aquarium (see page 18).

CASTLE WILLIAMS
Governor's Island

Impressive in appearance, imposing in size, this red sandstone bastion, when completed in 1811, was an armed gauntlet bristling with more than 100 cannons. Its impenetrable walls—eight feet thick—were one of the reasons the British fleet did not attempt an assault on New York during the war of 1812. Castle Williams is situated on the northwest point of the island and was designed and built by Lt. Col. Jonathan Williams, who had been put in charge of the defenses of New York in 1805.

CHURCH OF THE TRANSFIGURATION
1 East 29th Street

This modest Gothic Revival church stands in a quiet garden fenced off from the busy street. Built of warm red brick and brownstone trim, the original one-story building was completed in 1849. Four additions were later included. The church has been known as The Little Church Around the Corner since 1870 when the actor Joseph Jefferson, unable to arrange a funeral for another actor, was directed here. Under this sobriquet the church has become famous in verse and plays and its bond with the arts continues to the present.

CITY HALL
Broadway and City Hall Park

An architectural symbol of civic pride for more than 150 years, City Hall was designed in the Federal style, modified by French influence. It was the result of the collaboration of an American, John McComb, Jr. and a French architect, Joseph Mangin. The interior is dominated by a magnificent rotunda, whose domed space encloses a grand double stairway (see page 33).

THE COOPER UNION FOUNDATION BUILDING
Astor Place and East 7th Street

This pioneer building, the brainchild of the great philanthropist Peter Cooper, employed some of the first wrought-iron beams ever used in New York City. This large six-story brownstone building was built in the Anglo-Italiante style. The round-arched windows were a conspicuous feature of this style and two handsome round-arched porches are at the north and south ends.

THE DAKOTA APARTMENTS
1 West 72nd Street

Architect Henry Janeway Hardenbergh designed this first luxury apartment building in New York. Begun in 1880 and completed in 1884, this imposing structure of eight stories reflects the romanticism of the German Renaissance style. Massively constructed of yellow colored brick with stone trim and terra cotta ornament, it has the grandeur of a large European chateau.

JAMES B. DUKE MANSION
1 East 78th Street

324

The impressive splendor of this mansion is achieved through the simple grandeur of the French Classical style of Louis XV. It was designed in 1909 by architect Horace Trumbauer of Philadelphia. He modeled it after the Labottiere Mansion in Bordeaux, which had been designed by Laclotte in the eighteenth century. The mansion is constructed of limestone and, as viewed from the street, appears to be only two stories high, since the attic story is hidden by an imposing stone balustrade above the roof cornice. James B. Duke grew up on a farm in North Carolina, learned how to grow, cure and sell tobacco and later formed the American Tobacco Company. The mansion is now the New York University Institute of Fine Arts.

DYCKMAN HOUSE
Broadway and West 204th Street

This is the last Dutch Colonial farmhouse left on Manhattan Island. Built of fieldstone, brick, and clapboard, this eighteeenth century house replaced one of 1748 which was destroyed by the British in the Revolutionary War. Rebuilt in 1783, the house has a few features and details that suggest that some of the materials salvaged from the 1748 house were used in this farmhouse. The dwelling has a sweeping low-pitched gambrel roof, curved out over a full porch.

85 LEONARD STREET BUILDING

This is the last remaining building in New York City by James Bogardus, self-described inventor of cast-iron buildings. Completed in 1861, it is one of the few extant buildings of cast iron designed in the so-called "sperm candle" style, which uses classical elements in combination with non-classical emphasis on verticality, lightness, and openess.

FEDERAL HALL NATIONAL MEMORIAL
28 Wall Street

Designed as the New York Custom House by Town & Davis and completed in 1842 by Samuel Thomson and John Frazee, this imposing Greek Revival building now houses a museum devoted to the history of New York City (see page 30).

FIRST SHEARITH ISRAEL GRAVEYARD
55-57 St. James Place

This small graveyard of the Sephardic Jewish congregation dates back to 1683. Handsome headstqnes are interspersed with marble sarcophagi with flat slab tops.

FLATIRON BUILDING
Fifth Avenue & 23rd Street

The triangluar site where this French Renaissance skyscraper was built gave to it a special character and a poetic quality. It is covered with ornament, not one square inch remaining flush and plain. It derived its name from its shape which was similar to a laundress' flatiron. It was completed in 1902 and designed by D. H. Burnham, a Chicago architect.

FORT JAY
Governor's Island

Reminiscent of an eighteenth century French fortification with its dry moat and star shaped plan, Fort Jay is a dramatic reminder of the early defenses erected in New York harbor to protect the city from invasion. The pentagonal breastworks occupy a knoll and dominate the northern end of the island. The first permanent fortification on Governor's Island was begun in 1794 because of a threat of war with France. Fort Jay was extensively rebuilt in 1806 with stronger materials.

FOURTEENTH WARD INDUSTRIAL SCHOOL
256-258 Mott Street

325

Built in 1888 for the Children's Aid Society, this striking example of Victorian Gothic architecture was designed by Vaux & Radford. Four stories high, the building was constructed of selected common and pressed Philadelphia brick, laid with red mortar and trimmed with Gatelaw Bridge stone and terra cotta ornamental panels. A two-story oriel window dominates the facade, and the structure is crowned by an impressive crow-stepped gable.

FRAUNCES TAVERN
54 Pearl Street

This three-story brick building contains the notable "Long Room" where George Washington said farewell to his officers in 1783. Originally built in 1719 as a residence for Etienne Delancey, it was restored in 1907 by architect William H. Mersereau (see page 24).

FRIENDS MEETING HOUSE AND FRIENDS SEMINARY
15 Rutherford Place, Stuyvesant Square

Charles T. Bunting, a member of the meeting and a builder, was responsible for the construction and probably also the design for the three-story brick meeting house built in 1861. It is conservative in design, with a simple pedimented entrance porch. The T-shaped seminary building, built as nearly similar to the meeting house as possible with entrance porch and gable, also faces Rutherford Place.

GRACE CHURCH
800 Broadway

Begun in 1843 under the direction of architect James Renwick, Jr., this outstandingly beautiful church marked the advent of the Gothic Revival style in New York. Built of sparkling white Sing Sing marble, the building is crowned by a tower with flamboyant Gothic spire. Looking north on Broadway the well-proportioned church terminates the vista where the street changes direction at Tenth Street.

OLIVER GOULD JENNINGS RESIDENCE
7 East 72nd Street

This residence is an especially opulent and handsome example of a Beaux-Arts town house. Designed in 1898 by the Paris trained architects Ernest Flagg and Walter B. Chambers, the house harmonizes very effectively with the adjoining Sloane residence. Jennings was a director of several large corporations. The house is three stories high and made of Indiana limestone and is one of the few richly detailed Beaux-Arts town houses remaining in New York.

GRACIE MANSION
East End Avenue and 88th Street

Located in Carl Schurz Park on the East River this is one of the finest Federal style country houses remaining. Archibald Gracie, a wealthy merchant, purchased the site from the Jacob Walton heirs in December 1798 and in 1800 built his country seat and entertained lavishly. Among his illustrious guests were John Quincy Adams, Dewitt Clinton, and Alexander Hamilton. In 1891 the city purchased the house and restored it in 1927. Mayor Fiorello H. LaGuardia was the first to occupy Gracie Mansion, and it is now the official residence of the Mayor.

GRAND CENTRAL TERMINAL
Vanderbilt Avenue and 42nd Street

This is one of the great buildings in America. It combines distinguished architecture with a brilliant engineering solution, wedded to one of the most famous railroad terminals of our time. Monumental in scale, this great building functions as well today as it did when built. In style it represents the best of the French Beaux-Arts. It was completed in 1913 by architects Warren & Wetmore from designs by Reed & Stem. The great windows, the monumental columns and sculptured details represent a skillful combination of architectural elements of timeless grandeur.

326

HALL OF RECORDS
31 Chambers Street

This grand building was designed by John R. Thomas and built in 1899. Its opulent interiors are characteristic of the lavish Beaux-Arts style. The Hall of Records was conceived and planned to serve as a repository of municipal records but now also stands as a magnificent architectural symbol of the prosperity, importance and achievement of New York.

JOHN HENRY HAMMOND HOUSE
9 East 91st Street

This grand residence was designed by Carrere & Hastings in 1902. The Hammond House is a fine example of High Renaissance style inspired by Roman sixteenth century palazzo design. The five-story house has a limestone facade with entrance doors of wrought iron. Hammond was a lawyer and banker and married to Emily Vanderbilt Sloane.

EDWARD S. HARKNESS HOUSE
1 East 75th Street

This imposing residence in the style of an Italian Renaissance palazzo is outstanding for excellence of design and beauty and for subtle richness of detail. It is five stories high and made of Tennessee marble. This residence, built in 1907, was designed by Hale & Rogers for Edward S. Harkness, a son of one of the six original partners of the Standard Oil Company.

THE HARLEM COURTHOUSE
170 East 121st Street

Of the many historic buildings erected in Harlem around the turn of the century and still extant, this courthouse is the most significant and impressive. Begun in 1891 and designed by Thom & Wilson, it is handsomely picturesque in Romanesque Revival style with Victorian Gothic overtones. The building achieves much of its beauty by a judicious use of brick, stone and terra cotta.

E.V. HAUGHWOUT BUILDING
488-492 Broadway

One of the largest and most handsome examples of the commercial, cast-iron buildings of New York City, this five-story structure was designed in the Anglo-Italianate manner in 1857 by architect J.P. Gaynor, with iron components by James Bogardus. Its arched windows set between columns are reminiscent of Sansovino's great library in Venice. Originally used as a store, it was the first building in New York to have a passenger elevator for customers.

INDIA HOUSE
1 Hanover Square

Built for the Hanover Bank between 1851 and 1854, this brownstone building has played an important part in the commercial life of the city. It served as the Cotton Exchange between 1870 and 1886 and later became the offices of W.R. Grace & Co. Today it is mainly a clubhouse. Its handsome doorway, cornice and pedimented windows illustrate Anglo-Italianate architecture at its finest.

327

JUDSON MEMORIAL CHURCH
Washington Square South at Thompson Street

This small rectangular church built in 1892, with a sharply defined gable roof, is a superb example of Italian Renaissance Eclectic architecture. With the adjacent tower of Judson Hall, the church completes an architectural composition designed by McKim, Mead, and White. An outstanding feature of this church is the two-story entrance doorway set between the tower and the church proper.

OTTO KAHN HOUSE
1 East 91st Street

Built for Otto H. Kahn, banker, philanthropist and patron of the arts, this imposing residence, begun in 1913, was designed by the noted British architect J. Arm-
strong Stenhouse with C.P.H. Gilbert acting as associate architect. In its grand
scale, distinguished design and superb construction, the house is the finest Italian
Renaissance style mansion in New York City. It is four stories high above a deep
basement and built of gray limestone. It provided a gracious home for one of the
best known financiers of the period and a splendid setting for his magnificent
art collection.

METROPOLITAN MUSEUM OF ART
Fifth Avenue at 82nd Street

The Metropolitan Museum of Art occupies an imposing complex of buildings.
This first Victorian Gothic building was designed in 1877 by Calvert Vaux and
Jacob Wrey Mould, working with the building committee of the museum which
consisted of Richard Morris Hunt, James Renwick, and Russell Sturgis. Vaux and
Mould, architects of Central Park bridges and structures, also devised a master
plan for the future expansion of the museum. Other wings were designed by
McKim, Mead and White. Hunt, one of the founders of the American Institute of
Architects, designed a grand structure based on classical Roman prototypes
(see page 116).

EDWARD MOONEY HOUSE
18 The Bowery

The only town house surviving in Manhattan that dates from the period of the
American Revolution, this house was built between 1785 and 1789 in Early
Federal style. This three-story red-brick structure stands on its original site.

PIERPONT MORGAN LIBRARY
29-33 East 36th Street

The original building of the Morgan Library, designed in the Italian Renaissance
Eclectic style by architects McKim, Mead & White, was built in 1906 to house
Morgan's collection of paintings, sculpture and his library. In 1928, the adjoining
Annex was built by architect Benjamin Wister Morris in a Florentine Renaissance
design in harmony with the original library. The library walls were constructed of
"dry masonry," a remarkable method of construction in which the marble blocks
are joined so evenly that no mortar is necessary to bind them. This type of construction was used in the Parthenon and Erechtheum in Greece (see page 51).

NATIONAL ARTS CLUB
15 Gramercy Park South

This 1874 building represents the height of Victorian Gothic residential architecture. It displays a wealth of unusual details such as bands of stonework decorated
with leaves and flowers interspersed with the heads of famous authors. The Club

328 was originally two brownstones, remodelled for Samuel J. Tilden by Calvert Vaux,
architect of the Jefferson Market Courthouse in Greenwich Village. Tilden ran for
the presidency against Rutherford B. Hayes and lost. Tilden's library was part of
the nucleus of the great collection of the New York Public Library.

NEW YORK CITY MARBLE CEMETERY
52-74 East 2nd Street

The cemetery, begun in 1831, was the second nonsectarian burial ground in the
City opened to the public and was considered a fashionable burial place. It is
surrounded by a high brick wall and by houses and tenements, but may be readily

seen through a handsome iron fence. The grounds contain 256 vaults. The cemetery has the remains of many important New Yorkers and some national figures.

NEW YORK PUBLIC LIBRARY
Fifth Avenue and 42nd Street

This majestic marble building is one of the masterpieces of the Beaux-Arts style of civic architecture. It sits regally on a terraced plateau, displaying urns, fountains, flagpoles, sculpture, and ornament. It was designed by Carrere & Hastings and was completed in 1911 (see page 56).

OLD MERCHANT'S HOUSE
29 East 4th Street

This three-story brick town house completed in 1832 was one in a row of six. Joseph Brewster built the houses and lived in No. 29 until it was sold to Seabury Tredwell in 1835. The building is preserved in its original state, inside and out. The house is a unique document of its period and shows, with unrivaled authenticity, how a prosperous merchant of the 1830's lived. It is a fine example of Greek Revival (see page 39).

OLD ST. PATRICK'S CATHEDRAL
Mott Street at Prince Street

This early Gothic Revival church was begun in 1809 under the direction of architect Joseph F. Mangin. Although the church was gutted by a fire in 1886, it was restored and today the massive stone facade facing Mott Street is still impressive.

PAYNE-DAVIDSON BLOCKFRONT
Park Avenue and 68th Street

This is an outstanding group of neo-Federal town houses extending along the west side of Park Avenue. Designed by McKim, Mead and White, 680 Park Avenue (Percy R. Pyne House) was built in 1909. Fifteen years later they designed 684 Park (Oliver D. Filley House). In 1916 Delano & Aldrich built 686 (William Sloane House). Also in 1916 Walker and Gillette built 690 Park (Harry P. Davidson House). The Mrs. J. William Clark House at 49 East 68th Street is compatible with its neighbors and forms an integral part of this distinguished group. It was built in 1913 by Trowbridge and Livingston.

THE PLAYERS
16 Gramercy Park

This building was remodeled in 1888 from a Gothic Revival town house built in 1848. The front porch of the Players, with its handsome iron railings and gorgeous wrought-iron lamps, is the work of Stanford White. Executed in the Italian Renaissance Eclectic style, this porch displays a fine series of Tuscan columns.

THE PLAZA HOTEL
Fifth Avenue and 59th Street

This building occupies one of the finest sites in the city and is the most elegant of the great New York hotels. Although the detail and decoration are in a style that the architect described as French Renaissance, the boldness of mass and good scale of this eighteen-story, white brick and marble structure make the Plaza the outstanding example of American hotel architecture of the first decade of the twentieth century. It was designed in 1905 by architect Henry Janeway Hardenborgh, a pioneer in the field of luxury hotel and apartment houses. He also designed the Dakota Apartments.

SARA DELANO ROOSEVELT MEMORIAL HOUSE
47-49 East 65th Street

This dignified Georgian-style double town house was designed by Charles A. Platt and built in 1908. It was commissioned by Sara Delano Roosevelt, with number 47 to be occupied by her and number 49 by her son and daughter-in-law, Franklin and Eleanor Roosevelt. The family lived here whenever they were in New York. This five-story, brick trimmed with limestone, double residence was the scene of Roosevelt's heroic struggle with and recovery from poliomyelitis.

THEODORE ROOSEVELT HOUSE
28 East 20th Street

This handsome brownstone town house displays much fine detail of the Gothic Revival period. Built in 1848, it was remodeled in 1923 by architect Theodate Pope Riddle. Theodore Roosevelt was born in this house in 1858, and lived here until he was 14 (see page 43).

ST. JAMES CHURCH
32 St. James Steeet

This handsome monument in the Greek Revival style is attributed to Minard Lefever. One of the oldest Roman Catholic churches in Manhattan, this 1835 structure has a recessed porch with two columns. On either side of the porch are enclosed stairs with their own doors opening onto the street. The entire front is crowned by a low gable.

ST. MARK'S-IN-THE-BOWERY
Second Avenue at 10th Street

Being on the oldest site of continuous worship in the city, St. Mark's represents contruction over a considerable period of time. The main body of the church, with fieldstone walls of the Georgian tradition, was erected in 1799. The steeple of 1828 is pure Greek Revival; the cast-iron porch belongs to the Italianate style of the 1850's. Under the church lies the Stuyvesant Vault, where the remains of Peter Stuyvesant and his heirs are interred.

ST. MICHAEL'S CHAPEL OF OLD ST. PATRICK'S CATHEDRAL
266 Mulberry Street

Built in 1858 as a chancery office and designed by James Renwick, Jr., in association with William Rodrique, this is a fine example of Gothic Revival architecture. The most prominent feature of this small red brick, three-story building is the central projecting stone entrance vestibule with pointed arch doorway.

ST. PATRICK'S CATHEDRAL
Fifth Avenue and 50th Street

This cathedral represents the epitome of the Gothic Revival in New York City. It was designed by the architect James Renwick, Jr. A marvel of architectural design for its day, its rich marble exterior sits squarely on a handsome granite base. Its most conspicuous feature is the two identical towers which rise to 330 feet with octagonal spires decorated with flame-like tracery. The main entrance door is the focal point. The interior length is 306 feet. The cornerstone for St. Patrick's was laid on August 15, 1858.

ST. PAUL'S CHAPEL AND GRAVEYARD
Broadway and Fulton Street

Among the few eighteenth century buildings which remain today, St. Paul's is the most notable both architecturally and historically. It is the oldest existing church edifice in New York. The architect Thomas McBean designed the church to face the river, with its back to Broadway. It was built in1764 of rough-dressed local stone cut in cobblestone-size blocks. The most notable feature of this historic church is its spire which was built in 1794 by James Crommelin Lawrence. This church represents the epitome of the Georgian Period of architecture. It is the only church in New York in which George Washington worshipped.

SALMAGUNDI CLUB
47 Fifth Avenue

This grand mansion in the early Italianate style was built in 1852-53 for Irad Hawley, president of the Pennyslvania Coal Company. One of the first buildings to have a facade entirely of brownstone, its imposing entrance is richly framed in stone ornament. The first floor rooms, with original carved marble chimney pieces, rosewood doors and arcaded Corinthian screen separating the front and back parlors have been carefully preserved by the Salmagundi Club, known for its association with fine arts.

SCHERMERHORN ROW
2-18 Fulton Street

Known as Schermerhorn Row, these commercial buildings consist of a group of twelve red brick warehouses all erected at the same time in 1811 by Peter Schermerhorn. These structures as well as 91 and 92 South Street, with their high pitched roofs, form a unique architectural entity, reflecting the mercantile expansion of New York City dating back to the era when the harbor was a port of sailing ships. This block is the only remaining complex of commercial buildings in the Federal style of architecture still standing in New York City. All retain their original four stories and pitched roofs. Schermerhorn ran a ship chandler's business at number 243 Water Street.

SEA AND LAND CHURCH
Market Street and Henry Street

This attractive Georgian-Gothic church is similar to St. Paul's although it was built in 1817, almost fifty years later. It is a survival of the Georgian architectural tradition built in Federal times with the introduction of Gothic windows and doors. Henry Rutgers, a Revolutionary War patriot, donated land for the church.

SEVENTH REGIMENT ARMORY
643 Park Avenue

Begun in 1877, this fortified castle-like structure was designed by the eminent architect Charles W. Clinton. The military character of the building is expressed in the crenellated parapets crowning the towers and other details typical of medieval battlements. The designer used materials and techniques of his era to express the building's function in an efficient way. Thus, the armory has great historical value in providing an example of two conflicting tendencies of nineteenth century architecture, the romantic military and expressive functionalism.

331

HENRY T. SLOANE RESIDENCE
9 East 72nd Street

The prominent architectural firm of Carrere & Hastings was commissioned in the early 1890's to design this large town house for the merchant prince Henry T. Sloane. This elegant house is an especially fine example of the French Beaux-Arts style. By 1900, East 72nd Street was lined with mansions and town houses. Only a handful of these grand houses survive today, among them the Sloane house, which serves as an important reminder of the architectural splendor of late nineteenth century America.

SMALLPOX HOSPITAL
Roosevelt Island (opposite East 52nd Street)

Located at the southern tip of Roosevelt Island, this fine Gothic Revival structure was originally used for the treatment of the "loathsome malady," smallpox. It is now a picturesque ruin. The original hospital was built in 1854 and designed by James Renwick, Jr.

STATUE OF LIBERTY
Liberty Island

This world-famous Liberty monument intended to symbolize Franco-American friendship was a gift from the French and was the work of Alsatian sculptor Frederic Auguste Bartholdi and engineer Gustave Eiffel. The imposing pedestal was designed by New York architect Richard Morris Hunt (see page 16).

WILLARD STRAIGHT HOUSE
1130 Fifth Avenue

This is an outstanding example of early twentieth century residential architecture designed in the best tradition of the American town house. This six story brick house is in Federal style. This large dwelling on a corner lot was admirably suited for the domestic city life of a socially prominent family. It was owned by Willard D. Straight, diplomat, financier, and publisher of *The New Republic* (see page 155).

STUYVESANT-FISH HOUSE
21 Stuyvesant Street

This three-story brick Federal-style building was begun in 1803. A unique example of a fine urban dwelling of the period, the house is rich in historical associations. It was built by a great-grandson of Peter Stuyvesant for his daughter Elizabeth, at the time of her marriage to Nicholas Fish, who served at Valley Forge.

STUYVESANT POLYCLINIC HOSPITAL
137 Second Avenue

This handsome building was designed in a modified version of the neo-Italian Renaissance style by the architect William Schickel and built in 1883. The facade is of Philadelphia pressed brick, now painted white, above a stone basement. Especially notable is its sculptural detail which includes a series of portrait busts of famous physicians and scientists.

TRINITY CHURCH AND GRAVEYARD
Broadway at Wall Street

The present Trinity Church, completed in 1846, is the third edifice of this Episcopal parish, founded in 1697, to stand on this prominent site, closing the vista at the end of Wall Street. The church is Gothic Revival and was executed in brownstone by the noted ecclesiastical architect Richard Upjohn in a free rendering of English Gothic. Its spire is the most notable feature. The old burying ground which surrounds the Church holds the remains of Alexander Hamilton, Robert Fulton, and Francis Lewis.

332

265 HENRY STREET

This handsome Federal three-story town house, built in 1827, retains much of its original appearance, including its doorway and iron railings in front. This building is the central one of three houses which form the famous Henry Street Settlement founded by Lillian Wald in 1893.

UNITED STATES CUSTOM HOUSE
Bowling Green

The seven-story stone Custom House was designed in the Eclectic French Renaissance style. This is a truly monumental structure with four sculptured groups, heroic in size, representing the four continents. The keystones of the main windows are carved with heads typifying the eight races of mankind. Mercury, the ancient God of Commerce, appears on each of the capitals of the forty-four columns which encircle the building. It is the work of Cass Gilbert who designed the building in 1901 and is a monumental achievement of this period.

UNITED STATES GENERAL POST OFFICE
Eighth Avenue and 31st Street

This is one of the few public buildings that can be seen from all sides. Its majestic colonnade of twenty Corinthian columns creates a great architectural effect. These, along with the sweep of the front steps, are overpowering. It was designed in 1910 by McKim, Mead & White and is an outstanding example of the Roman Classic style notable for its monumental scale.

THE UNIVERSITY CLUB
1 West 54th Street

This huge granite building resembles a sixteenth century Italian Renaissance palazzo and was designed in 1897 by architects McKim, Mead & White. The University Club was established for the purpose of maintaining a library, reading room and gallery of art. It is monumental in scale and it is unlikely that a building of this type will ever again be built in the United States.

STEPHEN VAN RENSSELAER HOUSE
149 Mulberry Street

This is a small early nineteenth century Federal style house that followed the design pattern well established by the 1820's. It is two stories high with an attic and low basement and the main floor raised above street level has an entrance door at one side of the front. The stone stoop, seven steps high, retains some of its original wrought-iron handrailings.

WATCH TOWER
Mount Morris Park and 122nd Street

This fire lookout tower is a remarkable four-story octagonal structure, the last remaining of several such towers which once stood in Manhattan. This tower is an open cast-iron structure composed of three tiers of fluted columns superimposed on one another. A large alarm bell hangs from the second level. Fire watch towers were discontinued after 1878.

JAMES WATSON HOUSE
7 State Street

This brick Federal town house, the last of the row of elegant town houses which once lined State Street, is three stories high, set on a stone basement. Its right portion was completed in 1793, the left portion in 1806. Its design is attributed to John McComb, Jr. The building was restored in 1965. The unusual feature of this house is the great portico which follows the street curve.

GERTRUDE RHINELANDER WALDO MANSION
867 Madison Avenue

At the turn of the century, the upper East Side was lined with elegant town houses and great mansions. Today only a few survive. This elaborate neo-French

Renaissance limestone residence built in 1895 was designed by architects Kimball & Thompson for Mrs. Gertrude Rhinelander Waldo who never lived in the house. It is an exceptionally large and imposing structure based on the sixteenth century chateaux of the Loire Valley.

PAYNE WHITNEY HOUSE
972 Fifth Avenue

This superb mansion stands out on the last remaining blockfront of imposing town houses on Fifth Avenue. The gracious curve of the gray granite front rises five stories and is emphasized by entablatures. The house was designed in 1902 in style of the neo-Italian Renaissance by McKim, Mead & White. The house was the town residence of Payne Whitney, a financier, and is now occupied by the cultural office of the French Government.

STATEN ISLAND

ALICE AUSTEN HOUSE
2 Hylan Boulevard

The Austen House began as a one room frame dwelling built between 1691 and 1710. Standing on waterfront property overlooking the Narrows, this original structure expanded with gradual additions and alterations. John Austen purchased the property in 1844 and his friend James Renwick is credited with the Gothic Revival character of the house. Alice Austen, pioneer woman photographer, lived in the house for 75 years. It is now being converted into a museum.

BASKETMAKER'S SHOP
3741 Richmond Road

This house, built in 1810, is a typical small country cottage, one-and-one-half stories with a cellar kitchen which was also the basketmaking shop of John Morgan. The house is frame, clapboarded with a shingled front (see Richmondtown Restoration, page 311).

BATTERY WEED
Hudson Road, Fort Wadsworth Reservation

Located at the water's edge on the Narrows beneath the Verrazano Bridge, this massive masonry fortification was built between 1847 and 1861. Constructed of solid slabs of granite, the sea wall of Battery Weed is six feet thick. The fort is laid out in the form of an irregular shaped trapezoid. At the height of its glory it was one of the most powerful forts on the eastern seaboard and is still an extraordinary example of military architecture of the period (see page 303).

BILLIOU-STILLWELL-PERINE HOUSE
1476 Richmond Road

334

The original portion of the house, built in 1679, is distinctive for its steep medieval type roof and immense Dutch fireplace with a huge chimney head supported on two wooden posts, unique in this country. The house was built by Captain Thomas Stillwell and was subsequently owned by Nicholas Britton and the Perine Family (see page 304).

BOEHM-FROST HOUSE
43 Arthur Kill Road

This house, built in 1770, is a good example of a clapboard frame house with brick end chimneys, one of which has its stonework exposed to the weather at the first floor (see Richmondtown Restoration, page 310).

THE CHURCH OF ST. ANDREW
Old Mill Road and Arthur Kill Road

The church, with its picturesque outline and steeply pitched gable roofs, reflects the character of the austere and simple English parish churches of the twelfth century. The original small stone church was built in 1709 and was enlarged several times, the last in 1872 by architect William H. Mersereau. Many gravestones dating back to the colonial period are scattered throughout the graveyard, the oldest dating to 1733 (see Richmondtown Restoration, page 310).

CONFERENCE HOUSE
Foot of Hylan Boulevard

The most imposing surviving seventeenth century manor house on Staten Island is a magnificent two-and-a-half story fieldstone residence built between 1680 and 1688. The stone masonry is characteristic of the medieval influence in some early Colonial architecture. The manor house was built by Captain Christopher Billopp as the seat of the Manor of Bentley, a title conferred by Governor Thomas Dongan in 1676 (see page 316).

COOPER'S SHOP
3747 Richmond Road

The oldest section, built about 1790, was a simple clapboard one room house with a garret above. It was moved from Egbertville because it stood in the path of the Willowbrook Parkway. A one room extension was added later (see Richmondtown Restoration, page 310).

COUNTY CLERK'S AND SURROGATE'S OFFICES
303 Centre Street

This two-story brick office building dating from 1848, located on its original site, was built in a simplified Italianate style. It was renovated three times and turned over to the Staten Island Historical Society in 1933 for use as an Historical Museum (see Richmondtown Restoration, page 310).

CUBBERLY-BRITTON COTTAGE
3737 Richmond Road

The earliest section of this house, the stone center portion, was built in 1670 on the "Governor's Lot" as the "Town House" of Staten Island to serve court and government functions. It is an outstanding example of civil and domestic architecture. Nathaniel Britton who had lived in the English colony of Long Island before 1660 acquired the stone cottage in 1695. Issac Cubberly bought the property in 1761. The cottage is on a lawn adjacent to the mill pond (see Richmondtown Restoration, page 310).

335

ERNEST FLAGG HOUSE
209 Flagg Place

Together with its gatehouse and gate, this is an example of Dutch Colonial revival style on a monumental scale. Ernest Flagg designed and constructed his own thirty-two room mansion in 1898. The facade of the fieldstone mansion has a two level veranda supported by Doric columns. The gambrel roof is topped by a captain's walk. Flagg designed the first notable Manhattan skyscraper, the Singer Building.

FORT TOMPKINS
Hudson Road, Fort Wadsworth Reservation

Fort Tompkins is the oldest continuously manned military installation in the United States. Completed in 1861, it is built into the crest of the hill above Battery Weed overlooking the Narrows. A simple blockhouse built by the Dutch in 1636 was destroyed by the Indians and replaced in 1663. After this, a sandstone fort stood on the site until 1847 when the federal government constructed the present granite fort (see page 304).

KREUZER-PELTON HOUSE
1262 Richmond Terrace

The original colonial cottage with garret, erected in 1722, was constructed of random fieldstone and shows Dutch influence. It was built in three sections. It was first constructed by Cornelius Van Santvoord, a native of Holland, then additions were made by Cornelius Kreuzer and later by Daniel Pelton, Sr., who purchased the house in 1835. It is an interesting architectural example of historic continuity.

LAKE-TYSEN HOUSE
3711 Richmond Road

Erected about 1740 by Joseph Guyen, this house was moved when threatened with destruction by a developer. It is an outstanding example of Dutch Colonial style. This one-and-a-half story shingled-sided, gambrel roof house with dormers is one of the earliest known with a curved roof line (see Richmondtown Restoration, page 310).

NEVILLE HOUSE
806 Richmond Terrace

Built about 1770 of red, quarried sandstone, this impressive residence is one of the few large pre-revolutionary country houses still standing in New York City. An unusual feature is the long two-story veranda supported on six square posts. The imposing two-and-a-half story structure was built for Sea Captain John Neville. It was once a tavern called "The Old Stone Jug."

THE PARSONAGE
74 Arthur Kill Road

This structure built about 1855 in Gothic Revival style, stands on its original site. It is a two-story frame building sheathed with clapboards, originally built as a parsonage for the Dutch Reformed Church of 1808 (see Richmondtown Restoration, page 310).

SAILORS' SNUG HARBOR
Richmond Terrace

These monumental buildings, started in 1831 by architect Martin E. Thompson, form one of the most notable groups of Greek Revival buildings in the United States. Such unified results were rarely achieved in this country in terms of scale, extent, quality and use of materials. The different fronts of the five buildings contribute to the success of the group. Each relates and is joined by enclosed galleries that link the buildings and form interior corridors from end to end. For more than a century these buildings provided a home for retired sailors.

336

SCOTT-EDWARDS HOUSE
752 Delafield Avenue

The sandstone and clapboard Dutch Colonial house was built in 1730 on a parcel of the Old Governor Dongan grant of 1677. Greek Revival alterations were made during the 1840's when the residence became the home of Judge Ogden Edwards, a descendant of Jonathan Edwards and a cousin of Aaron Burr.

SLEIGHT FAMILY GRAVEYARD
Arthur Kill Road and Rossville Avenue

Set among trees in a narrow strip of land that rises between a highway and a steep bank leading to a salt meadow are the remains of some of Staten Island's earliest settlers. Gravestones date from 1750 and include descendants of Pieterse Wynant, Sr., who started the first permanent settlement on Staten Island in 1661.

STEPHENS HOUSE AND GENERAL STORE
297 Centre Street

This house and the attached General Store are located on their original site. The house, built in 1837 by Stephen D. Stephens, is in the Greek Revival style. It is a two-and-a-half story clapboarded structure with low attic windows set in smooth fascia boards (see Richmondtown Restoration, page 310).

SYLVANUS DECKER FARM
435 Richmond Hill Road

Encroachments and time have done little to diminish the simple, rugged character of this 1810 clapboard and shingle farmhouse. Sylvanus Decker left the small farm to the Staten Island Historical Society to be operated as a farm museum portraying nineteenth century farm life. It is located near Richmondtown Restoration.

THIRD COUNTY COURTHOUSE
302 Centre Street

This imposing courthouse is located in a dominant position on its original site. It was built in 1837 in Greek Revival style and has a pedimented portico with four unfluted Doric columns (see Richmondtown Restoration, page 310).

390 VAN DUZER STREET HOUSE

This 1830 frame house built in modified Greek Revival style is located in Stapleton, a village developed by William J. Staples and Minthorne Tompkins, whose father Daniel Tompkins was vice president in the Monroe administration and Governor of New York state. The house is a fine example of a style of architecture indigenous to Staten Island.

TREASURE HOUSE
37 Arthur Kill Road

This house, on its original site, is so called from British coins found in the walls in the 1850's. The earliest section was built in 1700 by Samuel Grasset, who operated a leather business. It is an interesting example of early domestic architecture, of frame and rubble stone construction with clapboard sides (see Richmondtown Restoration, page 310).

337

VAN PELT-REZEAU CEMETERY
Tyson Court

This cemetery is one of the very few remaining "Homestead Graves" on Staten Island. These were private cemeteries set aside on a remote part of a farm for family burials. This plot was used by the family which occupied the Voorlezer's House after it ceased to be used as a school (see Richmondtown Restoration, page 310).

VOORLEZER'S HOUSE
59 Arthur Kill Road

The "Voolezer's House, standing on its original site, was built by the Dutch Church in 1695 as a church, school, and house for their Voorlezer, a Dutch word meaning lay reader, clerk or teacher. This is the oldest school building in the United States. It is a two-story clapboard structure, original except for its restored exterior (see Richmondtown Restoration, page 310).

BRONX

BARTOW-PELL MANSION
Shore Road, Pelham Bay Park

This elegant country house of local stone with cast-iron balconies was designed in 1836 in the Federal style. The interior is typical of the Greek Revival style, with a freestanding staircase in the hall and twin parlors overlooking Long Island Sound. A terraced garden, stone stables and a small cemetery are some of the interesting features of the estate (see page 252).

ROBERT COLGATE HOUSE
5225 Sycamore Avenue

"Stonehurst" was built in 1860 for Robert Colgate, the merchant and philanthropist who was the eldest son of William Colgate, pioneer soap manufacturer. This grey Maine granite, Anglo-Italianate style mansion is magnificently situated along the Hudson River in Riverdale, a favorite summer retreat for rich New Yorkers in the 1860's that still retains much of its original character as a suburban villa development within the city limits.

FONTHILL
West 261st Street and Palisade Avenue

This Gothic Revival style castle overlooking the Hudson was built for Edwin Forrest, the renowned Shakespearean actor, in 1846. Its grouping of six turrets forms a picturesque composition reminiscent of early medieval fortresses. Constructed of stone with pointed arched windows, this little castle situated among beech trees is now used as Mt. St. Vincent college library.

FORT SCHUYLER
East of the Throgs Neck Bridge, Throgs Neck

Begun in 1833 and completed in 1856, this pentagonal fort, built of Connecticut granite, was designed for an armament of 312 guns. A fine example of military masonry construction, the massive fort, with Fort Totten which lies opposite, could protect New York City at the important juncture of Long Island Sound and the East River. Although it was abandoned in 1870, the fort was rehabilitated by the W.P.A. in 1934, and today serves as a Merchant Marine academy.

338

LORILLARD SNUFF MILL
New York Botanical Garden, Bronx Park

Built about 1800, this fieldstone with brick masonry trim early factory building stands adjacent to the Bronx River. Although completely altered to serve as a public cafeteria, the building, with its century old beams exposed showing where the machinery for the grinding stones had been attached, is a picturesque reminder of early factory construction (see page 240).

OLD WEST FARMS SOLDIER CEMETERY

2103 Bryant Avenue and 180th Street

The oldest public veterans' burial ground in the Bronx, this quiet cemetery is a modestly landscaped wire-fenced enclosure with the remains of forty veterans of four wars. A bronze statue of a Union Army soldier stands on a stone pedestal in the graveyard. The first interment was in 1815, the last that of a World War I veteran.

POE COTTAGE
Poe Park, 2640 Grand Concourse

This one-and-one-half story wooden farm cottage with attic and porch was built about 1812. Edgar Allan Poe lived here from 1846 to 1848, and is said to have written "Annabel Lee" in this cottage. It is a fitting memorial to its time and a tribute to the great poet (see page 237).

RIVERDALE PRESBYTERIAN CHURCH AND DUFF HOUSE
4765 Henry Hudson Parkway West

Designed by the noted architect James Renwick in 1863, this small stone parish church is a picturesque example of late Gothic Revival architecture. The building displays some fine architectural details, such as the handsome pointed-arch doorway with niche above and a steep slate roof. The church has served Riverdale since Civil War days.

ST. ANN'S CHURCH AND GRAVEYARD
295 St. Ann's Avenue at 140th Street

Situated amid rock outcroppings on irregular rising ground, this 1840 fieldstone country church was conceived by its donor, Gouverneur Morris, as a family memorial. It is a simple Gothic Revival building, with a Greek Revival vernacular tower. Morris' mother, a lineal descendant of Pocahantas, and Lewis Morris, signer of the Declaration of Independence, are interred in a large vault under the chancel.

ST. PETER'S CHURCH
2500 Westchester Avenue

These two picturesque Victorian Gothic style buildings in a quiet graveyard setting are a reminder of the rural past of the Bronx. The church, designed by Leopold Eidlitz, was completed in 1855. The clerestory was added and restored in 1879. Constructed of rough-cut stone, the church, with its steeply pitched roofs, bold profile, and towering spire, is the dominant feature of the neighborhood.

VAN CORTLANDT MANSION
Broadway and West 242nd Street, Van Cortlandt Park

This fine example of a Georgian country house was built in 1748 by Frederick Van Cortlandt. The mansion retains most of its original architectural features, and it is furnished with eighteenth century English and American furniture, some of which belonged to the Van Cortlandts (see page 229).

VALENTINE-VARIAN HOUSE
3266 Bainbridge Avenue at East 208th Street.

This well-proportioned two-story fieldstone house is important historically because it is one of a small group of eighteenth century residences remaining in the city. A fine example of Georgian domestic architecture, the building is now a museum and headquarters for the Bronx Historical Society (see page 238).

WAVE HILL HOUSE

West 249th Street and Independence Avenue

This elegant stone manor house in a park-like setting overlooking the Hudson exhibits a masterful blending of diverse architectural styles. A number of distinguished residents have occupied the mansion, which is now a cultural and scientific center for environmental studies (see page 232).

QUEENS

RICHARD CORNELL GRAVEYARD
Adjacent to 1457 Greenport Road

Neglected and forgotten for many years, this little graveyard is named after Richard Cornell, who was an inn master in Flushing. He was born in 1625 in England and was the first white settler in the Rockaways. This is one of the oldest burial grounds in New York.

FLUSHING MUNICIPAL COURTHOUSE
137-35 Northern Boulevard

This small town hall is an example of the Romanesque Revival style popular in the United States prior to the Civil War. This 1862 structure, in an excellent state of preservation, has retained all of its exterior ornamental details.

FRIENDS MEETING HOUSE
137-16 Northern Boulevard

The Meeting House of the Religious Society of Friends in Flushing dates back to 1694 when a small frame structure was built and later enlarged. The edifice is in English Medieval style erected on a frame of forty foot oak timbers, each hand hewn from a single tree. This is the oldest house of worship standing in New York City and one of the oldest in the country (see page 290).

GRACE EPISCOPAL CHURCH AND GRAVEYARD
155-03 Jamaica Avenue

This is an impressive, bold, rugged English Gothic Revival church with a landscaped country churchyard dotted with small tombstones dating from 1734. The church was erected in 1861 from plans by Dudley Field. Grace Church dates its founding to 1702.

KING MANSION
Jamaica Avenue and 153rd Street

This distinguished colonial residence situated in King Park was named a National Historic Landmark in 1974. The huge two-and-a-half story house is both Georgian and Federal in style. The oldest section dates from 1730 (see page 297).

340

KINGSLAND HOMESTEAD
37th Avenue and Parsons Boulevard

This house, in the Dutch Colonial style, is a rare example of a type of house once common in western Long Island. Kingsland Homestead has special significance today as a middle-sized house of the Revolutionary Period (see page 292).

LAWRENCE FAMILY GRAVEYARD
20th Road and 35th Street

This private cemetery holds the remains of some of this country's great patriots and is important because of the history connected with those buried there. This includes twelve high ranking military officers whose service dates from Dutch rule in New York.

LENT HOMESTEAD
78-03 19th Road

The beauty of this simple Dutch Colonial farmhouse lies in its stone work and steeply sloping roof with overhang at front and back. The farmhouse dates from 1729 and was built by Abraham Lent, grandson of Abraham Riker.

REFORMED DUTCH CHURCH OF NEWTON AND FELLOWSHIP HALL
85-15 Broadway

This is one of the oldest (1831) wood churches in the city and it can be seen from three directions. It is a one-story, Greek Revival style structure with a pitched roof. The church cemetery, with its many remaining headstones, has the appearance of a small colonial village churchyard.

STEINWAY HOUSE
18-33 41st Street

This twenty-seven room Italianate country villa, occupied by the piano manufacturer, was originally built in 1840 for Benjamin Pike, in a rural setting overlooking the East River. This granite block structure typifies the merchant's country home of the mid-nineteenth century.

BROOKLYN

BROOKLYN BOROUGH HALL
209 Joralemon Street

This dignified civic structure, designed by architect Gamaliel King, is one of the city's finest Greek Revival buildings. This all-masonry building, built in 1846, is crowned by a handsome Georgian Eclectic domed cupola. The seat of government for the city of Brooklyn for nearly fifty years until its union with New York in 1898, the building also houses portraits of the former Mayors of Brooklyn in its lobby.

BROOKLYN POST OFFICE
271-301 Washington Street

The Post Office is an excellent example of the Romanesque Revival style, with a wealth of rich detail and doors and windows enframed in stone. The original portion of the building, begun in 1885, is only one-third the size of this imposing structure that now covers an entire block. This old structure is four stories high and has a steep, sloping roof with a high, square tower on the southwest corner.

COMMANDANT'S HOUSE
Hudson Avenue and Evans Street
New York Naval Shipyard

341

The only building in New York City attributed to the eminent architect Charles Bulfinch, this two-story frame mansion was built in 1805 for the chief officer of this important naval establishment. Representing the Federal style of architecture at its finest, the building boasts an outstanding cornice and an exceptional Federal doorway.

83RD POLICE PRECINCT AND STABLE

179 Wilson Avenue

Erected in 1894, this impressive Romanesque Revival station house is situated in the Bushwick section of Brooklyn. The prominent architect, William B. Tubby, designed the station house in the image of a medieval stronghold. Its corner tower and the polychromatic use of red, yellow and ochre brick on the facade distinguish this fine example of municipal architecture.

ELIAS HUBBARD RYDER HOUSE
1926 East 28th Street

This quaint 1834 farmhouse is situated in Gravesend, one of the six original townships of Kings County. The two-story wood frame structure, which makes use of Dutch Colonial elements such as the projected roof eave, remained in the possession on the Ryder family for over one hundred and thirty years.

ERASMUS HALL MUSEUM
Courtyard of Erasmus Hall High School
911 Flatbush Avenue near Church Avenue

Erected in 1786, this two-and-a-half-story clapboard Federal style building stands in the center of an ivy-towered quadrangle of Collegiate Gothic buildings. It began as a private academy in 1787, with funds contributed by John Jay, Alexander Hamilton and others. It was the first secondary school chartered by the Regents of New York State and is one of the oldest schools in the country.

FLATBUSH DUTCH REFORMED CHURCH
890 Flatbush Avenue at Church Avenue

This handsome Federal-style church is adorned by one of the most beautifully scaled church spires in the city. Begun in 1793 and completed in 1798 under the direction of architect Thomas Fardon, the church was built of local stone and Holland brick. Its walls rest on a foundation made from stones of an earlier church of 1699.

FLATLANDS REFORMED CHURCH
Kings Highway and East 40th Street

This stately Greek Revival church, built in 1848, stands at the head of an avenue of linden trees. It is constructed of clapboard and painted white, and is set in a spacious churchyard enclosed by a fine wrought-iron fence. In its ancient cemetery are buired the Reverend Ulpianus Van Sinderen, the Revolutionary War minister, and Pieter Claesen Wyckoff, founder of the first church in 1654.

GREENWOOD CEMETERY GATES
Fifth Avenue and 25th Street

342

One of the monuments of the Gothic Revival style, this impressive gateway was designed by Richard M. Upjohn & Son and completed in 1865. A flamboyant Gothic clock-tower flanked by two principal gates represents an ingenious plan. Many famous Americans are buried behind this imposing gateway.

THE GRECIAN SHELTER
Prospect Park near Parkside Avenue

This rectangular-shaped shelter is a masterpiece of neo-classical architecture. Designed by architects McKim, Mead & White, the Shelter was completed in 1905. The flowing rhythm of twenty-eight marble columns supporting a full ornate entablature evokes the grandeur of classical antiquity.

HOUSES ON HUNTERFLY ROAD
1698-1798 Bergen Street

The four houses on Hunterfly Road, built about 1830, form a unique enclave in what is now the Bedford Stuyvesant area. They constitute the only surviving group of houses built parallel to the line of a colonial road and are now in the middle of a city block. The frame buildings lie on the edge of Weeksville, which was the first major free black settlement in the area.

LEFFERTS HOMESTEAD
Prospect Park, Flatbush Avenue at Empire Boulevard

Built by Lieutenant Peter Lefferts between 1777 and 1783, this charming eighteenth-century Dutch Colonial farmhouse replaced the earlier Lefferts homestead which was burned in the battle of Flatbush in 1776. An attractive feature of this small house is the beautiful Federal door attributed to the architect Major L'Enfant (see page 264).

LITCHFIELD VILLA
Prospect Park West at 5th Street

A palatial Italianate mansion completed in 1856, this unique structure with two irregular shaped towers and tall turret attached to the main building forms a picturesque architectural composition. An interesting colonnade of wood flanks the castle to the right. An unusual feature of the mansion is found in the colonnade, decorated with native plants—corn and wheat.

MAGNOLIA GRANDIFLORA
679 Lafayette Avenue

This tree, a neighborhood symbol and focus of community pride, was developed from a seedling that Mr. William Lemken sent from North Carolina 85 years ago. Although the species rarely flourishes this far north, this particular magnolia grandiflora is distinguished for its beauty as well as its unusual hardiness. The three brownstone houses behind the tree have also been designated as landmarks.

NEW LOTS REFORMED CHURCH
630 New Lots Avenue

Constructed in 1824 during the late Federal Period, this small clapboard church displays Early Gothic Revival details. Its triple center window, Palladian-Gothic in design, is an architectural rarity. Provincial in character, this rustic church was erected by farmers of the New Lots area for a sum reputed to have been about $35.

NEW UTRECHT REFORMED CHURCH
18th Avenue at 83rd Street

This early Gothic Revival building was erected in 1828 with stone from an earlier church of 1699. The church has painted brick arches and a handsome stone tower with wooden Gothic pinnacles. Surrounded by old trees and some boxwood, its picturesque setting is enhanced by an old iron fence.

343

PIETER CLAESEN WYCKOFF HOUSE
Clarendon Road and Ralph Avenue

This is the oldest building standing in New York City and New York State. Built before 1641, it is a wooden, one-story farmhouse exemplifying the Flemish Medieval Revival and Dutch Colonial styles of architecture. The structure is sadly deteriorated and recent vandalism has contributed to its worsening condition. Funds to stabilize the building have been obtained and work to halt the building's deterioration is underway.

PUBLIC SCHOOL 39
417 Sixth Avenue

This richly detailed three-story brick with stone trim school building was built in 1876. It is transitional in style, combining features of the Italianate, such as its bold roof cornice, and the French Second Empire, exemplified by the mansard roofs to either side of the central bay. The structure is one of the few public schools of its period which continues to serve its original function.

PUBLIC SCHOOL 111
249 Sterling Place

This handsome brick school building is distinguished by the round arches characteristic of the early Romanesque Revival style. Designed in 1867 by Samuel B. Leonard, Superintendent of Buildings for the Board of Education of the City of Brooklyn for nearly 20 years, it is one of the few school buildings in this style extant.

ST. BARTHOLOMEW'S CHURCH
1227 Pacific Street

This picturesque Romanesque Revival building was designed by George P. Chappell and completed in 1890. The church, with rough-faced red granite base and red brick above, has a variety of effective elements, including a wide gable with a large stained glass window and a belfry tower.

SOLDIERS' AND SAILORS' MEMORIAL ARCH
Grand Army Plaza

Dedicated to the men who fought in the Union Army in the Civil War, the memorial occupies a commanding site at the entrance to Prospect Park. John Hemingway Duncan, the architect of Grant's Tomb, designed the arch, which was completed in 1892. The memorial is 80 feet wide and 80 feet high, enclosing an arch 50 feet high and 35 feet wide. It is richly ornamented with sculpture by leading American artists of that period.

STEELE HOUSE
200 Lafayette Avenue corner Vanderbilt Avenue

This imposing two-story frame house is a unique example of the Greek Revival style in Brooklyn. Dating from the second quarter of the nineteenth century, the house has a shuttered, octagonal cupola rising above the roof. A flight of wooden steps, complete with newel posts, turned spindles and a wide hand rail, projects from the front of the house.

STOOTHOFF-BAXTER-KOUWENHOVEN HOUSE
1640 East 48th Street

344

This rare survivor of colonial times is the type of farmhouse constructed by Flemish farmers who came to New York via Holland in the 1700's. Built in two sections, the older low wing is c. 1747, and the large main portion dates from 1811. This shingled house exhibits a picturesque profile with pitched roofs, projected eaves and end chimneys. The house has been moved twice, and is now set behind a white picket fence.

VAN NUYSE-MAGAW HOUSE
1041 East 22nd Street

This Dutch Colonial farmhouse built around 1800 is an unpretentious frame structure with some twentieth century modifications. A rectangular, two-and-a-half-story shingle-covered dwelling, it is distinguished by a gambrel roof with outsweeping curves that give the house a sharp profile. Erected by Johannes Van

Nuyse (1736-1826) at the west end of his father's 85 acre farm, the house is an attractive reminder of early Brooklyn history.

WYCKOFF-BENNETT HOMESTEAD
1669 East 22nd Street

This one-and-one-half-story frame dwelling is one of the few eighteenth century Dutch Colonial farmhouses still standing in Brooklyn. Built in 1766, the house is rectangular in plan, with an extension on the northern end containing a kitchen and a milk house. The house belonged to the Wyckoff family until 1835, when it was sold to the Bennetts, who continued to farm the land until the turn of this century.

FIVE HISTORIC DISTRICTS

PARK SLOPE HISTORIC DISTRICT

This district is roughly an L-Shaped area that extends along Prospect Park West to Grand Army Plaza. The Park Slope Historic District is one of the most beautiful residential neighborhoods in the city. Its history and development are closely related to that of Prospect Park. The wide sunny avenues and tree-lined streets with houses of relatively uniform height are punctuated by church spires which provide a living illustration of the nineteenth century characterization of Brooklyn as a city of homes and churches. This district has a cross-section of the important trends in American architecture of the time and includes some of the most outstanding buildings in the country.

SOHO CAST-IRON HISTORIC DISTRICT

Bounded by Canal Street, Broadway, Houston Street and West Broadway, this district contains the largest group of cast-iron structures in the world and is recognized internationally for its unique character. The use of cast-iron for structural as well as ornamental purposes was an important factor in the development of commercial building technology. The buildings illustrate a wide range of styles popular in the second half of the nineteenth century. In recent years, artists have been attracted by the loft space the buildings provide and have converted many into studios and galleries. Soho is an acronym for south of Houston (Street).

BROOKLYN HEIGHTS HISTORIC DISTRICT

The Brooklyn Heights area is an elevated plateau bounded on the west by the East River, on the north by Fulton Street, on the South by Atlantic Avenue and on the east by Court Street. The stately brick and brownstone houses on these tree-lined streets with stone sidewalks represent most of the principal architectural styles of the nineteenth century and stand almost unchanged as originally built. Of the 1,284 buildings in this Historic District, 684 were built before the Civil War and 1,078 before the year 1900.

COBBLE HILL HISTORIC DISTRICT

More than twenty-two city blocks are included in the Cobble Hill Historic District, the area generally between Atlantic Avenue, Court, Degraw and Hicks Streets, with Brooklyn Heights forming a southerly extension. This residential district began in the mid-1830's when attractive rows of Greek Revival town houses were built. Cobble Hill goes back to the 1640's when the Dutch governor William Kieft granted patents for farms north of Red Hook, extending inland from the East River shore to the Gowanus Valley.

GREENWICH VILLAGE HISTORIC DISTRICT

Greenwich Village, (one of the oldest sections of Manhattan) can be traced back to Indian days when it was called Sappokanican. Its boundaries extended from the Hudson River to Fourth Avenue and the Bowery, and from Houston to 14th Street. Laid out for development in the years after the American Revolution, it contains the greatest concentration of early New York residential architecture to be found anywhere in the country. Here one can see the major architectural styles of the early city displayed side by side, ranging from the most naive to the most sophisticated versions.

Alphabetical List of Museums

347